First World War

and Army of Occupation

War Diary

France, Belgium and Germany

24 DIVISION
72 Infantry Brigade
Queen's Own (Royal West Kent Regiment)
8th Battalion
29 August 1915 - 30 April 1919

WO95/2213/2

The Naval & Military Press Ltd
www.nmarchive.com
Published in association with The National Archives

Published by

The Naval & Military Press Ltd

Unit 10 Ridgewood Industrial Park,

Uckfield, East Sussex,

TN22 5QE England

Tel: +44 (0) 1825 749494

www.naval-military-press.com

www.nmarchive.com

Contents

Document type	Place/Title	Date From	Date To
Heading	WO95/2213/2		
Heading	24th Division 72nd Infy Bde 8th Bn The Queen's Own (Roy. West Kent Regt) Aug 1915-Apr 1919		
Heading	8th Battn. The Queen's Own (Royal West Kent Regiment). September (29.8.15 to 30.9.15) 1915 Apr 1919		
War Diary	Blackdown Camp	29/08/1915	29/08/1915
War Diary	Aldershot	29/08/1915	29/08/1915
War Diary	Southampton	30/08/1915	30/08/1915
War Diary	Havre	01/09/1915	30/09/1915
Heading	24th Division 8th R.W. Rest Vol I Nov 15		
War Diary	Houtkerque	31/09/1915	04/10/1915
War Diary	Reninghelst	05/10/1915	14/10/1915
War Diary	Spoil Bank-Canal Bank	15/10/1915	19/10/1915
War Diary	Reninghelst	20/10/1915	23/10/1915
War Diary	Trenches Voormezeele	24/10/1915	28/10/1915
War Diary	Reninghelst	29/10/1915	02/11/1915
War Diary	Dead Dog Farm	03/11/1915	07/11/1915
War Diary	Reninghelst	08/11/1915	12/11/1915
War Diary	Reninghelst	01/11/1915	02/11/1915
War Diary	Dead Dog Farm	03/11/1915	07/11/1915
War Diary	Reninghelst	08/11/1915	30/11/1915
Heading	24th Div 8th R. West Rest Vol 2 December 1915		
War Diary	Bonningues Les Ardres (Pas de C)	01/12/1915	31/12/1915
Heading	8th Battalion Royal West Kent Regiment. January 1916		
War Diary		01/01/1916	04/02/1916
Heading	8th Battalion Royal West Kent Regiment. February 1916		
War Diary		01/02/1916	29/02/1916
Heading	8th Battalion Royal West Kent Regiment. March 1916		
War Diary		01/03/1916	31/03/1916
Operation(al) Order(s)	72nd. I.B. Operation Order No. 31	19/03/1916	19/03/1916
Operation(al) Order(s)	72nd. Infantry Brigade Operation Order No. 32	23/03/1916	23/03/1916
Heading	8th Battalion Royal West Kent Regiment. April 1916		
War Diary	Front line trenches Right Sector	01/04/1916	30/04/1916
Heading	8th Battalion Royal West Kent Regiment. May 1916		
War Diary	Field	01/05/1916	14/05/1916
War Diary	Dranoutre	14/05/1916	14/05/1916
War Diary	Front Line Trenches	15/05/1916	31/05/1916
Heading	8th Battalion Royal West Kent Regiment. June 1916		
War Diary	Dranoutre	01/06/1916	05/06/1916
War Diary	Field	06/06/1916	30/06/1916
Heading	8th Battn. The Queen's Own (Royal West Kent Regiment). July 1916		
War Diary	Field	01/07/1916	31/07/1916
Heading	8th Battalion Queens Own (Royal West Kent Regiment) August 1916		
Heading	War Diary 8th (S) Battn Queen's Own (Royal West Kent Regiment) from 1st August 1916 to 31st August 1916 (Volume)		

War Diary	Saisseval	31/07/1916	31/07/1916
War Diary	Ailly Sur Somme	01/08/1916	01/08/1916
War Diary	Morlancourt	01/08/1916	01/08/1916
War Diary	Sandpit Area	01/08/1916	10/08/1916
War Diary	Front Line	10/08/1916	11/08/1916
War Diary	Briqueterie	12/08/1916	13/08/1916
War Diary	Front Line	15/08/1916	16/08/1916
War Diary	Crators Near Carnoy	17/08/1916	17/08/1916
War Diary	Front Line	18/08/1916	18/08/1916
War Diary	Briqueterie	20/08/1916	21/08/1916
War Diary	Citadel	22/08/1916	22/08/1916
War Diary	Near Morlancourt And Ville Sur Ancre	25/08/1916	27/08/1916
War Diary	Ribemont	27/08/1916	27/08/1916
War Diary	Delville Wood	30/08/1916	31/08/1916
War Diary	Front Line	31/08/1916	31/08/1916
Heading	8th Battalion Royal West Kent Regiment. September 1916		
Heading	War Diary of 8th (S) Battn Royal West Kent Regt. from 1st Sept 1916 to 30th Sept 1916 (Vol)		
War Diary	Front Line Trenches	01/09/1916	01/09/1916
War Diary	Reserve Line	02/09/1916	07/09/1916
War Diary	Vauchelles-Les-Quesnoy	08/09/1916	19/09/1916
War Diary	Sains-Les-Pernes	20/09/1916	26/09/1916
War Diary	Gouy-Servins	28/09/1916	30/09/1916
Heading	8th Battalion Royal West Kent Regiment. October 1916		
Heading	War Diary of 8th (Service) Battalion Royal West Kent Regiment In the field from 1st October 1916 to 31st October 1916 (Volume)		
War Diary		01/10/1916	31/10/1916
Heading	8th Battalion Royal West Kent Regiment. November 1916		
Heading	War Diary of 8th (S) Battn Royal West Kent Regt from 1st November 1916 to 30th November 1916 (Volume)		
War Diary		01/11/1916	30/11/1916
Heading	8th Battalion Royal West Kent Regiment. December 1916		
Heading	War Diary of 8th (S) Bn Royal West Kent Regt from 1st Dec 1916 to 31st Dec 1916 (Volume)		
War Diary		06/12/1916	30/12/1916
Heading	War Diary of 8th S Bn Royal West Kent Regt from 1st January 1917 to 31st January 1917 (Volume)		
War Diary		01/01/1917	29/01/1917
Miscellaneous	A.G's Office Maine	02/02/1917	02/02/1917
Heading	War Diary of 8th S Battn Royal West Kent Regt from 1.2.1917 to 28.2.1917 (Volume-3)		
War Diary	Trenches	01/02/1917	04/02/1917
War Diary	Philosophe	07/02/1917	07/02/1917
War Diary	Trenches	10/02/1917	12/02/1917
War Diary	Noeux-Les-Mines	13/02/1917	13/02/1917
War Diary	Line-of-March	13/02/1917	13/02/1917
War Diary	Busnette (Par Choque pas de Calais)		
War Diary	Busnette	14/02/1917	16/02/1917
War Diary	Busnette And Training area	17/02/1917	28/02/1917
War Diary	Busnette	18/02/1917	26/02/1917
Heading	War Diary of 8th & Battn Royal West Kent Regt B.E.F. from 1st March 1917 to 31st March 1917 (Volume)		

War Diary	Busnette (Nest area)	01/03/1917	04/03/1917
War Diary	Fouquereuil-Bully Grenay Front Line Trenches	04/03/1917	05/03/1917
War Diary	Trenches	08/03/1917	08/03/1917
War Diary	Bde Support Calonne	09/03/1917	14/03/1917
War Diary	Trenches	16/03/1917	20/03/1917
War Diary	Bully-Grenay	21/03/1917	25/03/1917
War Diary	Bully-Grenay	23/03/1917	23/03/1917
War Diary	Trenches	26/03/1917	26/03/1917
War Diary	Bully Grenay	26/03/1917	28/03/1917
Heading	8th Battn. Royal West Kent Regiment 72nd Infantry Brigade 24th Division April 1917		
Heading	War Diary of 8th S Bn Royal West Kent Regiment for the period 1st April 1917 to 31st April 1917 (Volume)		
War Diary		01/04/1917	29/04/1917
Heading	War Diary of 8th & Battn Royal West Kent Regt from 1st May to 31st. May 1917 (Volume 1)		
War Diary	Delette	01/05/1917	31/05/1917
Heading	War Diary of 8th (S) Battn. Royal West Kent Regiment. from 1st June 1917 to 30th June 1917 (Volume)		
War Diary		01/06/1917	30/06/1917
Heading	War Diary of 8th. (Service) Battalion "Queen's Own" (R.W. Kent Regt.,) from 1st. July 1917 to 31st. July 1917 (Volume)		
War Diary		01/07/1917	31/07/1917
Heading	War Diary of 8th (Service) Battalion Royal West Kent Regiment from 1st. Aug. 1917 to 31st. Aug. 1917 (Volume)		
War Diary		01/08/1917	31/08/1917
War Diary	War Diary of 8th. S. Battalion Royal West Kent Regt., from 1st. Septr to 30th Septr. 1917 (Volume 23)		
War Diary		01/09/1917	30/09/1917
Heading	War Diary of 8th (S) Battn. Royal West Kent Rgt., In-the-field, from 1st Octr. to 31st Oct. 1917 (Volume 24)		
War Diary		01/10/1917	31/10/1917
Heading	War Diary of 8th. S. Battalion Royal West Kent Regt., from 1st. November 1917 to 30th Nov., 1917 (Volume 25)		
War Diary		01/11/1917	30/11/1917
Heading	War Diary of 8th. S. Bn. Royal West Kent Regiment. From 30.11.17 to 31.12.17 Volume 26		
War Diary		01/12/1917	31/12/1917
Heading	War Diary of 8th S Bn. Royal West Kent Regt from 1st Jan 1918 to 31st Jan 1918 (Volume 27)		
War Diary		01/01/1918	31/01/1918
Heading	War Diary of 8th (S) Battalion. Royal West Kent Regiment from 1st. Feb. to 28th. Feb. 1918 (Volume 28)		
War Diary		01/02/1918	28/02/1918
Miscellaneous	Orders for Fighting Patrol. Appendix 1	25/01/1918	25/01/1918
Miscellaneous	Appendix 2	04/02/1918	04/02/1918
Miscellaneous	Battalion Operation Order No. 68 by Lieut-Col. H.J. Wenyon D.S.O. Commanding 8th. S. Battn. Royal West Kent Regiment. In-the-field 17.9.1918	17/09/1918	17/09/1918
Miscellaneous	Battalion Operation Order No. 69 by Lieut-Col. H.J. Wenyon D.S.O. Commanding 8th. S. Battn. Royal West Kent Regiment. In-the-field 20.09.18	20/09/1918	20/09/1918

Heading	8th Battalion Royal West Kent Regiment March 1918		
Heading	War Diary of 8th S. Bn. Royal West Kent Regt. March 1918 (Volume 29)		
War Diary		01/03/1918	31/03/1918
Miscellaneous	Appendix "A". War Diary March/April 1918 8th. (S) Battn. Royal West Kent Regt. Account of operations from 19th. March 1918 to 5th April 1918	08/04/1918	08/04/1918
Heading	8th Battalion Royal West Kent Regiment April 1918		
War Diary		01/04/1918	30/04/1918
Operation(al) Order(s)	Battalion Operation Order No. 1 by Captain R. P. Baker Commanding 8th. S. Battn Royal West Kent Regiment. In-the-field 16 April 1918	16/04/1918	16/04/1918
Heading	War Diary of 8th S.Bn. R.W. Kent Regt. from 1.5.18 to 31.5.1918 Volume		
War Diary		01/05/1918	31/05/1918
Operation(al) Order(s)	Battalion Operation Order No. 69 by Lieut-Col. H.J. Wenyon D.S.O. Commanding 8th. S. Battn. Royal West Kent Regiment.	01/05/1918	01/05/1918
Operation(al) Order(s)	Battalion Operation Orders No. 3 by Lieut.Col. H.J. Wenyon D.S.O. In the Field 8th May 1018	05/05/1918	05/05/1918
Operation(al) Order(s)	Battalion Operation Orders No. 4 by Lieut-Col H.J. Wenyon D.S.O. Commanding 8th. S. Bn. R. West Kent Regt.	12/05/1918	12/05/1918
Operation(al) Order(s)	Battalion Operation Order No. 5 by Lieut-Col. H.J. Wenyon D.S.O. Commanding 8th. S. Battn. Royal West Kent Regiment.	15/05/1918	15/05/1918
Operation(al) Order(s)	Battalion Operation Order No. 7 by Lieut-Col. H.J. Wenyon D.S.O. Commanding 8th. S. Battn. Royal West Kent Regt.	21/05/1918	21/05/1918
Operation(al) Order(s)	Battalion Operation Order No. 6 by Lieut-Col. H.J. Wenyon D.S.O. Commanding 8th S. Battn. Royal West Kent Regiment.	21/05/1918	21/05/1918
Miscellaneous	8th Royal West Kent Regt.	25/05/1918	25/05/1918
Operation(al) Order(s)	Battalion Operation Orders No. 8 by Lieut-Col. H.J. Wenyon D.S.O. Commanding 8th. S. Battn. Royal West Kent Regiment. In-the-field 27th May 1918	27/05/1918	27/05/1918
Heading	War Diary (1st-30th June 1918) 8th S Bn Royal West Kent Regt. (Vol 32)		
War Diary	Bully-Grenay	01/06/1918	03/06/1918
War Diary	St Pierre	04/06/1918	09/06/1918
War Diary	Forward Line	10/06/1918	14/06/1918
War Diary	Bolly-Grenay	15/06/1918	20/06/1918
War Diary	St Pierre	21/06/1918	26/06/1918
War Diary	Forward Line	27/06/1918	30/06/1918
Operation(al) Order(s)	Battalion Operation Order No. 9 by Lieut-Col. H.J. Wenyon D.S.O. Commanding 8th. S. Battn. Royal West Kent Regiment.	03/06/1918	03/06/1918
Operation(al) Order(s)	Battalion Operation Order No. 10 by Lieut-Col. H.J. Wenyon D.S.O. Commanding 8th. S. Battn. Royal West Kent Regt.	08/06/1918	08/06/1918
Operation(al) Order(s)	Battalion Operation Orders No. 11 by Lieut-Col. H.J. Wenyon D.S.O. Commanding 8th S. Battn. Royal West Kent Regiment.	13/06/1918	13/06/1918
Operation(al) Order(s)	Battalion Operation Orders No. 12 by Lieut-Col. H.J. Wenyon D.S.O. Commanding 8th. S. Battn. Royal West Kent Regiment.	19/06/1918	19/06/1918

Operation(al) Order(s)	Battalion Operation Order No. 13 by Captain R.P. Baker. M.G. Commanding 8th. Battn. Royal West Kent Regt.	26/06/1918	26/06/1918
Miscellaneous	Orders for Raid By 2 Officers & 3 Sections.	12/06/1918	12/06/1918
Miscellaneous	Report On Patrol.	13/06/1918	13/06/1918
Heading	War Diary of 8th S.Battn. Royal West Kent Regt from 1st. July. to 31st. July. 1918 (Volume)		
War Diary	Front Line Si Emile Lens	01/07/1918	02/07/1918
War Diary	Bolly-Grenay	03/07/1918	08/07/1918
War Diary	St Pierre	09/07/1918	14/07/1918
War Diary	Front Line	15/07/1918	15/07/1918
War Diary	St Emile Sector Lens Area	16/07/1918	20/07/1918
War Diary	Front Line	20/07/1918	20/07/1918
War Diary	Bully-Grenay	21/07/1918	26/07/1918
War Diary	St Pierre	27/07/1918	31/07/1918
Operation(al) Order(s)	8th Bn. Royal West Kent Regt. Operation Order No. 14	01/07/1918	01/07/1918
Operation(al) Order(s)	Battalion Operation Orders No. 15 by Major P.C. Esdaile Commanding 8th. S. Battn. Royal West Kent Regiment.	07/07/1918	07/07/1918
Miscellaneous	Table "A" Battalion Temporarily Reduced To Lower Establishment (900 Other Ranks).		
Operation(al) Order(s)	8th B. Bn. Royal West Kent Regiment. Order No. 16		
Operation(al) Order(s)	8th. S. Bn. Royal West Kent Regt. Order No. 17		
Operation(al) Order(s)	8th S. Battn. R.W. Kent Regiment. Order No.18	25/07/1918	25/07/1918
Operation(al) Order(s)	8th S. Battn. Royal West Kent Regt. Order No 19	31/07/1918	31/07/1918
Diagram etc			
Heading	War Diary of 8th S Battn. Royal West Kent Regt from 1.8.1918 to 31.8.1918 (Volume)		
War Diary		01/08/1918	31/08/1918
Diagram etc	Appendix VIII		
Miscellaneous	Battalion Organization	10/08/1918	10/08/1918
Operation(al) Order(s)	8th. S. Bn. Royal West Kent Regt. Order No. 20	06/08/1918	06/08/1918
Operation(al) Order(s)	8th. S. Bn. Royal West Kent Regt. Order No. 21	12/08/1918	12/08/1918
Operation(al) Order(s)	8th. S. Bn. Royal West Kent Regt. Order No. 22	18/08/1918	18/08/1918
Operation(al) Order(s)	8th S. Bn. Royal West Kent Regt. Order No. 23	24/08/1918	24/08/1918
Operation(al) Order(s)	8th. S. Bn. Royal West Kent Regt. Order No. 24	30/08/1918	30/08/1918
Heading	War Diary of 8th S. Battn. Royal West Kent Regt from 1.9.18 to 30.9.18 (Volume 35)		
War Diary	Front Line	01/09/1918	12/09/1918
War Diary	Bolly-Grenay	13/09/1918	18/09/1918
War Diary	Front Line	19/09/1918	30/09/1918
Operation(al) Order(s)	8th. S. Bn. Royal West Kent Regt. Operation Order No. 25.	01/09/1918	01/09/1918
Operation(al) Order(s)	8th. S. Bn. Royal West Kent Regt. Operation Order No.	11/09/1918	11/09/1918
Operation(al) Order(s)	8th. S. Bn. Royal West Kent Regt. Order No. 27	18/09/1918	18/09/1918
Operation(al) Order(s)	8th. S. Battn. Royal West Kent Regiment.	26/09/1918	26/09/1918
Operation(al) Order(s)	8th. (S). Bn. Royal West Kent Regt. Order No. 28	28/09/1918	28/09/1918
Operation(al) Order(s)	8th. (S). Bn. Royal West Kent Regt. Order No. 29	29/09/1918	29/09/1918
Miscellaneous	Report On Hostile Raid On Post At N. 8.D. 3.5.	24/09/1918	24/09/1918
Miscellaneous		25/09/1918	25/09/1918
Heading	War Diary of 8th S. Battn. Royal West Kent Regt from 1st Oct. 1918 to 31st October 1918 (Volume 36)		
War Diary	Su & St Leger	01/10/1918	06/10/1918
War Diary	Graincourt	07/10/1918	16/10/1918
War Diary	Cambrai	17/10/1918	31/10/1918
Operation(al) Order(s)	8th. (S). Battn. Rl. West Kent Regt. Order No. 30	05/10/1918	05/10/1918

Operation(al) Order(s)	8th Royal West Kent Regiment Operation Orders	17/10/1918	17/10/1918
Heading	War Diary of 8th S. Battn. Royal West Kent Regt from 1 Nov. 1918 to 30th Nov 1918 (Volume 37)		
War Diary	Avesnes	01/11/1918	02/11/1918
War Diary	Haussy	03/11/1918	03/11/1918
War Diary	Septmeries	04/11/1918	04/11/1918
War Diary	Wargnies	05/11/1918	05/11/1918
War Diary	Le Grand	06/11/1918	09/11/1918
War Diary	Fiegnies	10/11/1918	10/11/1918
War Diary	Pissotiau	11/11/1918	16/11/1918
War Diary	Septmeries	17/11/1918	17/11/1918
War Diary	Lourghes	18/11/1918	18/11/1918
War Diary	Bruille	19/11/1918	20/11/1918
War Diary	Masny	21/11/1918	24/11/1918
War Diary	Nomain	26/11/1918	30/11/1918
Operation(al) Order(s)	8th. S. Bn. Royal West Kent Regiment Order No. 53	01/11/1918	01/11/1918
Operation(al) Order(s)	8th. S. Battn. Royal West Kent Regiment Order No. 34	03/11/1918	03/11/1918
Operation(al) Order(s)	8th. S. Bn. Royal West Kent Regiment Order No.	10/11/1918	10/11/1918
Operation(al) Order(s)	8th. S. Bn. Royal West Kent Regiment Order No. 36	18/11/1918	18/11/1918
Operation(al) Order(s)	8th. S. Bn. Royal West Kent Regiment Order No. 37 In-the-field., 20th November 1918	20/11/1918	20/11/1918
Operation(al) Order(s)	8th. S. Bn. Royal West Kent Regiment Order No. 38 In-the-field., 24th November 1918 Appendix H 2	24/11/1918	24/11/1918
Miscellaneous	Appendix F	18/11/1918	18/11/1918
Miscellaneous	Appendix E	17/11/1918	17/11/1918
Operation(al) Order(s)	8th. S. Bn. Royal West Kent Regt. Order No. 39	25/11/1918	25/11/1918
Heading	War Diary of 8th S. Battn. Royal West Kent Regt from 1st Dec 1918 to 31st Dec 1918 (Volume 38)		
War Diary	Nomain	01/12/1918	17/12/1918
War Diary	Tournai	18/12/1918	31/12/1918
Miscellaneous	Battalion Order by Lieut-Col. H.J. Wenyon D.S.O. Commanding 8th. S. Battn. Royal West Kent Regiment. Appendix A	03/12/1916	03/12/1916
Operation(al) Order(s)	8th. S. Bn. Royal West Kent Regt. Order No. 40 Appendix B	17/12/1918	17/12/1918
Heading	War Diary of 8th S. Bn. R.W.Kent Regt. from 1.1.1919 to 31.1.1919 (Volume 39)		
War Diary	Tournai	01/01/1919	31/01/1919
Heading	War Diary of 8th S. Bn. Royal West Kent Regt for February 1919 (Volume 40)		
War Diary	Tournai	01/02/1919	28/02/1919
Miscellaneous	Presentation Of Colours on the Champs de Lanouvres Tournai	21/02/1919	21/02/1919
Miscellaneous	Roll of Cadre Establishment. 8th S. Bn. Royal West Kent Regiment.		
Heading	War Diary of 8th S. Bn. Royal West Kent Regt for March 1919 (Volume 41)		
War Diary	Tournai	01/03/1919	26/03/1919
War Diary	Lamain	27/03/1919	30/04/1919

24TH DIVISION
72ND INFY BDE

8TH BN THE QUEEN'S OWN
(ROY. WEST KENT REGT)
AUG 1915 - APR 1919

72nd Inf.Bde.
24th Div.

Battn. disembarked Havre from England 1.9.15.

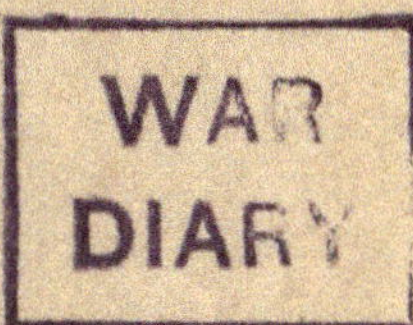

8th BATTN. THE QUEEN'S OWN (ROYAL WEST KENT REGIMENT).

S E P T E M B E R

(29.8.15 to 30.9.15)

1 9 1 5

6

apl 1919

VOLUME I

WAR DIARY
or
INTELLIGENCE SUMMARY
(Erase heading not required.)

8th R. West Kent

Army Form C. 2118

Instructions regarding War Diaries and Intelligence Summaries are contained in F. S. Regs., Part II. and the Staff Manual respectively. Title Pages will be prepared in manuscript.

Place	Date	Hour	Summary of Events and Information	Remarks and references to Appendices
BLACKDOWN CAMP. ALDERSHOT.	29th Aug.		Leave for SOUTHAMPTON.	
SOUTHAMPTON	30th		Stay at S'HAMPTON.	
HAVRE	1st Sept.		Arrive & stay 1 Day & 1 Night	
	2nd		Leave HAVRE for MONTREUIL	
	3rd		Arrive MONTREUIL & march to HUCQELIERS to Billets	
	4 – 20th		Training Carried on vigorously.	
	21st		Leave HUCQELIERS & march to ~~SO~~ BEUVRY via ISBERGUES.	
	25th		Arrive BEUVRY	
	26th		Attack HULLUCH, loose 3/4 of Battalion.	
	27th		Withdrawn to MOLLINGHEM.	
	28th		Arrive MOLLINGHEM.	
	29th 31st		MOLLINGHEM.	

W. Lewis Lt Adj.
8th R West Kent.

1875 Wt. W593/826 1,000,000 4/15 I.B.C. & A. A.D.S.S./Forms/C. 2118.

24th Division

72/114

8th R. W. Kent

Vol: I

121/7624

~~Sept.~~ Oct and to Nov 15

Vol: 11.

Instructions regarding War Diaries and Intelligence Summaries are contained in F. S. Regs., Part II. and the Staff Manual respectively. Title Pages will be prepared in manuscript.

WAR DIARY
or
INTELLIGENCE SUMMARY
(Erase heading not required.)

8/R. West Kent

Army Form C. 2118

Place	Date	Hour	Summary of Events and Information	Remarks and references to Appendices
HOUTKERQUE			The Battalion arrived from Wellingham & went into billets.	
	21/9/- to 4/10/-		Various Drafts were rec'd from 3rd & 9th Battalions. Re-organizing the Battalion & re-equiping. Nothing of note took place whatever. N.K.S.	
RENINGHELST.	5/10/- to 14/10/-		The Battalion moved into Tents & Huts here and work was Carried on, bombing & sniping having great attention, more drafts were rec'd also 8 officers reported for Duty. Major S. C. Parker took over Command of Battalion N.K.S.	
SPOIL BANK – CANAL BANK	15-19th		The Battalion moved from Reninghelst into Reserve Dugouts to Trenches 28 29 30. Instruction in Trenches & Fatigue & R.E. Carrying parties taking up most of the time. Four Casualties. N.K.S.	
RENINGHELST.	20-23rd		Return from Trenches. Work Carried on as before. Drafts require knocking into shape. N.K.S.	

1875 Wt. W593/826 1,000,000 4/15 J.B.C. & A. A.D.S.S./Forms/C. 2118.

Vol: II Cont.

Instructions regarding War Diaries and Intelligence Summaries are contained in F. S. Regs., Part II. and the Staff Manual respectively. Title Pages will be prepared in manuscript.

WAR DIARY
or
INTELLIGENCE SUMMARY

(Erase heading not required.)

8/ R. West Kents

Army Form C. 2118

Place	Date	Hour	Summary of Events and Information	Remarks and references to Appendices
Trenches. Voormezeele	24 - 28th		Took over Trenches from 1st N. Staffords. Nothing of note in our tour of duty in the Trenches. Very few Casualties. W.K.S.	
RENINGHELST.	29 - 2 Nov.		Return & Continue work reorganizing Bombers, Snipers etc. W.K.S.	
DEAD DOG FARM.	3rd - 7th		Took over from 9th Sussex Trenches P1. P2. P3. P4. Much rain, men had very bad feet. W.K.S.	
RENINGHELST.	8 - 12th		Work Continued, road making in the Camp & Transport lines. 1 Company at CANAL BANK on R.E. Carrying work. W.K.S.	

W. K. Sime Lt. Adj. 8/ Royal West Kents

1875 Wt. W593/826 1,000,000 4/15 J.B.C. & A. A.D.S.S./Forms/C. 2118.

Vol: III

Instructions regarding War Diaries and Intelligence Summaries are contained in F. S. Regs., Part II. and the Staff Manual respectively. Title Pages will be prepared in manuscript.

WAR DIARY
or
~~INTELLIGENCE SUMMARY~~
(Erase heading not required.)

8/ R. West Kents. Army Form C. 2118

Place	Date	Hour	Summary of Events and Information	Remarks and references to Appendices
RENINGHELST.	1-2 Nov:		Rest. WRD.	
DEAD DOG FARM. 2-7th			Took over trenches P1. P2. P3. P4 from 9th R. Sussex. Much Rain & Mud. Men had bad feet. Constant Re-building of trenches. WRD.	
RENINGHELST 8-12			Work continued on Rest Camp. Road & Path Making etc. 1 Company at CANAL BANK on R.E. Fatigue work. WRD.	

[illegible]
[illegible]
8/R. West Kents.

Vol: III. (Contd)

WAR DIARY
or
~~INTELLIGENCE SUMMARY~~
(Erase heading not required.)

8/R. West Kent. Army Form C. 2118

Instructions regarding War Diaries and Intelligence Summaries are contained in F. S. Regs., Part II. and the Staff Manual respectively. Title Pages will be prepared in manuscript.

Place	Date	Hour	Summary of Events and Information	Remarks and references to Appendices
RENINGHELST.	12th Nov:		Moved into Trenches at St ELOI taking over from 1st N. Staffords. [illegible]	
	17th		Relieved by 1st N: Staffords. Return RENINGHELST. [illegible]	
	18 / 19		RENINGHELST. Relieved by 2nd Suffolks.	
	20th		Move back to ~~EEXXX~~ EECKE. [illegible]	
	21st		EECKE.	
	22nd		Move to OCHTEZEELE.	
	23rd		〃 〃 HOULE. [illegible]	
	24th		Remain at HOULE	
	25th		Move to BONNINGUES. [illegible]	
	26th / 27th		BONNINGUES. In Rest billets	
	28th / 29th / 30th		Training. Re-fitting & Re-organizing Courses on Reorganising.	

[illegible] Lt. Col.
8/R. West Kents.

1875 Wt. W593/826 1,000,000 4/15 J.B.C. & A. A.D.S.S./Forms/C. 2118.

24th Div

8th R. West Kent

Vol. 2

December 1915

121
7928

2/6

Instructions regarding War Diaries and Intelligence Summaries are contained in F. S. Regs., Part II. and the Staff Manual respectively. Title Pages will be prepared in manuscript.

8th Queens Own R. West Kent Regt

WAR DIARY
or
INTELLIGENCE SUMMARY

(Erase heading not required.)

Army Form C. 2118

Place	Date	Hour	Summary of Events and Information	Remarks and references to Appendices
BONNINGUES to ARDRES (Pas de C.)	1st Dec: till 31st Dec.		The Battalion in Rest Area. Training of all kinds Carried on Continuously. Nothing of Note took place. W.K.T.	

W.K. [illegible] Capt. Adj
8/ R. West Kent Regt.
[illegible] 12. 15

1875 Wt. W593/826 1,000,000 4/15 J.B.C. & A. A.D.S.S./Forms/C. 2118.

24th Division
72nd Brigade.

8th BATTALION

ROYAL WEST KENT REGIMENT.

JANUARY 1 9 1 6

Instructions regarding War Diaries and Intelligence Summaries are contained in F. S. Regs., Part II. and the Staff Manual respectively. Title Pages will be prepared in manuscript.

WAR DIARY
or
~~INTELLIGENCE SUMMARY~~
(Erase heading not required.)

8th Royal West Kent Regt.

Army Form C. 2118

Place	Date	Hour	Summary of Events and Information	Remarks and references to Appendices
	1/1/16 to 4/1/16.		Rest Area. BONNINGUES les ARDRES. BKD	
	5th Jan:		Move to OUDERDOM. BKD	
	6th –		Take over Right of Right Sector HOOGE from 12th Manchester Regt. BKD	
	7 – 11th		Trenches, few casualties. BKD	
	12 – 14th		Battalion in Support CH: BELGE sheet 28. H23 b55. BKD	
	15 – 26th		Rest OUDERDOM & Divisional Reserve. Training Continued. BKD	
	27th – 31st		Take over left of left Sector HOOGE from 8th The Queens. BKD	
			While in trenches 2 casualties. Very quiet. BKD	
	1st – 4th Feby:			

B. K. Dave [illegible]
Capt: Adjt
8 R. West Kent Regt.

2. 2. 16

1875 Wt. W593/826 1,000,000 4/15 J.B.C. & A. A.D.S.S./Forms/C. 2118.

24th Division
72nd Brigade.

8th BATTALION

ROYAL WEST KENT REGIMENT.

FEBRUARY 1 9 1 6

Instructions regarding War Diaries and Intelligence Summaries are contained in F. S. Regs., Part II. and the Staff Manual respectively. Title Pages will be prepared in manuscript.

WAR DIARY
or
~~INTELLIGENCE SUMMARY~~
(Erase heading not required.)

8th Royal West Kent Regt.

Army Form C. 2118

Place	Date	Hour	Summary of Events and Information	Remarks and references to Appendices
	1st 4th	Febr:–	1½ Coys: in Rest. 2½ Coys: in support Railway Wood Trenches – in Ypres. WHD	
	5–	8th	A Take over Railway Wood + A1 A2 Trenches from 8th The Queens. Hold same till 8th Febr: WHD Relieved in this Sector on 8th Febr: by 2nd Leinster Regt. WHD	
	8th	15th	Rest in Camp C. WHD	
	16th		Move into support of Sanctuary Wood Trenches, at CH: BELGE Dugouts. WHD Taking over same from 6th The Buffs.	
	19th – 23rd		Take over + hold Sanctuary Wood Trenches from 8th The Queens. WHD	
	24/27th		CH: BELGE support Dugouts. WHD	
	29th		Take over Sanctuary Wood from 8th The Queens. WHD	

1875 Wt. W593/826 1,000,000 4/15 J.B.C. & A. A.D.S.S./Forms/C. 2118.

24th Division
72nd Brigade

8th BATTALION

ROYAL WEST KENT REGIMENT.

MARCH 1 9 1 6

Instructions regarding War Diaries and Intelligence Summaries are contained in F. S. Regs., Part II. and the Staff Manual respectively. Title Pages will be prepared in manuscript.

WAR DIARY

or

~~INTELLIGENCE SUMMARY~~

(Erase heading not required.)

8th Royal West Kent Regt.

Army Form C. 2118

Place	Date	Hour	Summary of Events and Information	Remarks and references to Appendices
1st March			CH. BELGE DUGOUTS & move to SANCTUARY WOOD to relieve 8th The Queens on 2nd March. [initials]	
2nd March	to 7th		SANCTUARY WOOD Trenches. Casualties slight. [initials]	
8th March			Take over Rest Camp A from 13th Middlesex Rgt. [initials]	
9 –	15th		CAMP A. Working parties by train to ASYLUM every night, work in Salient. [initials]	
March	12th		2/Lts FOWLER. J.H. COULDEN. E.O. GASCOYNE. W.L. BOWLING E.R. report for duty from 9th Battn	[initials]
"	13th		Capt WHEELER. H.B. reports for duty from 3rd Battn. [initials]	
March	16th		Move into SANCTUARY WOOD Support at CH: BELGE DUGOUTS. [initials]	
March	16/20		CH: BELGE. [initials]	
"	17th		2/Lt GASCOYNE wounded, suffering gas poisoning. [initials]	
March	20/21st		Relieved at CH. BELGE by 5th CANADIAN Mounted Rifles & move Camp F. [initials]	
March	22.		Move to BERTHEN (vide copy operation order 31 attached). [initials]	
	23rd/25		BERTHEN. Reconnoitre new Area. [initials]	
	26th		Move BRANOUTRE (vide operation order 32 attached). [initials]	
	27th		Move into Trenches at (Sheet 28) T5b. Trenches No C3. C4. D1 & D2 & 1 Coy support. Trenches taken over from 4th CANADIAN Battn	[initials]
	28 - 31st		In Trenches. Few Casualties. [initials]	

M. Kidson? Capt. Adj. 8th R. West Kent Rgt.

1875 Wt. W593/826 1,000,000 4/15 J.B.C. & A. A.D.S.S./Forms/C. 2118.

COPY.

72nd. I.B. Operation Order No.31.

Reference Maps
ø 1/40,000
Sheets 27 & 28.

19.3.'16.

MOVE. 1. The 72nd. Infantry Brigade will move to a new area on 21.3 '16. as shown in attached Table.

AREA. 2. Detail's of Units areas have already been issued.

ADVANCE PARTIES. 3. Advance parties will proceed to new area by bus from G.24.d.3.2. sheet 28 at 9 a.m.20.3.'16 returning from BERTHEN at 5 p.m.

SUPPLIES. 4. Guides for supply wagons on 21.3.'16 will be at WESTOUTRE at 11 a.m.

EXTRA TRANSPORT 5. Lorries for surplus baggage and blankets will be provided as follows on 21.3.'16 :-

NUMBER.	FOR.	AT.	TIME.	REMARKS.
2 lorries.	8th.R.W.Kent Regiment.	Camp F H.19.b.	8.30 a.m.	1 lorry for Blankets. 1 " " Baggage. The blanket lorry will make two journeys.

These lorries will proceed to Square,Poperinghe. They will join up there at 11 a.m. and proceed to BERTHEN, under an Officer to be detailed by 9th. Bn. East Surrey Regiment.

Units will have guides for these lorries at BERTHEN at 12 noon on 21.3.'16, who will guide them to their areas.

Blanket lorries will be unloaded at one central spot in each area, and will return at once to G.5.c.9.1. Sheet 28 and Camps E and F H 19.b. sheet 28 for a second load of blankets. This second load will then be taken to the unloading ground in each Unit's area..

6. Billetting parties will proceed to new areas on the morning of 21.3;'16.

7. The arrival of units in new area will be notified to Head quarters, 72nd. Infantry Brigade at R.19.d.6.5. Sheet 27.

8. On arrival in new area, units will send two orderlies to Headquarters, 72nd. Infantry Brigade.

(Signed). O.S.NELTHORPE
Captain.,
Brigade Major.,
72nd.Infantry Brigade.

MOUNTED COLUMN.(Table A)

UNIT.	STARTING POINT.	TIME.	ROUTE.	TO.	GUIDES FROM UNITS AT.
TRANSPORT. 8TH.ROYAL WEST KENT REGIMENT.	TRAIL TO BE CLEAR OF RENINGHELST SQUARE AT-	3.22 pm.	RENINGHELST- HEKSEN- WESTOUTRE- MT.KOKEREELE- BERTHEN.	R.20) R.21) R.22) R.27) R.28) R.33)	(27). R.22.a.5.0. (27).

DISMOUNTED COLUMN. (Table B)

UNIT.	STARTING POINT.	TIME.	ROUTE.	TO.	GUIDES FROM UNITS AT.
8th.ROYAL WEST KENT REGIMENT.	TRAIL TO BE CLEAR OF RENINGHELST SQUARE AT-	4.40 p.m.	RENINGHELST- HEKSEN- WESTOUTRE- MT.KOKEREELE- BERTHEN-	LE COQ. DE PAILLE. R.25. R.26. R.31 R.32 R.27 Sheet 27.	R.22.a.5.0. Sheet 27.

72nd. Infantry Brigade OPERATION ORDER NO.32.

23rd. March 1916.

1. The 72nd. Infantry Brigade will relieve the 1st. Canadian Infantry Brigade in the line between the 26th. and 28th. March 1916.

2. The 8th. (s) Bn. Royal West Kent Regt. will relieve the 4th. Canadian Battalion in the right trenches.

5. The Lewis Guns of the 72nd. Infantry Brigade will relieve as under:-

8th. Battn. Royal West Kent Regt's guns relieve the 4th. Canadian Battalion's guns in right front trenches.

6. The Grenadiers of the 9th. East Surrey Regt. and 8th. Royal West Kent Regt. will relieve on the morning of the 27.3.'16 under arrangements made by the Battalion Grenade Officers.

7. Battalions will take over and man all observation posts in their sector.

8. All trench stores, log books, maps, defence schemes and tables of work in hand and proposed, will be taken over, receipts to be forwarded to Headquarters, 72nd. Infantry Brigade.

9. 72nd. Infantry Brigade Headquarters will move to N.33.d.4.1 by 3.0 p.m. on 27.3.'16.

DATE.	UNIT.	FROM.	TO.	TIME.	ROUTE.	REMARKS
26.3.16.	8th. ROYAL WEST KENT REGIMENT.	REST AREA.	DIVISIONAL RESERVE. DRANOUTRE.	To arrive by 11 a.m. not to pass X.4.c.3.3. (27) before 7.45 a.m.	R.33.(27) X.4.a.7.6.(27) X.4.c.3.3.(27) R.35 central(27) St.JAN CAPEL. M.26.d.1.1.(28) S.9.a.6.7.(28) S.5.b.8.4.(28) DRANOUTRE.	In relief of 2nd. CANADIAN BATTALION.
Night 27/28th. March '16.	8th. ROYAL WEST KENT REGT.	DIVISIONAL RESERVE.	Right Trenches.	-----	-----	In relief of 4th. CANADIAN BATTALION.

NOTE-

TRANSPORT CAMPS ARE ALLOTTED AS UNDER:-

8th. ROYAL WEST KENT REGT. --- 2nd. CANADIAN BATTALION LINES.

DATE.	UNIT.	FROM.	TO.	TIME.	ROUTE.	REMARKS
27.3.'16.	8th. Battn. ROYAL WEST KENT REGT's Lewis Guns.	Rest area.	To Right Trenches. in relief of 4th. Canadian Battn's. Guns.		R.33 (27) X.4.a.7.6.(27) X.4.c.3.3 (27) R.35 central (27) ST.JAN CAPEL. M.26.d.1.1.(28) S.9.a.6.7.(28) S.5.b.8.4(28) DRANOUTRE.	

24th Division
72nd Brigade.

8th Battalion

ROYAL WEST KENTS REGIMENT.

APRIL 1916

8 West Kent
Army Form C. 2118
Vol 6

XXIV

Instructions regarding War Diaries and Intelligence Summaries are contained in F. S. Regs., Part II. and the Staff Manual respectively. Title Pages will be prepared in manuscript.

8th. Royal West Kent Regt.

WAR DIARY
or
~~INTELLIGENCE SUMMARY~~

(Erase heading not required.)

Place	Date	Hour	Summary of Events and Information	Remarks and references to Appendices
Front line trenches Right Sector	1/2 April.		Trenches at WULYERGHEM. C3. C4. D1. and D2. roughly T.6.b. Sheet 28 1/40,000.	
	2/3 April.		Para. 3. The 8th. Battn. The QUEENS Regt. will relieve the 8th. Bn. Royal West Kent Regt. in the right trenches on the night of 2/3 Apr. 1916. The 8th. Royal West Kent Regt. on relief will move into Brigade Reserve at "TEA FARM", "KANDAHAR" and "AIRCRAFT FARMS". The 8th Queens Regt. will not move in relief before midnight 2/3 April 1916.	72nd. I.B. Operation Order No. 33.
	8th. April.	5-20 am.	TEA FARM hit by 5.9 shell 8 Killed 5 Wounded. Headquarters moved to "KANDAHAR". FARM.	
			Para 3. The 8th. Royal West Kent Regt. will relieve the 8th. Queens in the right trenches on the night of 8/9 April 1916. Relief to be complete by 11 pm.	72nd. I.B. Operation Order No. 34.
	10th. April.		2/Lieut Eldridge wounded.	
			Para 2. The 8th. Battn. the Queens Regt. will relieve the 8th Battn. Royal West Kent Regt. in the right trenches on night 14/15 April 1916. The 8th. Royal West Kent Regt. will, on relief, move to Divisional Reserve DRANOUTRE.	72nd. I. B. Operation Order No. 35.

1875 Wt. W593/826 1,000,000 4/15 J.B.C. & A. A.D.S.S./Forms/C. 2118.

8th. Royal West Kent Regt.

WAR DIARY

or

~~INTELLIGENCE SUMMARY~~

(Erase heading not required.)

Army Form C. 2118

Instructions regarding War Diaries and Intelligence Summaries are contained in F. S. Regs., Part II. and the Staff Manual respectively. Title Pages will be prepared in manuscript.

Place	Date	Hour	Summary of Events and Information	Remarks and references to Appendices
	20/21 April 1916.		Para 2. The 8th. Battn. Royal West Kent Regt. will relieve the 8th. Battn. The Queens Regt. in the trenches on the night of 20/21 April 1916.	72nd I.B. Operation Order No. 36
	21st. to 26th.		Right Trenches.	
	22nd.		2/Lieut. Roscoe, Allworth, Willoughby, James report for duty.	
	26th.		2/Lieut. Flowers reports for duty.	
			Para. 2. The 8th. Battn. The Queens Regt. will relieve the 8th. Battn. Royal West Kent Regt. in the right trenches on the night 26/27 April 1916. The 8th. Battn. Royal West Kent Regt. on relief will move into Brigade Reserve.	72nd. I.B. Operation Order. No.37.
	27th.		Gas Alarm on account of prisoners reports."STAND TO" nightly 2-0 am.	
	27/30.		Brigade Reserve.	

1875 Wt. W593/826 1,000,000 4/15 J.B.C. & A. A.D.S.S./Forms/C. 2118.

24th Division
72nd Brigade.

8th BATTALION

ROYAL WEST KENT REGIMENT.

M A Y 1 9 1 6

8th Bn. Royal West Kent Regt.

Instructions regarding War Diaries and Intelligence Summaries are contained in F. S. Regs., Part II. and the Staff Manual respectively. Title Pages will be prepared in manuscript.

WAR DIARY
or
INTELLIGENCE SUMMARY
(Erase heading not required.)

Army Form C. 2118

XXIV 8 West Kent

Vol 7

Place	Date	Hour	Summary of Events and Information	Remarks and references to Appendices
Field	1/2 May		Brigade Reserve. Bus Farm. "Stand To" during Gas Alert period continued	
"	3/8th May		Front Line trenches. Right Sector Para II The 8th R.W. Kent Regt will relieve the 8th Queen's in the right trenches on the night of 2/3rd May 1916.	72 I B Operation Order No 39
"	6th May	8.10pm	St QUENTIN CABARET shelled with 5.9's. No damage. No casualties.	
"	9/14th May		In Divisional Reserve at Dranoutre.	
Dranoutre	11th May		Lieut. N.B. Green joined for duty + posted to 'D' Company	
	14th May		2/Lieut. B Vaughan and draft 19 other ranks joined for duty	
Front Line trenches	15th/19th		Para II The 8th R.W. Kent will relieve the 8th Queen's Regt in the right trenches on the night 14/15th May 1915	72 I B Operation Order No 42
do	17th	12.20 am	False Gas Alarm sounded. 'Stood To' for 20 minutes	
	18th		2/Lieut Woolley joined for duty + posted to 'C' Company	
	20th	12.25 am	Relieved by 8th Queen's Regt moved into Brigade Reserve at AIRCRAFT, KANDAHAR + N 33 central	
	21st		Para Major Whitty and party (100) 8th R.W. Kent Regt will move to farm M 36 a. 9½. 1½ by 6pm 22nd where the party will be billetted	72 I B Operation Order No 44

1875 Wt. W593/826 1,000,000 4/15 J.B.C. & A. A.D.S.S./Forms/C. 2118.

Army Form C. 2118

Instructions regarding War Diaries and Intelligence Summaries are contained in F. S. Regs., Part II. and the Staff Manual respectively. Title Pages will be prepared in manuscript.

WAR DIARY
or
INTELLIGENCE SUMMARY
(Erase heading not required.)

Place	Date	Hour	Summary of Events and Information	Remarks and references to Appendices
Front line Trenches	24/30th May		Para II The 8th Bn Royal West Kent Regt. will relieve the 8th Bn The Queens Regt. in the right trenches on the night 24/25th May 1916	72 SB Operation Order No 45
	31st May		Divisional Reserve at Dranoutre	
	31st	" 12-30 am	Captain W. Wood Commanding 'A' Company Killed.	
			2/Lieut Kenyon assumed command of 'A' Company	

[illegible] Lieut & Adjt.
8/R W Kent Regt

1875 Wt. W593/826 1,000,000 4/15 J.B.C. & A. A.D.S.S./Forms/C. 2118.

24th Division
72nd Brigade.

<u>8th BATTALION</u>

<u>ROYAL WEST KENT REGIMENT</u>

<u>J U N E 1 9 1 6</u>

Instructions regarding War Diaries and Intelligence Summaries are contained in F. S. Regs., Part II. and the Staff Manual respectively. Title Pages will be prepared in manuscript.

WAR DIARY or INTELLIGENCE SUMMARY

(Erase heading not required.)

Army Form C. 2118

XXIV

Vol 8.

June 1916

8th Bn. Royal W. Kent Regiment

Place	Date	Hour	Summary of Events and Information	Remarks and references to Appendices
Dranoutre	1st to 5th		Divisional Reserve.	
	2nd.		Draft of 175 other ranks joined.	
	4th		Lieut. E. R. Bowling killed.	
	Night of 4th/5th		Raiding party under Major H. S. White attempted to enter enemy's trenches at 28. N. 36. d. Attempt not successful owing to wire being insufficiently broken	
	5th		Captain ? Knox-Wright and Lieut. B/ M. Apperley joined for duty.	
Field.			Para. II ~~Bng~~ "The 8th Bn. R.W.Kent Regiment will relieve the 8th Bn. The Queen's Regiment in the right trenches on the night 5/6th June 1916"	73. I. B. Operation Order No. 47.
	6th to 13th		Front line trenches. Right Sector.	
	8th		Lieut. N. B. Green wounded.	
	9th		Draft of 12 other ranks joined	
			Para. II – The 8th Bn. The Queen's Regt. will relieve the 8th R.W.Kent Regt. in the right trenches on the night 13/14th June 1916.	73. I. B. Op. Order No. 48.
	14th to 18th		Brigade Reserve at Aircraft & Kandahar Farm and houses at 28 N 33 central.	
	16th.		Captain L.M. Kepp-Page and 15 Other ranks joined.	
	17th		At about 12.30 am Enemy released gas opposite sector held by 73rd Inf. Bde. Battalion moved to positions vide 73rd Inf. Bde. Defence Scheme. Casualties – 48	
			Para. II The 8th Bn. R. W. Kent Regt. will relieve the 8th Bn. Queen's Regt. in the right sector on the night 18/19th June 1916.	73. I. B. Op. Orders No. 50.
	18th to 30th		Front Line Trenches. Right Sector.	
	21st		Draft of 11 Other ranks joined.	

640/SP

1875 Wt. W593/826 1,000,000 4/15 J. B. C. & A. A.D.S.S./Forms/C. 2118.

Instructions regarding War Diaries and Intelligence Summaries are contained in F. S. Regs., Part II. and the Staff Manual respectively. Title Pages will be prepared in manuscript.

WAR DIARY
or
INTELLIGENCE SUMMARY
(Erase heading not required.)

Army Form C. 2118

June 1916 — 8th. Bn. Royal W. Kent Regt.

Place	Date	Hour	Summary of Events and Information	Remarks and references to Appendices
Field	28th	11.31 p.	Gas was released from our front and a raiding party of the 8th Queen's Regt. entered the enemy trenches, and inflicted several casualties. 5 prisoners were taken	
	29th		Enemy heavily bombarded our sector in retaliation for our gas discharges on the 28th. Our Casualties 40. Lieut. L. J. Vinecombe killed.	
			para II "On completion of the relief of the 8th R.W.Kent Regt on the night 30th June/1st July 1916 the Command of ~~ow~~ the C.R.D. trenches will pass to the B.G.C. 7th. Aus. Brigade.	72. I. B. Op. Order No. 55.
	30th		On relief the Battalion moved into Divisional Reserve to the 7th. Australian Brigade at KORTEPYP.	

Field
1. 7. 1916.

A. J. J. Mullen Lieut & Adjt.
for Lt. Colonel
Comdg. 8th R.W.Kent Regt.

1875 Wt. W593/826 1,000,000 4/15 J. B. C. & A. A.D.S.S./Forms/C. 2118.

72nd Inf.Bde.
24th Div.

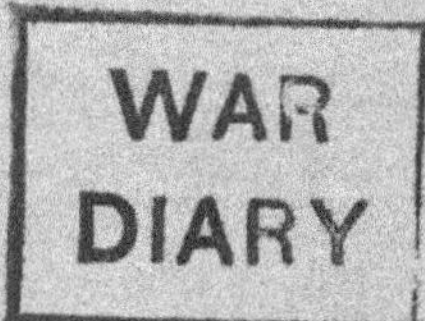

8th BATTN. THE QUEEN'S OWN (ROYAL WEST KENT REGIMENT).

J U L Y

1 9 1 6

Instructions regarding War Diaries and Intelligence Summaries are contained in F. S. Regs., Part II. and the Staff Manual respectively. Title Pages will be prepared in manuscript.

July 1916.

WAR DIARY or INTELLIGENCE SUMMARY

(Erase heading not required.)

8th Bn Royal W. Kent Regt.

Army Form C. 2118

24 July

Vol 9

Place	Date July 1916	Hour	Summary of Events and Information	Remarks and references to Appendices
Field	1st/3rd		Divisional Reserve at Kortepyp Huts to 7th Australian Brigade	
	1st		Capt. J. Knox-Wright joined 2nd Army Signal Coy. on probation.	
	2nd		Lieut. C. McCabe proceeded to Machine Gun School, Camiers, for Lewis Gun Course.	
"	4th	2.15pm	"On the 4.7.16 the 8th R.W.Kent Regt. will move from KORTEPYP to Rest Area METEREN. Camp vacated by 3rd Bn. Rifle Bde."	72nd I.B.O.O. No.56 d/ 1.7.1916
	4th/8th		Rest at Rest Area, Meteren.	
"	8th		"The 72nd Inf. Bde will relieve the 7th and 2nd Australian Brigades in the trenches on the night of 8/9th July 1916	
			"5. 8th R.W.Kent will move into reserve at KORTEPYP HUTS."	72nd I.B.O.O. No.56 undated (Comdrs 8.7.16)
"	9th/18th		Divisional Reserve at KORTEPYP HUTS	
"	18th		"The 8th R.W.Kent Regt. will relieve the 1st N. Staffs. Regt in the left trenches (138 – 141 (both incl)) on the night 18/19th July 1916 "Relief to be completed by 12 midnight."	72nd I.B.O.O. No.58 d/ 14.7.16
	19th/20th		Front Line, Trenches 138 to 141. Headqrs. FISHERS PLACE	
"	20th		"The 72nd Inf. Bde. will be relieved in the front line by a Brigade of the 20th Division on 19th and 20th July 1916	72nd I.B.O.O. No.62 d/ 19.7.16
			Night of 20th/21st relieved by 11th Bn. Rifle Bde. – relief complete 2.23am 21.7.16	
	21st	12.30am	Marched to BERTHEN. Arrived and settled down at 5.10 am.	
	21st/22nd		Rest Billets at BERTHEN and METEREN area	
	23rd		Lieut. B. Vaughan attached to 72nd Inf. Bde Machine Gun Company	
	24th		The 72nd Inf. Bde will entrain as shewn in Train Table No C.718 d/ 22.7.16"	
"			24.7.1916. 8th R.W.Kent Regt. Entrain at Bailleul West 5.28pm. Detrain at Longueau	72nd I.B.O.O. No.63 d/ 20.7.16 72nd I.B. letter No C/718 d/ 22.7.16

1875 Wt. W593/826 1,000,000 4/15 J.B.C. & A. A.D.S.S./Forms/C. 2118.

Army Form C. 2118

Instructions regarding War Diaries and Intelligence Summaries are contained in F. S. Regs., Part II. and the Staff Manual respectively. Title Pages will be prepared in manuscript.

WAR DIARY
or
~~INTELLIGENCE SUMMARY~~
(Erase heading not required.)

8th Bn Royal W. Kent Regt.

Place	Date July 1916	Hour	Summary of Events and Information	Remarks and references to Appendices
Field	25th	3am	Detrained at Longueau and marched through Amiens. Halted outside the city for breakfast and then marched to Saisseval, arriving at 10.20am. 1 man fell out, exhausted.	
	25th/31st		Billets at Saisseval. During this period the battalion continually practised attack, consolidation of trenches, various methods of signalling, practice firing for Lewis Gunners, and route marching.	
	30th		"The 72nd Inf Bde will move to the CORBIE - DAOURS area tomorrow 31.7.16"	72nd I.B.O.O. No. 64 of 30.7.16
	"	11.15pm	Transport moved by march route for MORLANCOURT.	
	31st	3pm	Battalion marched to AILLY - SUR - SOMME, but owing to train delay, could not entrain. Stayed night at AILLY STATION.	

Field 2.8.16

J. Mills. Lieut & Adjutant,
8th Bn. Royal W. Kent Regiment.

6238

1875 Wt. W593/826 1,000,000 4/15 J.B.C. & A. A.D.S.S./Forms/C. 2118.

24th Division
72nd Brigade

8th BATTALION

QUEENS OWN (ROYAL WEST KENT REGIMENT)

AUGUST 1916

Instructions regarding War Diaries and Intelligence Summaries are contained in F. S. Regs., Part II. and the Staff Manual respectively. Title Pages will be prepared in manuscript.

WAR DIARY
or
INTELLIGENCE SUMMARY
(Erase heading not required.)

Army Form C. 2118

Vol 10

Place	Date	Hour	Summary of Events and Information	Remarks and references to Appendices
			Confidential War Diary 8th (S) Battn Queen's Own (Royal West Kent Regiment) from 1st August 1916 to 31st August 1916 (Volume)	

1875 Wt. W593/826 1,000,000 4/15 I.R.C. & A. A.D.S.S./Forms/C. 2118.

Army Form C. 2118

Instructions regarding War Diaries and Intelligence Summaries are contained in F. S. Regs., Part II. and the Staff Manual respectively. Title Pages will be prepared in manuscript.

WAR DIARY
or
INTELLIGENCE SUMMARY
(Erase heading not required.)

Place	Date	Hour	Summary of Events and Information	Remarks and references to Appendices
SAISSEVAL.	31. 7. 16.	2pm.	Marched to AILLY-SUR-SOMME. Waited on Station from 4-30pm to 5'10am	
AILLY-SUR-SOMME	1st.	5am.	Entrained and proceeded to MERICOURT where the Battalion detrained and marched to billets at MORLANCOURT.	72nd. Inf Bde. O.O. No 65 of 30. 7. 16.
MORLANCOURT.	1st.	6pm.	Paraded and marched to SANDPITS near MEAULTE where the Battalion encamped.	O.O. No. 66. of 1. 8. 1916.
SANDPIT AREA.	1st. to 10th.		Practising new methods of attack. Training and organising battalion for the assault.	
	2nd.		2/Lieut. R.R. Rochat joined for duty.	
FRONT LINE.	10/11th.		The Battalion relieved the 1/5th. South Lancs Regt. in the front line, in front of Trones Wood.	O.O. No 70. 9.8.16.
BRIQUETERIE.	12/13th.		The 1st. Bn. N. Staffs. Regt. will relieve the 8th Bn. Royal W. Kent Regt in the front line trenches. On relief the 8th. Bn. RwKent Regt will be in Brigade Support. Captain Peulon and Lieut Farley wounded during tour.	O.O. No 72. 13. 8. 16.
FRONT. LINE.	15/16th.		The 8th. RwKent Regiment will relieve the 1st. North Staffs. Regiment in the front left trenches. Lieut. Dove killed during tour.	O.O. No 74. 14. 8. 16.
CRATORS near CARNOY.	17th.		Battalion relieved in front line and moved into reserve at Craters. Total Casualties during tour in Forward Area. 6 officers 146 other ranks.	
FRONT LINE.	18th.	7.30pm.	Battalion ordered to move up in relief of a battalion of the Northamptonshire Regt which had attacked during afternoon. A Company relieved in the front trench, outskirting Guillemont.	Brigade Wires.
BRIQUETERIE.	20/21st.		The 8th Queen's and 9th East Surreys will relieve the 8th. RwKent Regt in the trenches on the night 20/21st. On relief the 8th RwKent Regt. will move to BRIQUETERIE - DUBLIN TRENCH.	Bde. O.O. No 78.
CITADEL.	22nd.	6pm.	Brigade relieved in front line by 59th. Brigade. The Battalion relieved by the 11th. Rifle Brigade. On relief moved to camp at Citadel.	B.O.O. 80 of 22. 8. 16.
near MORLANCOURT and VILLE sur ANCRE	25th.	9.45am	Battalion marched (Brigaded) to camp (bivouacs) near VILLE sur ANCRE.	B.O.O. 81. 25. 8. 16
"	27th.	9am.	Brigade inspected by G.O.C. Division.	
RIBEMONT.	27th.	2.30pm.	Battalion marched to billets at RIBEMONT.	

1875 Wt. W593/826 1,000,000 4/15 J.B.C. & A. A.D.S.S./Forms/C. 2118.

Instructions regarding War Diaries and Intelligence Summaries are contained in F. S. Regs., Part II. and the Staff Manual respectively. Title Pages will be prepared in manuscript.

WAR DIARY
or
INTELLIGENCE SUMMARY
(Erase heading not required.)

Army Form C. 2118

Place	Date	Hour	Summary of Events and Information	Remarks and references to Appendices
DELVILLE WOOD	30th	6. am.	Battalion paraded at 6 a.m. to march to relieve in the front line. Arrived at Camp near Fricourt at 10.15 a.m. where the battalion rested and proceeded with relief at 6.30 p.m. Lt. Colonel Parker went to Field Ambulance sick and Major Whitty assumed Command of the Battalion.	Bde. O.O. No 83. of 28.8.16.
	30/31st.		Relieved 5th. K.S.L.I in front line of Delville Wood Trenches.	
FRONT LINE	31st.		Successfully repulsed counter attack by the Germans which was launched about 1.30 p.m. Casualties 2/Lieut. W. Flowers killed. 2 Officers wounded and 98 other ranks.	

Field.
12. 9. 16.

[signature] Lieut. A/Adjt.
8th Bn. RWKent Regiment.

1875 Wt. W593/826 1,000,000 4/15 J.B.C. & A. A.D.S.S./Forms/C. 2118.

24th Division
72nd Brigade.

8th. BATTALION

ROYAL WEST KENT REGIMENT.

SEPTEMBER 1 9 1 6

Instructions regarding War Diaries and Intelligence Summaries are contained in F. S. Regs., Part II. and the Staff Manual respectively. Title Pages will be prepared in manuscript.

WAR DIARY
or
INTELLIGENCE SUMMARY
(Erase heading not required.)

24

Army Form C. 2118

Vol 11

Place	Date	Hour	Summary of Events and Information	Remarks and references to Appendices
			SECRET WAR DIARY of 8th (S) Battn Royal West Kent Regt. From 1st Sept 1916 to 30th Sept 1916 (Vol)	

1875 Wt. W593/826 1,000,000 4/15 J.B.C. & A. A.D.S.S./Forms/C. 2118.

Instructions regarding War Diaries and Intelligence Summaries are contained in F. S. Regs., Part II. and the Staff Manual respectively. Title Pages will be prepared in manuscript.

WAR DIARY
or
INTELLIGENCE SUMMARY
(Erase heading not required.)

Army Form C. 2118

Place	Date	Hour	Summary of Events and Information	Remarks and references to Appendices
FRONT LINE TRENCHES.	1.9.16		FRONT LINE TRENCHES INNER TRENCH and EDGE TRENCH 2/LIEUT FLOWERS Killed in action " McCABE wounded. Shell Shock " B. VAUGHAN " " " APPERLEY wounded " HARVEY " 2/LIEUT JOHNSON, " BAKER, " MOFFAT, " HIGGINS, " ARNAUD } Joined for Duty. Relieved by 8th QUEENS.	
	2.9.16		Relief complete about 3.0 a.m.	
RESERVE LINE	2nd–5th 9.16		RESERVE TRENCHES CHECK LINE	
	4.9.16		2/LIEUT ROSCOE Died of wounds 2/LIEUT ORCHARDSON, " PROCTOR, HALL } Joined for Duty.	
	5.9.16		Relieved by 5th SOUTH LANCS. Relief complete about 6.45 p.m. Proceeded to camp near FRICOURT F.8.a 5.8.	72 I.B. O/O No 87 d. 4.9.16.
	6.9.16		Marched to Camp E.7.d. arriving about 1.0 p.m.	
	7.9.16	3.30 p.m.	Entrained at 3.30 p.m. EDGEHILL. Detrained LONGPRÉ 9.30 p.m. and marched to	72 I.B. O/O No 88 d. 6.9.16.
VAUCHELLES-LES-QUESNOY.	8.9.16		VAUCHELLES-LES-QUESNOY arriving 2.15 a.m. Transport came by Road arriving 6.20 p.m.	
	9th–18th 9.16		Training at VAUCHELLES-LES-QUESNOY	
	10.9.16.		2/LIEUT EWEN joined for Duty	
	12.9.16.		2/LIEUT T. R. GILBY rejoined for Duty.	
	13.9.16		LIEUT + ADJT. MILLS to Field Ambulance. 2/LIEUTS ALLWORTH, ROCHAT, JAMES + 150 O.R. proceeded to Rest Camp AULT.	
	17.9.16		Party returned from AULT.	
SAINS-LES-PERNES	19.9.16	4.45 a.m.	Entrained ABBEVILLE for move to 1st ARMY Area. Train left 4.45 a.m. Orders to detrain at BERGUETTE arrived BRYAS 9.30 a.m. recieved orders move to BERGUETTE cancelled ordered to detrain at BRYAS. Moved into Billets at SAINS-LES-PERNES.	72 I.B. O/O No 89.

1875 Wt. W593/826 1,000,000 4/15 J.B.C. & A. A.D.S.S./Forms/C. 2118.

Army Form C. 2118

Instructions regarding War Diaries and Intelligence Summaries are contained in F. S. Regs., Part II. and the Staff Manual respectively. Title Pages will be prepared in manuscript.

WAR DIARY
or
INTELLIGENCE SUMMARY
(Erase heading not required.)

Place	Date	Hour	Summary of Events and Information	Remarks and references to Appendices
SAINS-LES-PERNES	20th-24.9.16.		Training at SAINS-LES-PERNES	
	23.9.16.		2/LIEUT SMITH, 2/" FRENCH } Joined for Duty	
	20.9.16		CAPT. L. KEPP PAGE sick to FIELD AMBULANCE	
	24.9.16		Battalion with Transport moved off from SAINS-LES-PERNES 7.55 a.m. arrived new area at HAILLICOURT at 1 p.m.	
	26.9.16		Battalion with Transport moved off from HAILLICOURT 6.55 a.m. arrived new area at GOUY-SERVINS in DIVISIONAL RESERVE at 10 a.m. and took over Billets from unit of 9th DIVISION.	
GOUY-SERVINS	28.9.16		2/LIEUT HAYWARD joined for DUTY.	
	26-30.9.16		GOUY SERVINS. DIVISIONAL RESERVE	

3. 10. 16.

H. S. Brown Lieut. & A/Adjt.
8th Royal West Kent Regt.

1875 Wt. W593/826 1,000,000 4/15 J.B.C. & A. A.D.S.S./Forms/C. 2118.

24th Division
72nd Brigade.

8th BATTALION

ROYAL WEST KENT REGIMENT.

OCTOBER 1 9 1 6

Instructions regarding War Diaries and Intelligence Summaries are contained in F. S. Regs., Part II. and the Staff Manual respectively. Title pages will be prepared in manuscript.

WAR DIARY
or
INTELLIGENCE SUMMARY.
(Erase heading not required.)

24 Vol 12

Army Form C. 2118.

Place	Date	Hour	Summary of Events and Information	Remarks and references to Appendices
			Confidential. War Diary of 8th (Service) Battalion Royal West Kent Regiment. In the field From 1st October 1916 to 31st October 1916. (Volume)	

2353 Wt. W2544/1454 700,000 5/15 D. D. & L. A.D.S.S./Forms/C. 2118.

Instructions regarding War Diaries and Intelligence Summaries are contained in F. S. Regs., Part II. and the Staff Manual respectively. Title Pages will be prepared in manuscript.

WAR DIARY 8th Batt. Royal West Kent Regt. Army Form C. 2118

or

~~INTELLIGENCE SUMMARY~~

(Erase heading not required.)

Place	Date	Hour	Summary of Events and Information	Remarks and references to Appendices
October 1st 1916			Divisional Reserve GOUY SERVINS.	
2nd			Relieved 8th Bn Buffs in front line trenches. BERTHONVAL SECTION. RIGHT SUBSECTION. Relief complete 4.30 p.m.	72 Bde O.O. No 91 dated 29.9.16.
3rd			Second Lieutenants. F.G. YEO, C.L.A. HUTCHISON, J. PARFITT-BIGG joined for duty.	
8th			Second Lieutenants. H.W. LOVE, R.J. HILLMAN, H.T. DUNN joined for duty.	
			Second Lieutenant. E. SMITH to FIELD AMBULANCE SICK.	
10th			Relieved by 1st NORTH STAFFORDS in front line trenches relief complete 3.30 p.m.	
			Moved to Support line ZOUAVE VALLEY, COLISEUM, ALHAMBRA, CABARET ROUGE.	72 Bde O.O. No 92 dated 7.10.16.
15th			Second Lieutenant E. SMITH. died of sickness. Second Lieutenant R.R. ROCHAT wounded in action.	
18th			Relieved in Support Line by 9th ROYAL SUSSEX. Relief complete 5.40 p.m.	
			Moved on relief to Divisional Reserve GOUY SERVINS.	72 Bde O.O. No 93. dated 16.10.16.
24th			Relieved in Divisional Reserve by 1st CANADIAN INFANTRY BRIGADE. Moved to MAZINGARBE.	
25th			Relieved 14th H.L.I. in front line Trenches. RIGHT SUBSECTION. HULLUCH SECTION. Relief complete 12.15 p.m	72 Bde O.O. No 94 dated 22.10.16.
26th			Second Lieutenant F.G. YEO killed in action.	
27th			Second Lieutenant. T.R. GILBY to R.F.C.	
31st			Relieved in Front line trenches by 1st NORTH STAFFORDS. Relief complete 2.30 p.m.	
			Moved on Relief to Brigade Reserve. PHILOSOPHE.	72 Bde O.O. No 95 dated 29.10.16.

H S Brown Lieut and Adjt.
8th Royal West Kent Regt.

1875 Wt. W593/826 1,000,000 4/15 J.B.C. & A. A.D S.S./Forms/C. 2118.

24th Division
72nd Brigade.

8th BATTALION

ROYAL WEST KENT REGIMENT.

NOVEMBER 1 9 1 6

Instructions regarding War Diaries and Intelligence Summaries are contained in F. S. Regs., Part II. and the Staff Manual respectively. Title pages will be prepared in manuscript.

WAR DIARY
or
INTELLIGENCE SUMMARY.
(Erase heading not required.)

Army Form C. 2118.

Vol 13

Place	Date	Hour	Summary of Events and Information	Remarks and references to Appendices
			Confidential	
			War Diary	
			of	
			8th (S) Battn. Royal West Kent Regt.	
			from 1st November 1916 to 30th November 1916	
			(Volume)	

2353 Wt. W2544/1454 700,000 5/15 D. D. & L. A.D.S.S./Forms/C. 2118.

Instructions regarding War Diaries and Intelligence Summaries are contained in F. S. Regs., Part II. and the Staff Manual respectively. Title pages will be prepared in manuscript.

WAR DIARY
or
~~INTELLIGENCE~~ SUMMARY.
(Erase heading not required.)

Army Form C. 2118.

Place	Date	Hour	Summary of Events and Information	Remarks and references to Appendices
	1.11.16.		Brigade Reserve PHILOSOPHE	HSB
	6.11.16		Relieved 1st NORTH STAFFORDS in front line trenches RIGHT SUBSECTION, HULLUCH SECTION. Relief complete 4.15 p.m.	72nd I.B. O.O. No 96 dated 4.11.16. HSB
	10.11.16		Lieut H.S. BROWN sick to Field Ambulance.	HSB
	12.11.16		Relieved in front line trenches by 1st NORTH STAFFORDS. Moved on relief to BRIGADE SUPPORT. 10th AVENUE	72nd I.B. O.O. No 97 dated 9.11.16. HSB
	13.11.16		2/Lieut B. WADE and 2/Lieut K. PFEUFFAR joined for duty.	HSB
	18.11.16		Relieved 1st NORTH STAFFORDS in front line trenches. RIGHT SUBSECTION, HULLUCH SECTION.	72nd I.B. O.O. No 98 dated 15.11.16 HSB
	24.11.16		Relieved in front line trenches by 1st NORTH STAFFORDS. Moved on relief to BRIGADE ~~SUPPORT~~ RESERVE HSB. PHILOSOPHE	72nd I.B. O.O. No 99 dated 21.11.16 HSB
	28.11.16		Capt. L.M. KOPPA-PAGE evacuated to ENGLAND.	A.G's List No 59 dated 23.11.16. HSB
	30.11.16		Relieved 1st NORTH STAFFORDS in front line trenches. RIGHT SUBSECTION. HULLUCH SECTION.	72nd I.B. O.O. No 100 dated 27.11.16 HSB

H S Brown Capt. + Adjt
8th (S) Bn. Royal West Kent Regt.

2353 Wt. W2544/1454 700,000 5/15. D. D. & L. A.D.S.S./Forms/C. 2118.

24th Division
72nd Brigade.

8th BATTALION

ROYAL WEST KENT REGIMENT.

DECEMBER 1 9 1 6

Instructions regarding War Diaries and Intelligence Summaries are contained in F. S. Regs., Part II. and the Staff Manual respectively. Title pages will be prepared in manuscript.

WAR DIARY
or
INTELLIGENCE SUMMARY.
(Erase heading not required.)

Army Form C. 2118.

Vol 14

Place	Date	Hour	Summary of Events and Information	Remarks and references to Appendices
			SECRET War Diary of 8th (S) Bn Royal West Kent Regt. from 1st Dec 1916 to 31st Dec 1916 (volume)	

2353 Wt. W2544/1454 700,000 5/15 D. D. & L. A.D.S.S./Forms/C. 2118.

Army Form C. 2118.

WAR DIARY
or
~~INTELLIGENCE SUMMARY.~~
(Erase heading not required.)

Instructions regarding War Diaries and Intelligence Summaries are contained in F. S. Regs., Part II. and the Staff Manual respectively. Title pages will be prepared in manuscript.

Place	Date	Hour	Summary of Events and Information	Remarks and references to Appendices
	Dec			72nd Inf Bde
	6th		Relieved in right Subsection HULLUCH section by 1st N Staffs. Moved into Bde Support 10th avenue RPB	O.O. no 101
	12th		Relieved the 1st N. Staffs in right Subsection HULLUCH section RPB	O.O. no 102
	18th		Relieved by the 1st N Staffs in right Subsection HULLUCH section. Moved into Bde Reserve PHILOSOPHE RPB	O.O. no 103
	19th		2/Lt ROBERTS H.P.L. and 2/Lt TANNER D.F.W. joined for duty from Base RPB	
	24th		Relieved the 1st N Staffs in HULLUCH section right Subsection RPB	O.O. no 104
	30th		2/Lt GRIFFITH G.H. joined for duty from Base RPB	
	30th		Relieved in HULLUCH section right Subsection by 1st N Staffs. Moved into Bde Support 10th avenue RPB	O.O. no 105

RP Baker 2/Lt & a/adjt
8th (S) Battn Royal West Kent Regt.

2353 Wt. W2544/1454 700,000 5/15 D. D. & L. A.D.S.S./Forms/C. 2118.

Instructions regarding War Diaries and Intelligence Summaries are contained in F. S. Regs., Part II. and the Staff Manual respectively. Title pages will be prepared in manuscript.

WAR DIARY
or
INTELLIGENCE SUMMARY.
(Erase heading not required.)

Army Form C. 2118.

24

Place	Date	Hour	Summary of Events and Information	Remarks and references to Appendices
			Vol 15 SECRET War Diary of 8th S. Bn. Royal West Kent Regt. from 1st January 1917 to 31st January 1917 (Volume –)	

2353 Wt. W2544/1454 700,000 5/15 D. D. & L. A.D.S.S./Forms/C. 2118.

Army Form C. 2118.

Instructions regarding War Diaries and Intelligence Summaries are contained in F. S. Regs., Part II. and the Staff Manual respectively. Title pages will be prepared in manuscript.

WAR DIARY
or
~~INTELLIGENCE SUMMARY.~~
(Erase heading not required.)

8th (S) Bn Royal West Kent Regt.

Place	Date	Hour	Summary of Events and Information	Remarks and references to Appendices
	January 1917			72nd Inf Bde O.O.
	5		Relieved 1st N. Staffs Regt in HULLUCH Section, right subsection	no 106 RPB
	5		2/Lt E.G. BROWN rejoined from Hospl.	RPB
	8		2/Lt J.B. CRYER and 2/Lt H.J. LANAWAY joined on appointment, from Base	RPB
	10		2/Lt K. PFEUFFAR wounded, to Hospl.	RPB
	11		Relieved by 1st N Staffs in HULLUCH section: moved into Bde reserve PHILOSOPHE	no 107 RPB
	17		Relieved 1st N Staffs in HULLUCH section right subsection	no 109 RPB
	19		Lt. Col J. C. PARKER arrived from Base	RPB
	22		2/Lt F.A. ROBERTS Sick to Hospl.	RPB
	23		Relieved by 1st N Staffs Regt in right subsection HULLUCH section: moved into Bde support, 10th avenue	no 110 RPB
	23		2/Lt K PFEUFFAR rejoined from Hospl.	RPB
	25		Capt T.P.P. WALKER arrived from Base	RPB
	26		2/Lts DELHAM and MILLARD joined for duty with 24th Divnl Trng Battn, from Base	RPB
	29		Relieved 1st N Staffs HULLUCH Section, right subsection	no 113 RPB

RPBaker 2/Lt & a/adjt
8th Bn Royal West Kent Regt.

2353 Wt. W2544/1454 700,000 5/15 D. D. & L. A.D.S.S./Forms/C. 2118.

A G's Office, Base

Herewith War Diary for the month of January 1917.

S. J. K. Grant 2nd Lieut
Intelligence Officer
7/2/17 9th Bn East Surrey Regt.

Instructions regarding War Diaries and Intelligence Summaries are contained in F. S. Regs., Part II. and the Staff Manual respectively. Title pages will be prepared in manuscript.

WAR DIARY
or
INTELLIGENCE SUMMARY.
(Erase heading not required.)

Army Form C. 2118.

24

Vol 16

Place	Date	Hour	Summary of Events and Information	Remarks and references to Appendices

ORDERLY ROOM
No. C23
28 MAR. 1917
8TH (SERVICE) Bn. QUEEN'S OWN ROYAL WEST KENT REGIMENT.

War Diary
of
8th S. Battn. Royal West Kent Regt.
from 1-2-1917 to 28-2-1917
(Volume - 3)

In the field
28. 3. 1917.

2353 Wt. W2544/1454 700,000 5/15 D. D. & L. A.D.S.S./Forms/C. 2118.

Instructions regarding War Diaries and Intelligence Summaries are contained in F. S. Regs., Part II. and the Staff Manual respectively. Title pages will be prepared in manuscript.

WAR DIARY

~~or~~

~~INTELLIGENCE SUMMARY.~~

(Erase heading not required.)

February 1917

Army Form C. 2118.

Place	Date	Hour	Summary of Events and Information	Remarks and references to Appendices
Trenches	1-4.2.17	-	In front lines trenches, Hulluch Section. Right sub-section	
	4th		Relieved in front line trenches, Hulluch Section, Right sub-section by 1st Bn North Staffordshire Regt.; on relief, the Battalion moved into Divisional Reserve billets at PHILOSOPHE.	72nd Inf. Bde Operation Order No. 114. RPB
			The Battn. Comdr Lieut-Col. J.C. PARKER proceeded to attend 'C.O's' special conference at BOULOGNE; Major N.I. WHITTY assumed Command of the Battalion.	First Army letter No. 401/1 (G) dated 29.1.1917 RPB
PHILOSOPHE	4th	9am.	Party, consisting of 40 other ranks under 2nd Lieut. F. PROCTOR, proceeded to join 24th Divisional Training Battalion, ALLOUAGNE, for period of rest.	24th D.H.Q. letter G.X. 443/1 dated 1st Feby. 1917. RPB
Trenches.	10th	-	Battn. relieved 1st Bn. North Staffordshire Regt in front line trenches, Hulluch Section, Right sub-section. Weather condition :- Frosty.	72nd Inf Bde. Operation Order No. 115 RPB
Trenches	12th		Relieved in front line trenches. Hulluch Section, right sub-section by 13th Bn. Kings Royal Rifle Corps, 111th Brigade, 34th Division. - On relief the Battalion proceeded, by platoons, to occupy billets in NOEUX-LES-MINES. Route:- front line trenches - NORTHERN UP C.T. - PHILOSOPHE - SAILLY LABOURSE - NOEUX-LES-MINES.	72nd Inf Bde Operation Order No. 116 RPB
NOEUX-LES-MINES	13th	9.30 am.	Battalion paraded to proceed to Divisional Rest Area. Transport in rear of Battalion. Halted on outskirts of ALLOUAGNE at 12.30 pm for mid-day meal.	

2353 Wt. W2544/1454 700,000 5/15 D. D. & L. A.D.S.S./Forms/C. 2118.

Army Form C. 2118.

Instructions regarding War Diaries and Intelligence Summaries are contained in F. S. Regs., Part II. and the Staff Manual respectively. Title pages will be prepared in manuscript.

WAR DIARY
or
~~INTELLIGENCE SUMMARY.~~
(Erase heading not required.)

Place	Date	Hour	Summary of Events and Information	Remarks and references to Appendices
LINE-of-MARCH	13th	2-4.40 pm.	Proceeded on line of march about 2pm. following route via HAUT RIEUX-BAS RIEUX, thence to BUSNETTE (Battalion rest area) arriving at billets at 4.40 pm.	continuation of 42nd Inf. Bde Operation Order No. 116. RPB
BUSNETTE (par CHOQUE-pas de CALAIS)			Lieut.-Col J.C. PARKER returned from C.O's Conference and assumed command of the Battalion. Major N.I. WHITTY assumed duties of 2nd in Command of the Battalion.	
BUSNETTE	14th		Re-arranging and inspection of billets; cleaning of clothes, arms and equipment.	
BUSNETTE	15th		Billets made as comfortable as possible; inspection of kit, arms, equipment and clothing by Platoon Commanders etc.	
BUSNETTE	16th		Frost ceased and heavy thaw set in. Thaw scheme operated upon. Battalion re-organized.	2nd D.H.Q. letter Q.5459 dated 20th Jany. 1917. RPB
BUSNETTE and Training Area.	17th to 28th		Training: physical drill; close order drill; musketry drill; bayonet fighting; care of arms; extended order drill; Company drill; range firing; Battalion route marches (marching order); Company route marches; lectures on sanitation - prevention of espionage etc., General elementary training; 'specialist' training, etc, etc,	
BUSNETTE	18th		Captain Sir H.C.W. HAWLEY Bart; rejoined Battalion on relinquishing duties as Railhead Cash Disbursing Officer	

2353 Wt. W2544/1454 700,000 5/15 D. D. & L. A.D.S.S./Forms/C. 2118.

Army Form C. 2118.

WAR DIARY

or

~~INTELLIGENCE SUMMARY.~~

(Erase heading not required.)

Instructions regarding War Diaries and Intelligence Summaries are contained in F. S. Regs., Part II. and the Staff Manual respectively. Title pages will be prepared in manuscript.

Place	Date	Hour	Summary of Events and Information	Remarks and references to Appendices
BUSNETTE	19th		A/C.S. Major R.N. KILLICK, 6th Bn. Royal West Kent Regiment, having been nominated for Commission, reported as 2nd Lieut. from Cadet School, St. Omer and took up duties as such in "C" Company.	
			Party of 40 other ranks under 2nd Lieut. F. PROCTOR rejoined from period of rest at 24th Divisional Training Battalion.	
BUSNETTE	24th		Captain H.J. WENYON left Battalion for attachment to 14th Infantry Brigade Headquarters as "Staff Learner". Lieut. H.L. LEWIS "C" Company assumed Command of "D" Company	
BUSNETTE	25/26th		Major N.I. WHITTY proceeded on 18 days special leave to England.	
			Total casualties for month:-	
			Officers -- NIL. Other Ranks:- 1 slightly wounded - remained at duty	
			1 acc. wounded - since rejoined Battn.	

R.M. Baker 2nd Lieut. & A/Adjutant

8th (S) Battn. Royal West Kent Regiment

28.3.1917

2353 Wt. W2544/1454 700,000 5/15 D. D. & L. A.D.S.S./Forms/C. 2118.

Army Form C. 2118

Instructions regarding War Diaries and Intelligence Summaries are contained in F. S. Regs., Part II. and the Staff Manual respectively. Title Pages will be prepared in manuscript.

WAR DIARY
or
INTELLIGENCE SUMMARY
(Erase heading not required.)

Vol 17

Place	Date	Hour	Summary of Events and Information	Remarks and references to Appendices

War Diary

of

8th S Battn. Royal West Kent Regt

B.E.F.

from 1st March 1917 to 31st March 1917

(Volume.-)

In the field. 1st April 1917.

1875 Wt. W593/826 1,000,000 4/15 J.B.C. & A. A.D.S.S./Forms/C. 2118.

Instructions regarding War Diaries and Intelligence Summaries are contained in F. S. Regs., Part II. and the Staff Manual respectively. Title Pages will be prepared in manuscript.

WAR DIARY

or

~~INTELLIGENCE SUMMARY~~

(Erase heading not required.)

Army Form C. 2118

Place	Date	Hour	Summary of Events and Information	Remarks and references to Appendices
BUSNETTE (rest area)	1st 2nd		Continuation of training.	
	3rd	9.30 am.	Battalion left 'rest area' and marched from BUSNETTE to FOUQUEREUIL via CHOQUES.	72nd Inf Brigade Operation Order No. 118 RPB
	3/4th		Billetted for night in billets at FOUQUEREUIL	
FOUQUEREUIL - BULLY GRENAY. FRONT LINE TRENCHES	4th	9.30 am.	Battalion left FOUQUEREUIL and marched to BULLY GRENAY following route - FOUQUERIERS - DROVIN - NOEUX - les - Mines - PETIT - SAINS - BULLY GRENAY, arriving later place about 1pm; remained in billets until 6pm. then proceeded into front line trenches, Left sub-section, CALONNE II relieving 14th Candian Battn.	
			Capt H.G. LOCK proceeded on special leave to England - 2nd Lieut E.G. BROWN M.C., assumed command of 'B' Company.	
	4/5th		2nd Lieuts E.B.A. HARVEY and H.G. WOOLLEY rejoined Battn. for duty.	
	5th		Capt Sir H.C.W HAWLEY Bart. took up duties of Town Major BULLY GRENAY.	
TRENCHES	8th		Battn. relieved by 1st Bn. N.R. Staffordshire Regt in front line system CALONNE II left sub-section. On relief the Bn. (less "D" Coy) moved into Bde. Support billets at CITE CALONNE. "D" Company took up billets in MAROC as Bde. support Company.	72nd Inf Brigade Operation Order No 119. RPB
Bde Support CALONNE	9th 13th		Battn. supplied working and carrying parties daily.	
	14th		The Battn. relieved the 1st Bn. N.R. Staffordshire Regt in the front line trenches Left sub section CALONNE II.	72nd Inf Brigade Operation Order No 120. RPB

1875 Wt. W593/826 1,000,000 4/15 J.B.C. & A. A.D.S.S./Forms/C. 2118.

Instructions regarding War Diaries and Intelligence Summaries are contained in F. S. Regs., Part II. and the Staff Manual respectively. Title Pages will be prepared in manuscript.

-2-

WAR DIARY ~~or~~ ~~INTELLIGENCE SUMMARY~~

(Erase heading not required.)

Army Form C. 2118

Place	Date	Hour	Summary of Events and Information	Remarks and references to Appendices
TRENCHES	16		2nd Lieut. C C BARING reported for duty.	
	18/19th	4 a.m.	Attempted raid by Germans on DOUBLE CRASSIER - left of Battn. front - raid repulsed without casualties to us. 4 Germans known to be killed including 1 Officer. No 8514 4C A DENT awarded Military Medal for exceptional coolness in dealing with the raiders.	
	19th		Major N I WHITTY returned from leave to England and assumed duties of Second-in-Command.	
TRENCHES	20th/21st	12 45 am.	Relieved by 1st Bn. N.S. Staffordshire Regt. in front line trenches, Left sub Section CALONNE II. On being relieved the Battn. moved into Division at Reserve billets BULLY GRENAY.	42nd Inf Brigade Operation Order No. 123 RPB
	20th		2nd Lieut. W J EWEN admitted to Field Ambulance.	
BULLY-GRENAY	21st		2nd Lieut. C R H ALLWORTH admitted to Field Ambulance.	
	21st to 25th		Working and carrying parties supplied daily - one Company employed each night wiring the Reserve Line.	
			During the period in Divisional Reserve all ranks passed through Box Respirator drill; also through test gas where necessary.	
BULLY-GRENAY	23rd		Capt. W G LOCK rejoined Battn. from leave to England and assumed duties as Officer Commanding 'B' Company.	
TRENCHES	26th		Battn. relieved the 1st Bn. N.S. Staffordshire Regt. in front line trenches - Left sub section - CALONNE II. Left of the Bn. frontage extended to M 4 d. 40. 60 (sheet 36 c S W 1) to include the DOUBLE CRASSIER taken over from 16th Brigade 6th Division	42 I B O. Order 125; 42nd I B wire "BM 65" RPB

1875 Wt. W593/826 1,000,000 4/15 J.B.C. & A. A.D.S.S./Forms/C. 2118.

Instructions regarding War Diaries and Intelligence Summaries are contained in F. S. Regs., Part II. and the Staff Manual respectively. Title Pages will be prepared in manuscript.

-3-

WAR DIARY
or
INTELLIGENCE SUMMARY
(Erase heading not required.)

Army Form C. 2118.

Place	Date	Hour	Summary of Events and Information	Remarks and references to Appendices
BULLY GRENAY	26th	NOON	Training Platoon, Instructors and 1 Officer, under 2nd Lieut. S A FRENCH proceeded to join the 24th Divisional Training Battalion at ALLOUAGNE.	
	24th to 31st		In front line trenches, Left sub section CALONNE II	
	24th		Lieut. H L LEWIS proceeded on special leave to England. 2nd Lieut. F PROCTOR assumed command of D Company.	
	28th		2 more Lewis Guns received from Ordnance Stores. This completes establishment, i.e. 16 per Battalion.	
			Casualties during month:-	
			Officers - Nil. Other Ranks - Killed i/a 1	
			Killed acc. 1	
			Wounded i/a 15	
			Wounded acc. 4	
			Wounded S.I. (at duty) 4	

1.4.17.

R B Baker 2nd Lieut.
A/Adjt. 8th S. Bn. Royal West Kent Regiment.

1875 Wt. W593/826 1,000,000 4/15 J.B.C. & A. A.D.S.S./Forms/C. 2118.

8th BATTN. ROYAL WEST KENT REGIMENT

72nd INFANTRY BRIGADE

24th DIVISION

APRIL 1917

Instructions regarding War Diaries and Intelligence Summaries are contained in F. S. Regs., Part II. and the Staff Manual respectively. Title pages will be prepared in manuscript.

WAR DIARY
or
INTELLIGENCE SUMMARY.
(Erase heading not required.)

Army Form C. 2118.

Vol 18

Place	Date	Hour	Summary of Events and Information	Remarks and references to Appendices
			War Diary of the 8th S By Royal West Kent Regiment for the period 1st April 1917 to 31st April 1917 (Volume - -) ORDERLY ROOM No. C114 4 MAY 1917 8TH [illegible] QUEEN'S OWN ROYAL WEST KENT REGIMENT.	

A7092). Wt. W12839/M1293 750,000. 1/17. D. D & L., Ltd. Forms/C2118/14.

Instructions regarding War Diaries and Intelligence Summaries are contained in F. S. Regs., Part II. and the Staff Manual respectively. Title pages will be prepared in manuscript.

WAR DIARY
or
~~INTELLIGENCE SUMMARY.~~
(Erase heading not required.)

Army Form C. 2118.

Ref. Map 1/10000 LENS 36 C SW1 Edition 8 a.

Place	Date	Hour	Summary of Events and Information	Remarks and references to Appendices
	April 1		Relieved in CALONNE II by 1st Bn N. Staffs Regt. On relief moved into Brigade Support in Cité CALONNE	72nd I.B. Op. order no 126
	2nd to 6th		In Brigade support. Working parties daily under 103rd RE on CALONNE defences. Supplied nightly carrying parties for medium and light T.M. ammunition.	
	7th		Moved into CALONNE II, relieved 1st N Staffs. C Coy holding double CRASSIER, D Coy in Centre, B on right A Coy in Support.	no 128
	8th		Attitude of enemy quiet. Patrols sent out nightly, but unable to enter enemy trenches undetected.	
	12th		Raid carried out on the triangle M14d, N of the CRASSIERS by 2nd York & Lancaster Regt. Cooperation by C Coy from N. CRASSIER with rifle grenades. Zero hour 10 pm	no 130
	13th		2/Lt M HOLMES and 2/Lt F M CROWE joined for duty on appointment. At 4.45 pm strong patrols were pushed out from C D & B Coys and entered the enemy line. Capt T.P.P WALKER and 2/Lt K PFEUFFAR wounded by a Sniper. Enemy front and support lines occupied without opposition. Two prisoners of 35th Fusilier Regt captured. Patrols pushed forward as far as railway M10c to M11a, the three Coys taking up a line in the German support trench, left flank resting on CRASSIER in touch with 6th Divn, right in touch with 9th E Surreys. The following moves took place on the night 13/14th. Batt Hq to locality B. A Coy from Support to front line trench. Bde support coy of 1st N Staffs to CRASSIERS. Bde Reserve Coy of the 8th Queens to Front line trench. C D & B Coys advanced further & occupy German 3rd line CORPORAL, CORD, CORSAIR	
	14th		8th Bn Queens passed through our line to continue the advance through CITÉ ST PIERRE Batt Hq moved up to FOSSE 16. A coy moved up to CORSAIR from Support	no 132

A7092). Wt. W12839/M1293 750,000. 1/17. D. D & L., Ltd. Forms/C2118/14.

Instructions regarding War Diaries and Intelligence Summaries are contained in F. S. Regs., Part II. and the Staff Manual respectively. Title pages will be prepared in manuscript.

WAR DIARY
or
~~INTELLIGENCE SUMMARY.~~
(Erase heading not required.)

Army Form C. 2118.

Ref Map 1/10000 LENS 36 C S W 1 Edition 8a

Place	Date	Hour	Summary of Events and Information	Remarks and references to Appendices
	14th		working party of 120 men on digging + improving trench on Eastern Boundary M11d.	
			Capt W.G. LOCK wounded, at duty.	72nd Inf Bde op. order no 133
	15th	6.30am	Batt Hq moved forward to CORSAIR TRENCH. Patrols of B+D Coy ordered to push forward in attempt to make good enemys trench M13 central to PUITS 12 Bis at M12 b 8 6. The enemy were found to be holding the strong point M13 central, with the SE end of COLLEGE Trench filled in. COLLEGE trench occupied by us as far as N13 a 6,9. The 8th Queens were working forward on our left. Our disposition at 9.45pm was: two coys in COLLEGE + COWDEN trench one coy in CORKSCREW. one coy in trench running NW from CORKSCREW at M11 d 4,1.	
	16th		Coy HQ in tunnel under railway embankment was blown in by direct hit of heavy shell. All C Coy officers casualties. 2/Lt R.C. VAUGHAN 'C' Coy, 2/Lt N. JOHNSON 'A' Coy killed in this dugout at M12 d 6 9½ and their bodies not recovered, with those of 3 O R's. Also wounded by same shell 2/Lt H.J. LANAWAY; 2/Lt M. HOLMES; 2/Lt H G WOOLEY.	
			2/Lt E.S.A. HARVEY killed in action. Capt W.G. LOCK wounded at duty.	
			Advance continued in conjunction with 1st Bn N. Staffs	no 134
		9am	Preliminary bombardment of objective by Artillery of Left Group. Batt Adv. Hq established under Major N I WHITTY at Junction of COWDEN with railway. Two guns of 72nd M G Coy brought up. No progress made as it was not found possible to advance without becoming seriously engaged. Enemy snipers + M. Guns in houses along COMBAT trench.	
		9pm	Relief started, by 9th E Surreys; relief took all night. On relief the Battn occupied the Support line CORSAIR-CORPORAL.	
			2/Lt R W BROTHERS joined for duty on appointment.	

Instructions regarding War Diaries and Intelligence Summaries are contained in F. S. Regs., Part II, and the Staff Manual respectively. Title pages will be prepared in manuscript.

WAR DIARY
or
INTELLIGENCE SUMMARY.
(*Erase heading not required.*)

Army Form C. 2118.

Ref: Map 1/10000 LENS 36 C SW1
Edition 8.a.

Place	Date	Hour	Summary of Events and Information	Remarks and references to Appendices
	17th		Work of consolidating the second line of defence proceeded with; "localities" were selected. Ammunition + bombs were brought up + dumps formed.	op. order no 135
			Cité St PIERRE was shelled intermittently all day.	
			2/Lt E.G. WOOLLEY died of wounds in 33rd C.C.S.	
	18th		work of consolidation continued.	
			Relieved after dark by 4th Bn Leicester Regt, 138th Bde. Relief complete at 12.20 am of 19th.	no 136
	19th		On relief moved into Billets in Fosse 10. Arrived in at 3.30 am.	
			Capt H.L. LEWIS from leave. Assumed command of C Coy.	
			Major C.P. KINGSLAND from 4th (T) Reserve Battn joined for duty.	
	~~20~~ 19th		Battn moved from Fosse 10 to LOZINGHEM; order of march HQ B, C, D, A. arrived in at 4.30 pm	no 136/1
	20th		Move from LOZINGHEM to LIGNY-LEZ-AIRE. Start 9am. Order of march HQ, D C B A arrived in at 1.15 pm. Blankets taken by 3 lorries.	
	21st		Day spent in cleaning up. Capt Sir H HAWLEY returned to duty from Divn Burials Office.	
	22nd		Church Parades.	
	23.		Baths in mine building at FLECHINELLE	

A7092). Wt. W12839/M1293 750,000. 1/17. D. D & L., Ltd. Forms/C2118/14.

Instructions regarding War Diaries and Intelligence Summaries are contained in F. S. Regs., Part II. and the Staff Manual respectively. Title pages will be prepared in manuscript.

WAR DIARY

or

~~INTELLIGENCE SUMMARY.~~

(Erase heading not required.)

Army Form C. 2118.

Place	Date	Hour	Summary of Events and Information	Remarks and references to Appendices
	24th		At LIGNY-LEZ-AIRE. Inspection of Coys by C.O.	
			2/Lt C.R.H ALLWORTH from Hspl.	
	25th	9am	Battn moves to DELETTE order of march A B C, D, Hq arrive in at 12.40 pm.	
	26th		Cleaning up + kit inspections.	
	27th		Training in progress. 2/Lt W.J. EWEN from Hspl.	
	29th		Church Parade.	

Casualties for the month:

	Officers	O. R's
Killed	3	13
died of wds	1	4
wounded	4	41
wounded SC, at duty	1 (twice)	5

R.O. Baker ?/Lt. & a/Adjt
8th (S) Bn R. W. Kent Regt.

A7092). Wt. W12839/M1293 750,000. 1/17. D. D. & L. Ltd. Forms/C2118/14.

Instructions regarding War Diaries and Intelligence Summaries are contained in F. S. Regs., Part II. and the Staff Manual respectively. Title pages will be prepared in manuscript.

WAR DIARY
or
INTELLIGENCE SUMMARY.
(Erase heading not required.)

Army Form C. 2118.

Vol 19

Place	Date	Hour	Summary of Events and Information	Remarks and references to Appendices
			Secret.	
			War Diary	
			of	
			8th S. Battn Royal West Kent Regt	
			from 1st May to 31st May 1917.	
			(Volume -)	

A7092). Wt. W12839/M1293 750,000. 1/17. D. D & L., Ltd. Forms/C2118/14.

Instructions regarding War Diaries and Intelligence Summaries are contained in F. S. Regs., Part II. and the Staff Manual respectively. Title pages will be prepared in manuscript.

WAR DIARY
or
~~INTELLIGENCE SUMMARY.~~

(Erase heading not required.)

Army Form C. 2118.

8th (S) Battn Royal West Kent Regt

Place	Date	Hour	Summary of Events and Information	Remarks and references to Appendices
DELETTE	May 1		The Battn still in rest at DELETTE. Training continued. Inspection by the Corps Commander of Coys in the attack, and of all officers	RPB
	2		Inspection by ADMS for P B men.	RPB
	3		Continuation of training. Inspection of the arms of the Battn by Bde armourer	RPB
	4		All box respirators tested in gas chamber	RPB
	6		Baths	RPB
	7		Withdrawal of first blankets and winter clothing	RPB
	8		Practice trench attack by Battn. Party sent to 1st Army Rest Camp	RPB
	9		Training continued	RPB
	10		Move to WITTES. Start 9 am arrive in 4.10 pm. 2½ hrs halt at midday for dinners. Route via THEROUANNE and REBECQ	72 I.B. O.O. No 138 RPB
	11		at WITTES Inspection by 24th Divnl Commander	RPB
	12		Move from WITTES to BOESCHEPE area. Start 5.30 am via STEENBECQUE HAZEBROUCK STEENVOORDE Halt for 2½ hours for dinners. Very hot day. All in at 7.15 pm Capt G E W POWELL, Lt A J PORTER, 2/Lt G S BOWEN, 2/Lt W E BRISLEY } from 2/1st Kent Cyclist Battn joined for duty	72 I.B. O.O. No 139 RPB
	13		Continued on march, moved off 10 am via POPERINGHE to BRANDHOEK area. Occupied DOMINION Camp, in at 4.30 pm then moved into EERIE CAMP at 9.30 pm. Hot day	RPB 72 I.B. O.O. No 140 RPB
	14		Moved out of camp at 9.45 pm entrained at BRANDHOEK at 10.40 pm. Detrained in YPRES and occupied billets in Infantry Barracks, Brigade Reserve. Relieved 8th York and Lancs all in at 1 am, 14/15th	72 I.B. O.O. No 141 RPB

A7092). Wt. W12839/M1293 750,000. 1/17. D. D & L., Ltd. Forms/C2118/14.

Instructions regarding War Diaries and Intelligence Summaries are contained in F. S. Regs., Part II. and the Staff Manual respectively. Title pages will be prepared in manuscript.

WAR DIARY
or
INTELLIGENCE SUMMARY.
(Erase heading not required.)

Army Form C. 2118.

Place	Date	Hour	Summary of Events and Information	Remarks and references to Appendices
	May 14		Major N I WHITTY, with 13 officers and 230 O.R's left in transport lines.	RPB
	15		In Bde Reserve, YPRES. Details moved into TORONTO Camp.	RPB
	16		Details attached to APM, 2nd Can Tunnelling Coy and 129th R.E.	RPB
	17			RPB
	19		In Brigade Reserve, YPRES.	7.1.8 O.O. No 142
	20		Relieved the 8th Queens in Right Subsection HOOGE I. Start 9.30 pm from LILLE GATE. CBA in front line, D Coy in Support.	RPB
	21		Capt H.S. BROWN and party to 2nd Army Rest Camp. Major N I WHITTY and party of instructors to Divnl Training Battn STEENVOORDE area. 2/Lt ORCHARDSON wounded. Lt G. BULLEN (from 1st Bn) joined for duty, from Base. 2/Lt C CLARKE (from 8th Bn). Lt W.R.C. HODGE (2/1 Cyclists Bn).	RPB
	22		Registration by hostile artillery on front and support lines.	RPB
	23		Hostile minnie bombardment during the morning. At 7pm intense artillery and minnie bombardment on our trenches. SOS signal sent up from our front line and our artillery opened up at once. Enemy fire ceased at 8.55pm but reopened at 9.30pm mostly on Support and C.T's till 11pm. Our artillery opened at once. Our own trenches were badly knocked about and had many blocks in them. It is believed that the enemy contemplated a raid. Our total casualties were 7 killed and 31 wounded. 2/Lt C CLARKE Shell Shock. One Coy of the Queens moved up into close support and one Coy moved up to ZILLEBEKE dugouts. During the early hours of night 23/24 a Russian escaped prisoner shot in front of our lines. A German NCO came over. Major N I WHITTY called back from training battalion.	RPB

A7092). Wt. W12839/M1293 750,000. 1/17. D. D & L. Ltd. Forms/C2118/14.

Instructions regarding War Diaries and Intelligence Summaries are contained in F. S. Regs., Part II. and the Staff Manual respectively. Title pages will be prepared in manuscript.

WAR DIARY
or
INTELLIGENCE SUMMARY.
(Erase heading not required.)

Army Form C. 2118.

Place	Date	Hour	Summary of Events and Information	Remarks and references to Appendices
	May 24		D Coy, from Support, relieved B in the front line. Working party of the Queens at work during night 24/25 on the damaged trenches.	RPB
	25		Draft of 50 from Base. Working party of 9th E Surreys worked on the trenches on night of 25/26	RPB
	26		Relieved by 8th Queens and moved into Bde Reserve in the Barracks YPRES. A Coy left up in close support in WELLINGTON CRESCENT and RITZ ST. Relief complete at 1.20am. Draft of 22 OR's from Base	72 I B OO 143 RPB
	27		Carrying party of 250 OR's for gas bombs carrying up to CRAB CRAWL. Working party of 100 at work on ZILLEBEKE - HELLFIRE CORNER road. 4 of the carrying party wounded	RPB
	28		Relieved by the 2nd Bedfords 89th Bde. On relief proceeded by train from YPRES on night of 28/29th. Asylum and Station heavily shelled. Detrained at HOPOUTRE and went into Camp at HOPOUTRE Area. Lt Col J.C PARKER wounded (at duty). Details attached 129th RE and Town Major rejoined.	72 I B OO 144 RPB
	29		Kit inspections. Details attd 2nd Can Tunnelling Coy rejoined.	RPB
	30		Commenced training. One limbered cart issued to complete establishment.	RPB
	31		Baths in POPERINGHE. Continue training. Total casualties for month Killed officers NIL OR's 16 / wounded " 3 OR's 38	RPB

R P Baker Capt & Adjt
8th Bn Royal West Kent Regt

A7092). Wt. W12839/M1293 750,000. 1/17. D. D & L., Ltd. Forms/C2118/14.

Instructions regarding War Diaries and Intelligence Summaries are contained in F. S. Regs., Part II. and the Staff Manual respectively. Title pages will be prepared in manuscript.

WAR DIARY

or

~~INTELLIGENCE SUMMARY.~~

(Erase heading not required.)

Army Form C. 2118.

Vol 20

Place	Date	Hour	Summary of Events and Information	Remarks and references to Appendices
			W A R D I A R Y of 8th.(S) Battn.Royal West Kent Regiment from 1st.June 1917 to 30th. June 1917. (Volume........)	

ORDERLY ROOM
No. C198
-3 JUL. 1917
8TH (SERVICE) Bn. QUEEN'S OWN ROYAL WEST KENT REGIMENT.

A7092). Wt. W12839/M1293 750,000. 1/17. D. D & L., Ltd. Forms/C2118/14.

Instructions regarding War Diaries and Intelligence Summaries are contained in F. S. Regs., Part II. and the Staff Manual respectively. Title pages will be prepared in manuscript.

WAR DIARY
or
~~INTELLIGENCE SUMMARY~~.
(Erase heading not required.)

Army Form C. 2118.

8th Bn Royal West Kent Regt

Place	Date	Hour	Summary of Events and Information	Remarks and references to Appendices
	JUNE 1		In camp in the HOPOUTRE Reserve area. Training in Progress	RPB
	2		working party 50 men ABELE station unloading shell. Training.	RPB.
	4		Training. 'W' day of 2nd Army offensive; the division in X Corps Reserve	RPB
	5		Moved out of HOPOUTRE camp to 'N' camp, Brigade assembly Area. Arrived in at 2.15 am on 6th 'Y' day. Transport remained at Devonshire camp	0.0147 RPB.
	6		Moved forward from N camp into billets in DICKEBUSCH Village; arrived at 2 am 7th. Zero hour 3 am. Situation quiet in the billets.	0.0147 RPB.
	7		moved at 1pm into G.Hq 2nd line CAFÉ BELGE; in dugouts: X Corps Reserve.	RPB
	8		remained in GHQ 2nd line: slight shelling	RPB
	9.		advance parties reconnoitred line. Moved off by Coys in the evening to take over trenches in Bde Reserve MOUNT SORREL section from 70th I. Bde. Relieved 9th KOYLI in STAFFORD Trench. Relief over at 2.15 am, 10th	RPB 00. 150.
	10		Shelled by hostile artillery: 2/Lt J.N. KILLICK W 1/a. Relieved 70th I Bde in left subsection Mt SORREL Section. Batt Hq in HEDGE St dugouts. ACD in line, B in support.	RPB.
	11		intermittent artillery fire from N.E.	RPB
	13		moved into Bde Support, relieved the 9 E. Surreys: Shelled all the time, especially on MAPLE Trench.	00 152 RPB.
	14.		shelled: aerial activity hostile	RPB.
	15.		hostile shelling: Consolidating by night.	RPB.
	17		relieved the 8th Queens in left subsection Mt SORREL Section: 8th Queens took over from us.	00 154
	19.		Relieved in left subsection by 1st R Fusiliers. On relief proceeded to MICMAC camp, arrived in at 6 am. Bde withdrawn into Divisional Reserve. 2/Lt G.H. GRIFFITH and 2/Lt S.A. FRENCH wounded.	00 155 RPB

A7092). Wt. W12839/M1293 750,000. 1/17. D. D & L., Ltd. Forms/C2118/14.

Instructions regarding War Diaries and Intelligence Summaries are contained in F. S. Regs., Part II. and the Staff Manual respectively. Title pages will be prepared in manuscript.

WAR DIARY
or
~~INTELLIGENCE SUMMARY.~~
(Erase heading not required.)

Army Form C. 2118.

Place	Date	Hour	Summary of Events and Information	Remarks and references to Appendices
	JUNE			
	21		Interior Economy in Camp.	RPB
	22		interior economy: gas helmet testing. Inspection by Corps Commander	RPB
	23		Relieved 73rd Bde in right subsection. The Battn took over from 2nd Leinsters in Reserve at Brewery Camp DICKEBUSCH. B Coy in the Triangle, had 6 casualties going in. Camp was shelled during the night	00 156 RPB
			2/Lt H.W. FARLEY and 2/Lt L.R.Y. SMITH joined for duty.	RPB.
	24.		Lt Col PARKER on leave. Major N.I. WHITTY. DSO, in command.	RPB
	25.		2/Lt A.B. RICHARDSON joined for duty	
	26		moved out of camp at DICKEBUSCH at 8 pm and relieved the 8th Queens in the left subsection BATTLE WOOD. A, B & C. Coys in front line, D Coy in support	00 157 RPB.
	27.		intermittent shelling round Batt Hq and tracks leading to front line, day and night. Part of transport sent off to LUMBRES rest area by road.	RPB
	28		Post held by A Coy bombed by enemy, by night: they were driven off. Support positions held by D Coy shelled.	RPB
	29		Relieved by 8th YORKS Regt, 69th Inf Bde: completion of relief at 2.20 am. Quiet night with comparatively little shell fire. On relief proceeded to MICMAC camp. Part of transport entrained and sent off.	00 158 RPB
	30		Moved out of MICMAC camp at 11.45 am proceeded to RENNINGHELST, entrained and travelled as far as LUMBRES, march to SENNINGHEM. Billeted in the village, 8 pm	RPB

Casualties for month of JUNE

	Officers	O R's
Killed	0	23
Wounded	3	53

A7092). Wt. W12839/M1293. 750,000. 1/17. D. D & L., Ltd. Forms/C2118/14.

R P Baker 2/Lt [illegible] 8th (S) Battn Royal West Kent Regt.

Instructions regarding War Diaries and Intelligence Summaries are contained in F. S. Regs., Part II. and the Staff Manual respectively. Title pages will be prepared in manuscript.

WAR DIARY
or
~~INTELLIGENCE SUMMARY.~~
(Erase heading not required.)

Army Form C. 2118.

Vol 21

Place	Date	Hour	Summary of Events and Information	Remarks and references to Appendices
			SECRET.	

W A R D I A R Y

of

8th. (Service) Battalion "QUEEN's OWN" (R.W.Kent Regt.,)

from 1st.July 1917 to 31st.July 1917.

(Volume ....).

A7092). Wt. W12839/M1298 750,000. 1/17. D. D. & L., Ltd. Forms/C2118/14.

JULY. **WAR DIARY** *or* ~~INTELLIGENCE SUMMARY~~. Army Form C. 2118.

Instructions regarding War Diaries and Intelligence Summaries are contained in F. S. Regs., Part II, and the Staff Manual respectively. Title pages will be prepared in manuscript.

(Erase heading not required.)

8th Bn Royal West Kent Regt.

Place	Date JULY	Hour	Summary of Events and Information — Ref maps { HAZEBROUCK 5a, ZILLEBEKE trench map 1/10,000	Remarks and references to Appendices
	1		In rest at SENINGHEM, LUMBRES area, having arrived the evening of June 30th.	RAB
	2nd to 3rd		Interior economy, kit inspections.	RAB
	4		Training for offensive operations. Rifle range constructed.	RAB
	5th to 12		Training was carried out according to table of work. The area was mainly under cultivation with standing crops and not particularly suitable.	
	13th		Practice attack by 1st N Staffs & 8th Queens witnessed by all officers.	RAB
	14		Bttn Sports	RAB
	15 to 16		Continuation of training	RAB
	17		March out from SENINGHEM, 2.45 am proceeded to RENESCURE area. Packs were carried in lorries	72 Inf Bde O.O. 160. RAB
	18		Moved out of RENESCURE, 4.35 am resumed march via STAPLE, HONDEGHEM to CAESTRE area	O.O. 160 RAB
	19		Moved out of billets at 7.45 am, marched to billets in EECKE area. Advance party sent on to prepare camp in RENINGHELST area	O.O. 160 RAB
	20		Moved out of billets at 5.5 am, marched via BOESCHEPE to RENINGHELST area, camp in field in bivouacks	O.O. 160 RAB.
	21		Moved out of camp at 7.30 am and marched via OUDERDOM to MICMAC Camp.	
	22		Proceeded to the line, took over from 10th W. Riding Regt in reserve, 69th Inf Bde, in 23rd Divnl area. Batt Hq in LARCH WOOD, A Coy in BATTERSEA FARM, B in THE DUMP, C and D SCOTTISH WOOD. Relief complete 1.15 am	O.O. 161 RAB.
	23			
	24		Draft of 151 other ranks arrived from base. Relieved the 9th E Surrey Regt on the 72nd Inf Bde Battle front. A & B in front line, C in Support D in reserve in METROPOLITAN trench. Relief complete 11 30 pm	O O 162 RAB / RAB / O O 163 RAB
	25		Working on the 72nd Inf Bde assembly trenches. Barrage rations carried up by working parties	RAB
	26.		Work on assembly trenches. Raid conducted on enemy strong point JOBS POST by 2/Lt E. G BROWN under cover of practice barrage at 5.30 pm. 12 enemy captured. During the night 4 more captured by B Coy. 2/Lt B WADE, Shell Shock.	RAB
	27		C Coy relieved A Coy in front line. Intermittent shelling during day and night.	RAB
	28		B Coy relieved by D Coy, B Coy going back into METROPOLITAN TRENCH. Intermittent shelling continues Major G. F W. POWELL 2/1st Kent Cyclist Bttn, att'd 8th R W. Kent killed i/a by shell fire. Draft 18 OR's	RAB
	29		C Coy relieved in front line by a Coy of 1st N. Staffs Regt; D Coy by Coy of 8th Queens. Relief complete by 4 15 am 30th. On relief C & D, also B Coy from METROPOLITAN LEFT, moved into the assembly positions for Support Bn in old German front & support lines, N of railway cutting	OO 166 / RAB

A7092). Wt. W12839/M1294 750,000 1/17. D. D & L., Ltd. Forms/C2118/14.

Instructions regarding War Diaries and Intelligence Summaries are contained in F. S. Regs., Part II. and the Staff Manual respectively. Title pages will be prepared in manuscript.

WAR DIARY
or
INTELLIGENCE SUMMARY.
(Erase heading not required.)

Army Form C. 2118.

Place	Date JULY	Hour	Summary of Events and Information — Ref map ZILLEBEKE trench map 1/10,000	Remarks and references to Appendices
	30		Battn in assembly position, Support Battn to the Brigade. 1st N Staffs in the front line on the left and 8th Queens on the right. Movement by day was restricted as much as possible. Work was continued on the dugouts in the area. 200 cans of water carried up to front line Battns.	RAB
	31		Zero day of 5th Army Offensive. The Battn supplied a carrying party of 2/Lt TANNER, PROCTOR and SMITH with 135 men to carry Stokes ammunition, who went over with the assaulting battalions. 2/Lt L.P.Y. SMITH was wounded by shell fire on this party. Raining weather set in making progress very ~~pad~~ bad.	00165 RAB
			Total casualties for the month were	
			Killed: Officers 1, ORS 3	
			Wounded (all causes): Officers 2, ORS 52	

R.A. Baker 2/Lt Adjt
8th Bn Royal West Kent Regt.

A7092). Wt. W12839/M1293 750,000. 1/17. D, D & L., Ltd. Forms/C2118/14.

Instructions regarding War Diaries and Intelligence Summaries are contained in F. S. Regs., Part II. and the Staff Manual respectively. Title pages will be prepared in manuscript.

WAR DIARY

or

~~INTELLIGENCE SUMMARY.~~

(Erase heading not required.)

Army Form C. 2118.

Vol 22

Place	Date	Hour	Summary of Events and Information	Remarks and references to Appendices
			W A R D I A R Y of 8th. (Service) Battalion Royal West Kent Regiment from 1st.Aug.1917 to 31st.Aug.1917. (Volume .-) To:- D.A.G., Base through 72nd.Inf.Bde H.Qs.	

A7092). Wt. W12839/M1294 750,000. 1/17. D. D & L., Ltd. Forms/C2118/14.

Ref Trench Map ZILLEBEKE 6 a 1/10000

Instructions regarding War Diaries and Intelligence Summaries are contained in F. S. Regs., Part II. and the Staff Manual respectively. Title pages will be prepared in manuscript.

WAR DIARY
or
~~INTELLIGENCE~~ SUMMARY.
(Erase heading not required.)

8th (S) Battn Royal West Kent Regt

Army Form C. 2118.

Place	Date	Hour	Summary of Events and Information	Remarks and references to Appendices
	August 1		Zero + 1 day of 5th Army offensive. The Battn still occupied their assembly trenches as on July 30th as Support Battn of 72nd Inf Bde. Carried up rations for 8th Queens. Supplied a large party from D Coy to carry down wounded from front line, under shell fire. B Coy moved out of IMMOVABLE Support and went into METROPOLITAN TRENCH to let in a Company of 9th E Surreys, who also took over the front line from 8th Queens and 1st N. Staffs. All the trenches very wet	72nd I.B O.O. 167
			2/Lt H.R. JAMES rejoined from Base	RPB.
	2		Intermittent shelling: more rain	RPB
	3		Extension of Brigade frontage to J25 d 15,80. A Coy took over front line from 13th Middlesex. D Coy + Batt Hq in CANADA St tunnels. C Coy in MT SORREL, old enemy front and support lines. B Coy in METROPOLITAN TRENCH	O.O. 168 RPB.
	4.		A Coy in front line. Ground very wet	RPB
	5		Improvement in weather conditions. A Coy opened fire on attacking party of enemy, raiding trenches held by 9th E. Surreys on the right. Heavy bombardment at 11 pm when D Coy were on their way up in relief of A.	RPB
	6		D Coy in front line	RPB
	7		Relief by 8th Buffs, night 7/8th complete by 4 30 am. B Coy relieved by 12th Sherwoods, A Coy by 1st R.F.	O.O. 170 RPB

A7092). Wt. W12839/M1293 750,000. 1/17. D. D & L., Ltd. Forms/C2118/14.

Ref. Trench Map
ZILLEBEKE 6A 1/10000

Instructions regarding War Diaries and Intelligence Summaries are contained in F. S. Regs., Part II. and the Staff Manual respectively. Title pages will be prepared in manuscript.

WAR DIARY
or
INTELLIGENCE SUMMARY.
(Erase heading not required.)

Army Form C. 2118.

Place	Date	Hour	Summary of Events and Information	Remarks and references to Appendices
	8		In huts MICMAC Camp. Kit inspection and interior economy	RMB
	9		Baths and gas helmet testing	RMB
				RMB
	10		Major N. I. WHITTY sick to F.A	OO 171 RMB.
	11		Moved to DICKEBUSCH. Brigade in Support	RMB
	13		2/Lt K. PFEUFFAR reported for duty from Base	RMB
	15		To trenches, right Subsection SHREWSBURY FOREST. Relief complete 10.30 pm B+C Coy in front line. Capt WENYON rejoined for duty as 2nd i/c, from Divn.	OO 173 RMB
	16		In trenches, Attack on 5th Army Front on left of the Battn. Zero at 4.45 am	RMB
	17		Intercompany relief during night	RMB
	18		2/Lts H.W. BEATTIE, F. CARVILLE, A.G. FULLER, A.F. POPE, B. STEPHENS, H C WALTON joined from Base for duty	RMB
	19		Relieved by 3rd RB. Complete by 10 50 pm. Proceeded to MICMAC	OO 174 RMB
	20 to 22		Interior economy and training	RMB
	23		Brigade moved up to DICKEBUSCH area, in Support. Took over camp from 2nd Leinsters.	RMB
	24		The Battn moved at 5 pm to CHATEAU SEGARD in support to 24th Divn, in consequence of an SOS	RMB
	25		Returned to H camp	RMB.

A7092). Wt. W12839/M1293. 750,000. 1/17. D. D & L., Ltd. Forms/C2118/14.

Ref. Trench Map ZILLEBEKE 6a. 1/10000

Instructions regarding War Diaries and Intelligence Summaries are contained in F. S. Regs., Part II. and the Staff Manual respectively. Title pages will be prepared in manuscript.

WAR DIARY

or

~~INTELLIGENCE~~ ~~SUMM~~ARY.

(Erase heading not required.)

Army Form C. 2118.

Place	Date	Hour	Summary of Events and Information	Remarks and references to Appendices
	26		2/Lts. H.E. OUTRAM, C.G. TILEY J H B WARDEN joined from Base for duty	RAB
	27		Relieved 7th Northants in right subsection. Heavy shelling during relief, following an SOS, but no casualties.	OO 177 RAB
	29.		2 prisoners of the 6th R.I.R brought in. D relieved A in the front line	RAB
	30		Major N I WHITTY rejoined from Hspl for duty	RAB
	31.		Relieved in front line trenches by 8th Buffs. Proceeded to MICMAC Camp.	OO 178 RAB

R l Baker Capt. Adjt
8th Bn R. West Kent Rgt.

A7092). Wt. W12839/M1293 750,000. 1/17. D. D & L., Ltd. Forms/C2118/14.

Army Form C. 2118.

Instructions regarding War Diaries and Intelligence Summaries are contained in F. S. Regs., Part II. and the Staff Manual respectively. Title pages will be prepared in manuscript.

WAR DIARY
or
INTELLIGENCE SUMMARY.
(Erase heading not required.)

Vol 23

Place	Date	Hour	Summary of Events and Information	Remarks and references to Appendices

SECRET.

WAR DIARY

of

8th.S.Battalion Royal West Kent Regt.,

from 1st.Septr. to 30th.Septr.1917.

(Volume .-)

To:-
D.A.G.? Base
(through 72nd.I.B.H.qs.)

A7092). Wt. W12839/M1293 750,000. 1/17. D. D & L., Ltd. Forms/C2118/14.

Instructions regarding War Diaries and Intelligence Summaries are contained in F. S. Regs., Part II. and the Staff Manual respectively. Title pages will be prepared in manuscript.

WAR DIARY
or
~~INTELLIGENCE SUMMARY.~~
(Erase heading not required.)

Army Form C. 2118.

Place	Date	Hour	Summary of Events and Information	Remarks and references to Appendices
	Sept 1		In MICMAC Camp, HUBERTSHOEK Refitting	RAB
	2		Lt Col J.C. PARKER sick to Hospital Major N I WHITTY left in Command with Capt H.J WENYON as Second in Command	RAB
	3		Moved up to Camp H. DICKEBUSCH. Brigade in reserve. Took over from 9th R Sussex	72 I.B. O.O. 20179 RAB
	4		Reconnoitred front line astride YPRES-MENIN road, in front of INVERNESS COPSE weather conditions improving	RAB
	5		Lieut G BULLEN, (O.C. B Coy) left for transfer to R.F.C. Lieut E.G BROWN took over B Coy	RAB
	6		Training by platoons continued	
	7		Moved up to front line left Subsection in front of INVERNESS COPSE. C B D Coys held posts in front line A Coy in Support in tunnels under MENIN road Relief took place by daylight without any hostile shelling. B Coys detached posts took over after dark. Relieved 2nd Leinsters and 7th Northants	O.O. no 180 RAB.
	8		Enemy attitude quiet, with occasional shelling of STIRLING CASTLE and MENIN tunnel entrances. Worked at night on NEW CUT Support line.	RAB
	9		Hostile attack on line of posts in INVERNESS COPSE. Bombardment started [illegible] Enemy attacked with Sturmtruppen and Flammenwerfer and succeeded in effecting an entry into C Coys posts and capturing 15 O.R's. Attack on B Coys front failed, due to our L.G. fire and intensity of our own S.O.S barrage. Capt H J WENYON organized counter attack which was carried out after preliminary barrage of rifle grenades and bombs. 2/Lt K PFEUFFAR and 2/Lt H W BEATTIE each led counter attacking parties, which with cooperation of Lewis guns and rifle grenades evicted the enemy, recapturing the posts, and taking 15 prisoners. Fire from Lewis Guns of D Coy from left flank accounted for many enemy casualties	RAB

A7092). Wt. W12839/M1293 750,000. 1/17. D. D & L., Ltd. Forms/C2118/14.

Instructions regarding War Diaries and Intelligence Summaries are contained in F. S. Regs., Part II. and the Staff Manual respectively. Title pages will be prepared in manuscript.

WAR DIARY
or
~~INTELLIGENCE SUMMARY.~~
(Erase heading not required.)

Army Form C. 2118.

Place	Date Sept	Hour	Summary of Events and Information	Remarks and references to Appendices
	9		During hostile bombardment at 4 am 2/Lt H.C. WALTON killed i/a. Lieut W R C HODGE w/a. Enemy attitude quiet for rest of day	RRB
	11		Relieved by 1st Bn Royal Fusiliers. On relief proceeded to MICMAC Camp.	O.O. 181 RRB
	12 13		Baths and refitting. Box respirators tested.	RHB
	14		Withdrawal of 24th Division. Entrained into busses and motor lorries and moved into MERRIS area. Billets in farms near MERRIS	O.O. 182 RRB
	15 17		Training according to programme by Companies + platoons.	RRB
	18		Capt T. P.P. WALKER rejoined from England and took over C Coy from Capt H.L. LEWIS Major N.I. WHITTY leave to Engl. Inspection of Battn by G O C. Capt H.J. WENYON temporarily in command of Battn	RRB
	20		The 24 Divn commenced move to Third Army IV Corps. Part of 72 I B commenced entraining at CAESTRE Station. B Coy detailed as entraining Coy for the Brigade	RRB.
	21.		The Battn marched off at 5 30 am and entrained at CAESTRE, with transport. 32 officers and 627 OR'S. Detrained on arrival at BAPAUME by night and marched, followed by transport to Camps at BEAULENCOURT arriving in at 5am on 22nd. A halt was made on the road for tea. Now in Third Army.	O.O. 183 RRB
	22.		Short Company Parades in Camp	RRB
	23.		2/Lts J.S. CRIGHTON, S.F. HOLLIDAY, F.J. JANAWAY joined from Base on appointment	RRB.

A7092). Wt. W12839/M1293. 750,000. 1/17. D. D & L., Ltd. Forms/C2118/14.

Ref Maps 57C + 62C 1/40000

Instructions regarding War Diaries and Intelligence Summaries are contained in F. S. Regs., Part II. and the Staff Manual respectively. Title pages will be prepared in manuscript.

WAR DIARY
or
~~INTELLIGENCE SUMMARY.~~
(Erase heading not required.)

Army Form C. 2118.

Place	Date	Hour	Summary of Events and Information	Remarks and references to Appendices
	Sept 25		Brigade march to Camps around HAUT ALLAINES and MOISLAINS. The Battn moved out of camp at 6.40 am with Transport. Distance marched about 9 miles	OO 184 RMB
	26		Reconnoitred front line	
	27		Moved by motor bus from HAUT ALLAINES Camp to ROISEL, the Brigade relieving the 102nd Bde of 34 Divn in Reserve. Billets in ROISEL village arriving in 11.30 am.	OO 185 RMB
	28		Moved up into trenches Left Support Battn of Centre Brigade. Night relief took over from 9th Northumberland Fusiliers.	OO 185 RMB
	29		Following officers from Base joined for duty 2/Lt's W.L.H. WALSH L.C. BAKER J BOWSKILL H.G. MICHIE.	RMB
			Working party 200 OR's on CTS. for 4 hours work at night. Fine weather.	RMB
	30		2/Lt's J.E. ARGENT P.C. BRUNGER R.A. WALKER from Base joined for duty. Major N.I. WHITTY from leave re-assumed Command of Battn. Same working parties. C Coys trenches shelled by 5.9's when engaged in counter battery work resulting in two casualties. Otherwise all quiet	RMB

R M Baker Capt. Adjt
8th (S) Bn Royal West Kent Regt.

A7092). Wt. W12839/M1293 750,000. 1/17. D. D & L., Ltd. Forms/C2118/14.

Instructions regarding War Diaries and Intelligence Summaries are contained in F. S. Regs., Part II. and the Staff Manual respectively. Title pages will be prepared in manuscript.

WAR DIARY
or
INTELLIGENCE SUMMARY.
(Erase heading not required.)

Army Form C. 2118.

Place	Date	Hour	Summary of Events and Information	Remarks and references to Appendices
			Vol 24	

S E C R E T.

WAR DIARY

of

8th.(S) Battn. Royal West Kent Rgt.,
In-the-field,
from 1st.Octr. to 31st.Oct.
1917.

(Volume .-)

A7092). Wt. W12839/M1293. 750,000. 1/17. D. D & L., Ltd. Forms/C2118/14.

Instructions regarding War Diaries and Intelligence Summaries are contained in F. S. Regs., Part II. and the Staff Manual respectively. Title pages will be prepared in manuscript.

Army Form C. 2118.

WAR DIARY
or
~~INTELLIGENCE SUMMARY.~~
(Erase heading not required.)

8th (S) Bn R. W. Kent Regt

Place	Date	Hour	Summary of Events and Information	Remarks and references to Appendices
Oct	1		In Brigade support left Subsection HARGICOURT. Major N I WHITTY in command of Battn, Capt H J WENYON second in command	RPB
	2		working parties on nightly, on ~~Sup~~ CT's. Baths.	RPB
	3		moved up to front line left subsection, to relieve 9th E Surreys. ABC Coys in front line, D in support. Daylight relief	RPB. O.O.186. 72 I.B.
	4–8		Enemy attitude quiet. Rain on 6th made trenches very wet & muddy.	RPB
	9		Relieved in front line by 9th E Surreys daylight relief, over at 5 pm moved into left Support COTE WOOD	OO 186 RPB.
	10.		Lt Col J C PARKER rejoined from Hspl. Major N I WHITTY to Corps Reinforcement Training Camp.	
	11. –15		working parties on CT's, gumboot stores, TM carrying parties nightly.	RPB
	16		To front line left subsection HARGICOURT. Relieved the 9th E Surreys Compleate at 3.15 pm DBA in front line C in Support	OO 187 RPB.
	17		Side stepped one Coy front to the left taking over one Coy front from 2nd Leinsters. ADB – order in front line. Batt Hq moved.	OO 188 RPB.
	18		In front line enemy attitude quiet.	RPB
	19.		Capt H J WENYON to 72 I B Hq for duty.	RPB.

A7092). Wt. W12839/M1293 750,000. 1/17. D. D & L., Ltd. Forms/C2118/14.

Instructions regarding War Diaries and Intelligence Summaries are contained in F. S. Regs., Part II. and the Staff Manual respectively. Title pages will be prepared in manuscript.

WAR DIARY
or
~~INTELLIGENCE SUMMARY~~.
(*Erase heading not required.*)

Army Form C. 2118.

Place	Date	Hour	Summary of Events and Information	Remarks and references to Appendices
	20		In front line. Enemy very quiet, no artillery activity	RPB
	22		Relief by 9th E Surreys by day complete at 4 pm. Moved into Divisional Reserve in VENDELLES	OO187 RPB
	23		Baths	RPB
	24		Interior economy. Training + reorganization	RPB
	25		Training	RPB
	26		Moved up to front line left sub-section HARGICOURT and relieved 9th E. Surreys. Relief carried out by daylight in heavy rain. D C A in Front Line, B in Support	O.O.189 J.B.C.
	30		Slight enemy artillery retaliation for bombardment of BELLICOURT. No casualties or damage.	J.B.C.
	31		Relieved by 9th E. Surreys by day. Bn moved back into Support at COTE WOOD.	O.O.190 J.B.C.

J. B. Cooper ?/Lt
a/adjutant
8th. S. Bn. R. West Kent Regt.

A7092). Wt. W12839/M1293 750,000. 1/17. D. D & L., Ltd. Forms/C2118/14.

Instructions regarding War Diaries and Intelligence Summaries are contained in F. S. Regs., Part II. and the Staff Manual respectively. Title pages will be prepared in manuscript.

WAR DIARY

or

~~INTELLIGENCE SUMMARY~~

(Erase heading not required.)

Army Form C. 2118.

72/24

Place	Date	Hour	Summary of Events and Information
			W A R D I A R Y of 8th.S.Battalion Royal West Kent Regt., from 1st.November 1917 to 30th.Novr.1917. (Volume .-) -------------------------

A7092. Wt. W12839/M1293 ... 1/17 D. D. & L., Ltd. Forms/C2118/14.

Instructions regarding War Diaries and Intelligence Summaries are contained in F. S. Regs., Part II. and the Staff Manual respectively. Title pages will be prepared in manuscript.

WAR DIARY
or
~~INTELLIGENCE SUMMARY.~~
(Erase heading not required.)

Army Form C. 2118.

3

Place	Date	Hour	Summary of Events and Information	Remarks and references to Appendices
	Nov 1st		Battalion in Brigade Support in LOTE TRENCH, FERVAQUE and PRIEL WOOD trenches	J.B.C.
	Nov 2 / Nov 3rd		Lt. Col. J.C. PARKER proceeds to England for duty. Major H.J. WENYON D.S.O assumes command of Bn	J.B.C.
	Nov 5th/6th		R. boundary of Brigade altered from RUBY LANE to FISH LANE (inclusive).	72nd I.B.O. J.B.C.
	Nov 7th		Bn relieved 9th E SURREY REGT in left sub-section HARGICOURT	J.B.C.
	|		wiring of front line undertaken.	J.B.C.
	Nov 13th		Bn relieved by 9th E SURREY REGT and moved back to Divisional Reserve at VENDELLES	J.B.C.
			Baths interior economy etc	J.B.C.
	Nov 14th		A, B, D Coys on working parties. C Coy training	J.B.C.
	Nov 15th		Visit of Corps Commander.	
	Nov 16th		A, B, C Coys in working parties. D Coy training.	J.B.C.
	Nov 17		whole battalion engaged in training.	
	Nov 18th			
	Nov 19th		Training	J.B.C.
	Nov 20th		Relieved 9th E. SURREY REGT in Front Line. active patrolling during the night to ascertain whether the enemy had any intention of retiring. Enemy found to be vigilant and holding his line in normal strength	J.B.C. 72nd I.B.O. 190/1
	Nov 21st 22nd 23rd 24th		New trench to connect posts in BAIT TRENCH with the general line commenced	J.B.C.
	25th		Bn moved back into Support in LOTE, FERVAQUE and PRIEL WOOD trenches.	
			2/Lt H.J. DUNN K/a.	J.B.C.
			Major N.I. WHITTY D.S.O. assumes command of the Bn. Major H.J. WENYON second in command.	J.B.C.

Army. Wt. W12839/M1298 750,000 1/17 D. D & L., Ltd. Forms/C2118/14.

Instructions regarding War Diaries and Intelligence Summaries are contained in F. S. Regs., Part II. and the Staff Manual respectively. Title pages will be prepared in manuscript.

WAR DIARY
or
~~INTELLIGENCE SUMMARY.~~
(Erase heading not required.)

Army Form C. 2118.

4

Place	Date	Hour	Summary of Events and Information	Remarks and references to Appendices
	Nov 26th		—	
	27th		—	
	28th		—	
	29th		—	
	30th		Relief by units of the Fourth Cavalry Division cancelled owing to German attack on Division on our left	J. B. C.
			J. B. Coyle Lt. & Adjt. 8th (S) Bn Royal West Kent Regt.	

A5092. Wt. W2859/M1293 750,000. 1/17. D. D. & L., Ltd. Forms/C2118/14.

Army Form C. 2118.

Instructions regarding War Diaries and Intelligence Summaries are contained in F. S. Regs., Part II. and the Staff Manual respectively. Title pages will be prepared in manuscript.

WAR DIARY
or
INTELLIGENCE SUMMARY.

(Erase heading not required.)

Vol 26

Place	Date	Hour	Summary of Events and Information	Remarks and references to Appendices

ORDERLY ROOM
No. C2
1 JAN 1918
8TH (SERVICE) Bn. QUEEN'S OWN ROYAL WEST KENT REGIMENT.

WAR DIARY

of

8th.S.Bn.Royal West Kent Regiment.

From 30.11.17 to 31.12.17

volume

(A7092). Wt W12839/M1293. 75 ,0 0. 1/17. D. D. & L., Ltd. Forms/C.2118/14.

Instructions regarding War Diaries and Intelligence Summaries are contained in F. S. Regs., Part II. and the Staff Manual respectively. Title pages will be prepared in manuscript. Ref. 62C.

WAR DIARY
or
~~INTELLIGENCE SUMMARY.~~
(Erase heading not required.)

8th Bn R. W. Kent Regt Army Form C. 2118.

Dec 1917

Place	Date Dec	Hour	Summary of Events and Information	Remarks and references to Appendices
	1		Relieved 9th Bn E Surreys in front line HARGICOURT	72.I.B RMB
			600 gas projectors discharged by special RE on our right	0.0
	3		one platoon frontage taken over from right battn	194 RMB
	5		Capt T.P.P. WALKER to TANK Corps. Capt A J PORTER took over C Coy.	[illegible] RMB
	6		Capt S.G. THOMPSON (Yeomanry) joined for duty.	
			Capt E.G. BROWN to TANK Corps. 2/Lt B. HIGGINS took over B Coy.	RMB
	7		gas projectors discharged by special RE on our right	
	8		Relieved by 9th E. Surreys & moved to Reserve, VENDELLES	
			Raid attempted by D Coy, 2/Lts CARVILLE and HOLLIDAY:	
			unsuccessful owing to wire not being all cut	oo 198 RMB.
	9		in divnl reserve at VENDELLES Baths and interior economy	
	11		Training: working party daily on road making at JEANCOURT	RMB
	12			RMB
	13		Continued with training	
	14		Relieved the 9th E. Surreys in front line HARGICOURT	RMB
			A + D in front line, C support B reserve	RMB
	15		B Coy all wiring the support line	
	16		2/Lt S.F. HOLLIDAY wounded on wiring party. Snow fell.	RMB

(A7092) Wt W12839/M1293 75,0.0. 1/17. D. D. & L., Ltd. Forms/C.2118/14.

Instructions regarding War Diaries and Intelligence Summaries are contained in F. S. Regs., Part II. and the Staff Manual respectively. Title pages will be prepared in manuscript.

WAR DIARY

or

~~INTELLIGENCE SUMMARY~~.

(Erase heading not required.)

Army Form C. 2118.

Place	Date	Hour	Summary of Events and Information	Remarks and references to Appendices
			quiet in front line snow and frost	RPB.
	17		ditto: now in Fifth Army	RPB
	18		more frost: misty all quiet	RPB
	19		A Coy relieved by 20th Hussars, 5th Cav Bde, & moved out	
	20		to VRAIGNES	RPB
			Battn relieved by 8th Buffs 17 Inf Bde. Complete by 12.15 pm	60
	21		moved in lorries to camp in HANCOURT. Bde in reserve	195 RPB
			CO's inspection	RPB
	23		Training, Range practices. Continuance of cold weather.	RPB
	24		no training. Company dinners.	RPB
	25		Xmas day.	RPB
			Lt Col NI WHITTY DSO to England for duty with M.G. Corps	RPB
	26		Major HJ WENYON DSO in Command.	RPB
			2/Lt W.L.H WALSH & Lt. L WILLOUGHBY transferred to 6th Bn	RPB
	28		2/Lt L. WEST and Lt P.A. GEDGE join for duty	
	29		Church parades	RPB
	30		Training. Cold weather continues.	RPB
	31		Effective strength of Battn: 38 officers, 676 ORs: 294 OR's below Estt.	RPB

R P Baker Capt & Adjt
8th R.W. Kent Regt.

(A7092). Wt W12839/M1293 75,000. 1/17. D. D. & L., Ltd. Forms/C.2118/14.

4

Instructions regarding War Diaries and Intelligence Summaries are contained in F. S. Regs., Part II. and the Staff Manual respectively. Title pages will be prepared in manuscript.

WAR DIARY
or
INTELLIGENCE SUMMARY.
(Erase heading not required.)

Army Form C. 2118.

24

Vol 27

Place	Date	Hour	Summary of Events and Information	Remarks and references to Appendices
			Secret War Diary of 8th S. Bn. Royal West Kent Regt. from 1st Jany 1918 to 31st Jany 1918 (Volume.)	

(A7092). Wt W12839/M1293 75,0.0. 1/17. D. D. & L., Ltd. Forms/C.2118/14.

Army Form C. 2118.

WAR DIARY
or
INTELLIGENCE SUMMARY.
(Erase heading not required.)

8th (S) Bn Royal West Kent Regt

Instructions regarding War Diaries and Intelligence Summaries are contained in F. S. Regs., Part II. and the Staff Manual respectively. Title pages will be prepared in manuscript.

Ref HARGICOURT 1/10000 and FRANCE 62 C 1/40000

Place	Date	Hour	Summary of Events and Information	Remarks and references to Appendices
	Jan 1		In Reserve at HANCOURT, in huts. Inspection of Battn by B.G.C. Frost still holding.	RPB
	2		Move from HANCOURT to VENDELLES (Support)	72 IB O.O. No 201
			Major H J WENYON (in command) back from leave	RPB.
	3		Working party 250 ORS on B Switch line wiring at JEANCOURT	RPB
	4		Work as for 3rd. Frost still holding. Reconnoitred front line	RPB
	5		Moved up to front line right sub section HARGICOURT in relief of 2nd Leinsters. Start at 9am all in at 2.5pm. B Coy in front line, C in support D Support ii A in reserve at L10 a	72 IB OO 201 RPB
	6		Thaw commenced but frost at night 2/Lieuts E.C. ANDREWS J. MALBY C.P.H MANLEY joined for duty	RPB
	7		Trench work impossible owing to hardness of ground. All men from reserve & Support coys were employed on carrying up RE material. C Coy relieved B in front line	RPB
	8		Situation very quiet in front line. 6" of snow by night, then frost. Carried up large quantities of RE material and wire was put out	RPB
	9		B Coy to front line in relief of C. Freezing. Snow. good visibility	RPB
	10		Trenches got very bad owing to thaw all day. BELLICOURT was bombarded by the heavies	RPB

(A7092) Wt W12539/M1293 750,000 1/17. D. D. & L., Ltd. Forms/C.2118/14.

Army Form C. 2118.

Instructions regarding War Diaries and Intelligence Summaries are contained in F. S. Regs., Part II. and the Staff Manual respectively. Title pages will be prepared in manuscript.

WAR DIARY
or
INTELLIGENCE SUMMARY.

(Erase heading not required.)

Place	Date	Hour	Summary of Events and Information	Remarks and references to Appendices
	11		C Coy to front line in relief of B. A Coy revetted new trench between CURTAIN LANE and detached posts in BAIT TRENCH by night but work was very difficult owing to condition of ground. All trenches very wet. Patrol done by 2/Lt C.C. BARING. Our TM's conducted a shoot on RUBY WOOD	RPB
	12.		Trenches very wet and heavy. Work on new trench continued. Patrol done by D Coy.	RPB
	13.		Relieved during afternoon by 8th BUFFS and moved to MONTIGNY FARM. Bde in Support. Men in Adrian huts. Very incomplete camp.	72 T B 003 RPB
	14		Heavy rain. Worked in camp on improvements.	RPB
	15		Working party of 200 OR's for work on the Intermediate Line.	RPB
	16		D Coy Commenced digging practice trenches for proposed raid. From this date onwards to the 29th every man in the Battn was out on working parties, day or night. The working strength of the Battn started at 250 OR but decreased as D Coy were excluded in order to practice the proposed raid after they had dug their model trenches. Work was concentrated on the forward area, digging and	RPB

(A7092). Wt W12839/M1293 75,000 1/17. D. D. & L., Ltd. Forms/C.2118/14.

Instructions regarding War Diaries and Intelligence Summaries are contained in F. S. Regs., Part II. and the Staff Manual respectively. Title pages will be prepared in manuscript.

WAR DIARY
or
INTELLIGENCE SUMMARY.
(*Erase heading not required.*)

Army Form C. 2118.

Place	Date	Hour	Summary of Events and Information	Remarks and references to Appendices
	16 (ctd) to 29		wiring the Intermediate line and various switch lines and forward defensive works; digging in BOLSOVER TUNNEL, unloading RE material at various dumps: erection of huts at VERMAND. There were no men available for work round the camp except a few regimental employs. The huts were tarred and re-roofed, stoves fitted, 3 latrines erected and a considerable number of minor improvements carried out	RPB
	20		Practice taking up battle positions in HARGICOURT TRENCH	RPB
	23		2/Lt C TRENCHARD-DAVIS reported for duty	RPB
	26		a/Major W R CORRALL from 5th Buffs posted as 2nd in Command to the Battn	RPB
	28		Hostile aircraft bombing raid on MONTIGNY DUMP at night. One bomb fell close to hut occupied by A Coy, and 2 of their men were wounded and 1 sl wounded	RPB
	29		2/Lt P.H. TYLER joined for duty	RPB
	30		Moved to front line in relief of 2nd Leinsters. Start at 8.30 am, relief over at 2 pm. Moved by Track A. Trenches and tracks in a very bad state	RPB

(A7092). Wt. W12839/M1293. 75 ,0.0. 1/17. D. D. & L., Ltd. Forms/C.2118/14.

Instructions regarding War Diaries and Intelligence Summaries are contained in F. S. Regs., Part II. and the Staff Manual respectively. Title pages will be prepared in manuscript.

WAR DIARY
or
INTELLIGENCE SUMMARY.
(Erase heading not required.)

Army Form C. 2118.

Place	Date	Hour	Summary of Events and Information	Remarks and references to Appendices
	31.		In front line trenches. A Coy in front line, D in close support C in support at Batt Hq, B back in reserve at L. 10 a. Enemy more alert in this sector than formerly, firing darts and sniping at movement.	
			Command during Jan'y.	
			Major H J WENYON DSO. in command	
			Capt W J EWEN — A Coy.	
			" C.R.H. ALLWORTH — " B	
			2/Lt K PFEUFFAR M.C — C, till going on leave	
			Lt H.R. JAMES	
			2/Lt F CARVILLE — D.	
			"Fighting" strength at end of month 643 OR's.	
			R P Baker Capt. Adjt 8th (S) Bn R. W. Kent Regt.	

(A7092). Wt W12839/M1293 75,0 0. 1/17. D. D. & L., Ltd. Forms/C.2118/14.

Army Form C. 2118.

Vol 28

WAR DIARY
or
INTELLIGENCE SUMMARY.
(Erase heading not required.)

Instructions regarding War Diaries and Intelligence Summaries are contained in F. S. Regs., Part II. and the Staff Manual respectively. Title pages will be prepared in manuscript.

Place	Date	Hour	Summary of Events and Information	Remarks and references to Appendices

S E C R E T.

W A R   D I A R Y

of

8th.(S) Battalion Royal West Kent Regiment

from ... 1st.Feb. to 28th.Feb. 1918

(Volume .-   )

(A7092). Wt W12839/M1293. 75,0 o. 1/17. D. D. & L., Ltd. Forms/C.2118/14.

Ref. Map HARGICOURT Special Sheet 1/10,000

Instructions regarding War Diaries and Intelligence Summaries are contained in F. S. Regs., Part II. and the Staff Manual respectively. Title pages will be prepared in manuscript.

WAR DIARY
or
~~INTELLIGENCE SUMMARY.~~
(Erase heading not required.)

8th Battn R. West Kent Regt.

Army Form C. 2118.

Place	Date	Hour	Summary of Events and Information	Remarks and references to Appendices
	Feb 1.		In front line trenches HARGICOURT. A Coy in front line, D close support C in Support at Batt Hq, B at L10a in reserve. B Coy had 2 casualties from shell fire. RSM RANKIN hit by rifle bullet. Misty morning + frost. B + C supplied working parties for front line, draining and pumping	RPB
	2		Clear day. Wire cutting by 6" Newtons to make gaps in enemy wire for raid. Parties of D Coy reconnoitred No man's land at night, for raid.	RPB
	3.		Raid by D Coy on enemy trenches. No prisoners taken but casualties inflicted on enemy. 2/Lt F. CARVILLE W/a 2/Lt J.S. CRIGHTON wounded and prisoner. C Coy relieved A Coy in front line after midnight, and A went back to support	appendix 1 & 2 RPB.
	4		quiet day. Batt Hq shelled at intervals during the night by NAUROY group. A and B sent up to front line for work. The SOS was sent up on the divisional front in apprehension of a raid	RPB
	5		Extension of Battn frontage. B Coy took over one Coy frontage from the 1st N. Staffs after dark, the front now being RUBY LANE to CLUB LANE. B Coys position was an isolated one (posts) with access only after dark. D Coy still in POND SUPPORT and C Coy in front line. A Coy worked on ONION LANE	72nd I. Bde O.O. 511 RPB.
	6.		Enemy attitude very quiet. Trenches getting drier owing to improvement of weather. A Coy worked in front line at night, also a party of the 9th R. SUSSEX.	RPB.

(A7092) Wt W12839/M1293 750,000 1/17. D. D. & L., Ltd. Forms/C.2118/14.

Ref. HARGICOURT Special sheet 1/10000 and 62C NE 1/20000

Instructions regarding War Diaries and Intelligence Summaries are contained in F. S. Regs., Part II. and the Staff Manual respectively. Title pages will be prepared in manuscript.

WAR DIARY
or
INTELLIGENCE SUMMARY.
(Erase heading not required.)

Army Form C. 2118.

Place	Date	Hour	Summary of Events and Information	Remarks and references to Appendices
	7.		Relief by 8th Queens (17th Inf Bde). Moved by trains from TEMPLEUX to HANCOURT. Relief complete 7.15 pm. Draft of 125 OR's arrived from 3/4th Battn (T.F.). Lt J.H. SELFE, 2/Lt S.E.G. QUESTED, 2/Lt D.M. OLIVER joined for duty	72nd Inf Bde OO. 6 RPB
	8		In Camp at HANCOURT. Cleaning up and kit inspections.	RPB
	9		Whole Battn out at work on rear defences, digging GREEN LINE. Each man did a task of 80 cubic ft.	RPB
	10, 11,		} the Same	RPB
	12		the Same. Capt F.C NEEDHAM from 3/4th Battn joined for duty	RPB
	13		Moved up to Bde Support in COTE WOOD in relief of the SIALKOT dismtd Cav. Bde. By train from HANCOURT to TEMPLEUX. Relief complete at 7.7 pm. A and D Coy in FERVAQUE - COTE TRENCH. B and C in dugouts at L 10.a. One platoon A Coy at VILLERET	Bde OO. 7 RPB.
	14		Worked on INTERMEDIATE LINE	RPB
	15.		Same. C Coy supplied a party of 50 for work on NOSE TRENCH. Rest of the Battn	RPB
	16, 17		B Coy worked on NOSE TRENCH, A on VILIA and VIOLET posts. Rest of the Battn worked on FERVAQUE TR.	RPB
	18		Relieved by 9th E. Surrey Regt at COTE WOOD. Moved up to front line in relief of 1st N Staffs in Right Subsector. Hq at the EGG. Relief Complete at 7 pm. 2/Lt C.D. WHITBOURN from 3/4th Bn joined	Appendix 3 RPB

(A7092). Wt W12839/M1293 750,000 1/17 D. D. & L., Ltd. Forms/C.2118/14.

Ref HARGICOURT Special sheet 1/10000

Instructions regarding War Diaries and Intelligence Summaries are contained in F. S. Regs, Part II. and the Staff Manual respectively. Title pages will be prepared in manuscript.

WAR DIARY
or
INTELLIGENCE SUMMARY.
(Erase heading not required.)

Army Form C. 2118.

Sheet 62C NE 1/20000 : AMIENS 1/100,000

Place	Date	Hour	Summary of Events and Information	Remarks and references to Appendices
	20		Heavy retaliation for shoot on RUBY WOOD. Very slight damage done and no casualties.	RPB
	22.		Relief. A Coy relieved by 8th Queens, remainder by 9th E. Surreys. Relief complete at 7.10 pm. Proceed to billets in VENDELLES, and took over from 3rd R.B. Casualties for tour 1 OR K i/a 5 OR w i/a	Appendix 4 RPB.
	23.		Interior economy, baths. Reconnaissance of battle position in RED LINE various working parties on rear defences.	RPB
	24.		distribution of medal ribbons by CORPS Commander at MONTIGNY. Battn mess started. Football match with HORSE GUARDS. Draft of 67 OR'S (mostly young boys from Training Reserves)	RPB
	25.		CO's inspections. Advance parties moved off to CORBIE area	RPB.
	26.		Transport moved off to Rest area, under Capt NEEDHAM.	72 IB OO no 10
	27.		Relieved at VENDELLES by 2/7th Manchesters. Relief complete at 9.30 am Entrained at ROISEL at 12 noon, detrained at VILLERS BRETONNEUX at 4.40 pm. Marched to LA NEUVILLE, billets. Arrived in after dark in rain; billets not very Satisfactory. Draft 108 OR'S joined.	RPB. RPB
	28		Interior economy in billets.	RPB.

Command during Feb:–
Lt Col H.J. WENYON D.S.O.
Maj W.R. CORRALL (5th Buffs) on detachment

A Coy Capt W.J. EWEN
B " " CRH ALLWORTH
C " S.G. THOMPSON
D " F. PROCTOR.

R.P. Baker Capt & Adjt
8th (S) Bn R.W. Kent Regt.

(A7092) Wt W12839/M1293 75,0.0. 1/17. D. D. & L., Ltd. Forms/C.2118/14.

Orders for Fighting Patrol. Appendix 1

1. A fighting patrol will enter enemy front line, capture enemy post at G.1.d.90.22, kill or capture any garrison occupying dug-outs between G.1.d.88.23 and G.2.c.0.4., and destroy these dugouts.

2. **Wire cutting-** Gaps to be cut in advance by 6" Newtons at G.1.d.87.18 and G.1.d.95.43-

Other gaps are being cut by 6" Newtons at

G.7.b.88.65
G.7.b.90.87
G.2.c.05.95

Battalions in the line opposite these points to be asked to keep these gaps under persistent Lewis Gun and Rifle fire.

3. **Plan of Attack**

Enemy trench will be entered at 2 points :-

G.1.d.9.2 and G.2.c.00.42.

Patrol will be organised in parties, which will enter enemy trench or proceed to their stations outside the enemy trench, in the following order:-

	Party	Consisting of	Enter enemy trench at	Role
Enter simultaneously	1	2 N.C.O. & 3	G.2.c.00.41	Block enemy front line at G.2.c.05.45
	5	1 N.C.O. & 3	G.1.d.9.2.	Block enemy front line at G.1.d.88.10
	2	1 N.C.O & 4	G.2.c.00.41	Block enemy C.T. at G.2.c.10.41.
Enter simultaneously	3	1 Off. 2 N.C.Os. 5 men and two sappers.	G.2.c.00.40	Deal with posts & dugouts between point of entry and G.1.d.92.30
	4	1 Off. 1 N.C.O. 6 men and 2 sappers.	G.1.d.9.2.	Capture enemy post at G.1.d.90.22 & deal with dugouts and saps between point of entry and G.1.d.92.30.
	6	1 Off. 2 N.C.Os 6 men 2 sappers 4 stretcher Bearers divided into sections as follows:-		

Control Station.	(a)	1 Off. and 1 man with telephone 2 sappers with Bangalore torpedoes 4 stretcher bearers	remain at G.1.d.80.35 to control communications. Blow gap in wire at G.1.d.83.35 <u>after</u> patrol has entered enemy trench.
	(b)	1 N.C.O. & 2	Forming chain of connecting files between southern point of entry and Control Station.
	(c)	1 N.C.O. & 3	Forming chain of connecting files between northern point of entry and Control Station.

3. Plan of attack- continued-

Party	Consisting of	Enter enemy trench at	Role.
7.	5 runners		Forming chain of connecting files between control post and BAIT TRENCH at G.1.d.62.35.

The control Post will be connected by phone to Dug-out in POND TRENCH at G.1.d.38.18 which will be connected with :-
(i) Artillery direct.
(ii) Brigade Headquarters via Battalion H.Qs.

COMMENCEMENT OF PATROL- A Zero time will be fixed at which all parties will proceed from their assembly positions.

CONTINUATION OF PATROL- The parties will remain in position till their task is completed.

The pass word BOBBY will be used between men on the patrol to avoid difficulties if two parties meet.

CONCLUSION OF PATROL-

When the task is completed the Commander of the patrol will order parties 3 and 4 to return to our trenches. When these parties are out of the enemy trench the Commander of No.4 party will send two of his men to No.5 party with a small glass bottle with his name written on a paper inside.

The commander of No.3 party will similarly send two small glass bottles to No.1 and No.2 parties.

On receipt of these glass bottles the parties will return to our trenches.
Party 6 will remain in position until the whole of the parties in the enemy trench have returned.

If the glass bottle method fails, "The Cookhouse Door" Bugle call will be sounded from BAIT TRENCH.

If this fails a Green Rocket will be fired from BAIT TRENCH.

CODE WORDS.-

IN Enemy trench successfully entered.
Howitzers and 3" Stokes commence firing on selected points.
4.5 Hows. on G.2.c.14.67 and G.2.c.6.4.
3" Stokes on G.7.b.85.95.
[illegible] SKIN TRENCH

BUMP Box barrage from Artillery required.

PIG Prisoner. e.g. 4 Pigs = 4 Prisoners.

CAMP Patrol back in our trenches.

Our Casualties.

APPLE	Killed
PLUM	wounded
TURNIP	missing.

[signature]
.... Major,
25th.January 1918. Commanding 8th.S.Battn.Royal West Kent Regt.

Appendix 2

The raid on the enemy position at G.1.d.9.3. was carried out last night.

The Assembling of the parties in No Man's Land was carried out in good order as arranged, and the circumstances seeming to be favourable The Commander of each Party took all his men to forward assembly positions on the enemy wire within a few yards of the Gaps. This was completed by the Right Party at 9.55 p.m. and by the Left Party at about 10.5 p.m.

The Control Post had proceeded to its position at G.1.d.85.35. and Advanced Battalion Headquarters was in touch with 2/lieut JANAWAY by telephone from 9.0 p.m. until about 11.10 p.m.

At 9.55 p.m. 2/Lieut. CARVILLE led his party into the enemy trench at G.1.d.90.15. The wire had been perfectly cut and the entry was made without difficulty. The party then proceeded along the trench Northwards and reached a point about G.1.d.9.2. where an enemy post is normally held. This was found to be unoccupied and the party proceeded again towards the suspected dug-out at G.1.d.90.30. At this moment loud shouting was heard and a large party of the enemy appeared on the high bank which forms the parados of the trench at this point. Our men were very heavily bombed from this bank and further reinforcements in large numbers came across, probably from dug-outs in the bank at G.2.c.00.05. One of the enemy, either Officer or Warrant-Officer, dropped into the front line at about G.1.d.90.25 and made off North. 2/Lieut. CARVILLE at once pursued him an fired four revolver shots into him at close range. 2/Lieut. CARVILLE did not consider it possible to search this man as by this time the enemy party had been considerably reinforced, his party was hopelessly out-numbered and in great danger of being cut off.

It was impossible to scale the parados and the order was given for our party to throw all remaining bombs and return to their assembly positions in No Man's Land. One of the enemy stood up to throw a bomb and was shot by 2/Lieut. CARVILLE.

By this time 2/Lieut. CARVILLE had been twice wounded but he succeeded in getting his party back to shell-holes outside the enemy wire. From here he ordered the party to return to our trenches in small parties and finally returned himself at 10.45 p.m. The casualties in this party were several but not serious, but unfortunately a trench mortar fell among a party of six entering our trenches in CURTAIN LANE and killed or wounded them all.

. . .

The Left Party eneterd the enemy trenches at about 10.10 p.m. the (42. two blocking parties proceeded to their posts at G.2.c.10.60 and G.2.c.10. Two of the enemy retreated down the C.T. and were fired at by the blocking party.

. . . . .

2/Lieut CRIGHTON led his party to the 'T' head at G.1.d.95.42. This was found to be unoccupied but very fully stocked with bombs. The alarm was given by two men running Northwards behind the trench shouting 'English'. From the 'T' head our party made for the enemy trench and just as they were entering it 2/Lieut. CRIGHTON was shot. Men appeared to come out of about four dug-out entrances behind the trench as four patches of light could be seen and there was a good deal of shouting. A word like 'Mull' was passed down from mouth to mouth and our party was heavily bombed from the parados.

Sergt. VANNER had taken command of the party and all available bombs were thrown. The blocking parties co-operated. Sergt. VANNER then went to the blocking parties and gave the order to return through the enemy wire. He and Sergt. ALLEN stayed behind and attempted to get 2/Lieut CRIGHTON'S body away. They succeeded in dragging him some 15 yards towards the 'T' head but they were seen and fired at by several rifles from about 15 yards away. Another effort was made to move the body but Sergt. VANNER was then heavily bombed as well as fired at. They could not get the body any further. Sergt. ALLEN was hit slightly.

Outside the enemy wire two of our party were wounded and Sergt. VANNER. Sergt. ALLEN succeeded in getting them back to BAIT TRENCH. They were all reported in at 11.0 p.m.

2/Lieut JANAWAY was still at the CONTROL POST. He succeeded in gaining touch with the left party and kept me fully informed by telephone of their movements. He made four attempts to gain touch with the Right Party but was prevented by heavy volleys of bombs and darts which were put down by the enemy in front of his own wire. The enemy was continually bombing his wire just in front of the control post but 2/Lieut JANAWAY and the Sapper detailed for the work succeeded in exploding one Bangalore Torpedo in the wire.

After this the enemy trench mortared the Control Post, very severely wounded one of the stretcher bearers in 2/Lieut JANAWAY'S party and buried 2/Lieut JANAWAY. I then ordered 2/Lieut JANAWAY to return. With the help of Cpl. ANDREWS the wounded man got in with very great difficulty. 2/Lieut. JANAWAY finally returned to our line at 12 midnight, having been at his post in very difficult circumstances, constantly being bombed and later, trench-mortared, for three hours. His work in keeping touch with the left party and keeping me informed of what was happening, was of the greatest value.

It was quite impossible for either attacking party to get in touch with the enemy - and in both cases our party was considerably outnumbered. Asfar as possible in the case of each of these parties, as well as at the control post, the plans made were carried out.

The return to our trenches was carried out in orderly fashion. The Total casualties in the raiding party and the trench garrison were :-

1 Officer and 5 other ranks killed
1 Officer and 12 other ranks wounded.

Also two of the sappers attached were wounded. A large proportion of these casualties were caused through enemy trench mortars falling in one of the posts in our trenches and among the party of six men previously mentioned.

I would like to point out the very excellent work done by the following Officers and N.C.Os.

2/Lieut. CARVILLE	i/c Right Party.
2/Lieut. JANAWAY	i/c Control Post and connecting file.
Sergeant VANNER	i/c Left Party (after 2/Lieut.CRIGHTON had been killed)
Sergeant ALLEN	i/c Left Blocking Parties.
Corporal ANDREWS	i/c Forward Stretcher Bearers attached to 2/Lieut. JANAWAY's Party

Communication back and forward worked most excellently throughout. The wire out to 2/Lieut.JANAWAY fortunately held until after the return of the Left Parties.

The cutting of the enemy wire was perfectly done by 'Y' Battery of the 6" Newtons. Lieut HENNETT carried out the observed shooting necessary from an open forward trench during the two days previous. The trench from which he had to observe is the special mark for enemy retaliation when the 6" Newtons fire and the very greatest credit is due to Lieut. HENNETT for the fearless way in which he carried out the shooting. His position was being heavily trench-mortared at all times while observing, yet the perfection of the gaps made, speak fully for the thoroughness of his work.

(Sd) H.J. WENYON
Major.
Commanding 8th S. Bn. Royal West Kent Regt.

4th February 1918.

SECRET. Battalion Operation Order No.68 COPY NO. 3

by

Lieut-Col. H.J.WENYON, D.S.O.

Commanding 8th.S.Battn.Royal West Kent Regiment.

In-the-field, 17.9.1918.

Appendix 3

1. The Battalion will be relieved in Support by the 9th.E.Surrey Regt. on the afternoon 18/19th. inst, and on relief will take over the front line, Right Sector, from the 1st.North Staffordshire Regiment.

2. The 9th.E.Surrey Regt., will commence taking over from about 4 p.m. and onwards. Teas at 3.30 p.m. Companies will move off as soon as relieved to take up their positions in the line.

3. Blankets to be rolled and stacked at Battn.H.Qs. to await collection by Transport, and left in charge of one man.

4. Companies to make their own arrangements for moving trench bundles, dixies, etc., to their new H.Qs.

5. Advance parties- the usual advance parties to proceed in the afternoon early for taking over stores. They will make any arrangements required direct with the O's C.Companies of 1st.N.Staffords Rgt., as regards guides for posts.

6. Rations will be dumped at the Crater, HARGICOURT, at about 6.30 p.m.-("B" Coy's at their H.Qs) Companies to make their own arrangements for ration carrying and truck pushing. One water cart will come up nightly to the CRATER. "B" Company will be supplied nightly with 20 tins of Water from Transport Lines.

7. Trench Stores, Defence schemes, etc., to be handed over; a separate receipt to be taken for Iron Rations.

8. Relief by 9/E.Surrey's to be notified to Battalion Headquarters at COTE WOOD. "A" and "D" Companies are not to cross the open ground forward of COTE-FERVAQUE Trench.

(Sgd). J. B. C R Y E R, 2/Lieut.,

A/Adjutant, 8th.S.Battn.R.W.KENT REGIMENT.

Copies to:-

1. File
2.} War Diary.
3.}
4. O.C., 1st.N.Staffords Regt.,
5. O.C., 9th.E.Surrey Regt.,
6. O.C. "A" Company
7. O.C. "B" Company
8. O.C. "C" Company
9. O.C. "D" Company
10. Headquarters' Mess.
11. Quartermaster.
12. Signalling Officer.
13. A/R.S.Major.
14. Transport Sergeant.

SECRET. Battalion Operation Order No. 80 COPY NO......

by

Lieut-Col. H. J. WENYON, D.S.O.

Commanding 8th. S. Battn. Royal West Kent Regiment.

In-the-field, 20.2.1918.

- - - - - - - - - - - - - - - - Appendix 4

1. The following reliefs will take place tomorrow-

(a) "A" Company will be relieved by a Company of the 8th. Bn. The Queen's Regt., Relief to be complete by 12 noon.

(b) The remaining 3 Companies of the Battalion will be relieved by the 9th. Battn. E. Surrey Regt.,

All companies will proceed on relief to VENDELLES.

2. Route-

"A" Company - L.10.a. - COTE WOOD - FERVAQUE TRENCH - JEANCOURT. O.C. "A" Company will send a picquet in advance to ensure that all men enter the trench well below the crest.

"B" Company - Direct track to JEANCOURT.

"C", "D" & H.Qs. - L.10.a. - JEANCOURT.

3. Advance parties- Officers Commanding Companies will send down advance parties under an Officer during the morning to report to Captain R. P. BAKER at VENDELLES and take over billets.

Officers i/c Advance parties will be responsible for meeting their Companies and guiding them in.

4. Transport-

For "A" Company - L.10.a. at 1.30 p.m.
For "B" Company - Coy H.Qs at 7.30 p.m.
For "C", "D" & H.Qs.- CRATER at 8.0 p.m.

Two men per Company will be left in charge of Lewis Guns and stores and will proceed with Transport to VENDELLES.

5. Trench stores, maps, work in hand and proposed, Reserve Rations and 'S.O.S.' Rockets must be carefully handed over.

Receipts for all stores to be handed in to Orderly Room.

6. Completion of relief will be notified by wiring Company Commander's name.

Arrival at VENDELLES will be notified to Orderly Room by runner.

(Sgd). J. B. C R Y E R, 2/Lieut.,

A/Adjutant, 8th. S. Bn. ROYAL WEST KENT REGT.,

Copies to:-

1. File.
2.) War Diary.
3.)
4. O.C., 8th. Queen's (R.W.S.) Regt.,
5. O.C., 9th. East Surrey Regt.,
6. O.C. "A" Company
7. O.C. "B" Company
8. O.C. "C" Company
9. O.C. "D" Company
10. Headquarters' Mess.
11. Captain R. P. BAKER.
12. Quartermaster.
13. Signalling Officer.
14. A/R.S. Major.
15. Transport Sergeant.

72nd Brigade.

24th Division.

8th BATTALION

ROYAL WEST KENT REGIMENT

M A R C H 1 9 1 8

Appendix :-

Account of Operations 19.3.18 - 5.4.18.

B149 / 11

Mar 1918 — Army Form C. 2118.

Vol 29

Instructions regarding War Diaries and Intelligence Summaries are contained in F. S. Regs., Part II. and the Staff Manual respectively. Title pages will be prepared in manuscript.

WAR DIARY
or
INTELLIGENCE SUMMARY.
(Erase heading not required.)

Place	Date	Hour	Summary of Events and Information	Remarks and references to Appendices
			SECRET.	
			War Diary of 8th S. Bn. Royal West Kent Regt. March 1918. (Volume –)	

2353 Wt. W2544/1454 700,000 5/15 D. D. & L. A.D.S.S./Forms/C. 2118.

Instructions regarding War Diaries and Intelligence Summaries are contained in F. S. Regs., Part II. and the Staff Manual respectively. Title pages will be prepared in manuscript.

WAR DIARY
or
~~INTELLIGENCE~~ SUMMARY.
(Erase heading not required.)

Army Form C. 2118.

8th Battn Royal West Kent Regt.

Ref FRANCE 62 C

Place	Date	Hour	Summary of Events and Information	Remarks and references to Appendices
	March 1. 1918.		Marched out of LA NEUVILLE (CORBIE) at 4 am: entrained at VILLERS-BRETONNEAUX 9.30 am. Detrained at BRIE and marched to camp at DEVISE, took over Cavalry camp. All in at 4 pm. Transport came by road. Weather fine but cold. Snow in evening.	RPB
	2.		In camp at DEVISE at one hour notice	RPB
	3.		Interior economy. C O reconnoitred line	RPB
	4-5		Platoon training commenced. Constructed range and assault course.	RPB
	6.		Inter platoon football competition started	RPB
	7.		Training. Capt J R WOOD to England 1 month leave. 2/Lt JHB WARDEN sick to England	RPB
	8.		Battn parade ceremonial. Lt B. HIGGINS to Engl. 6 months duty.	RPB
	9.		Reconnoitred new sector. Battn parade	RPB
	10		Brigade parade Inspection by Commander XIX Corps.	RPB
	11.		To line. Moved by lorry to BIHECOURT, thence march to VADENCOURT in relief of units of 2nd dismtd Divn. A+C in outpost Zone. Relief complete 11.10 pm. B+D garrison of VADENCOURT. Patrols from 1 am to dawn. 2/Lt E. LEVEY reported for duty.	RPB
	12.		Capt A.E. JONES reported for duty. Defensive patrols out till dawn.	RPB

A7092). Wt. W12839/M1293 750,000. 1/17. D. D & L., Ltd. Forms/C2118/14.

Instructions regarding War Diaries and Intelligence Summaries are contained in F. S. Regs., Part II. and the Staff Manual respectively. Title pages will be prepared in manuscript.

WAR DIARY

or

INTELLIGENCE SUMMARY.

(Erase heading not required.)

Army Form C. 2118.

Place	Date	Hour	Summary of Events and Information	Remarks and references to Appendices
	March 11 1918		Map BELLENGLISE Special Sheet 1/10,000	
			The front of about 1600 yards taken over by the Battalion extended from the OMIGNON RIVER at M8 (Central) to M2.A.0.7.	
			The outpost zone was one of considerable depth and went back to MAREVAL and POINTRU Trenches R.11.D. & R.12.C.	
			The Right forward Company was disposed as follows – Coy HQ and 1 platoon POINTRU Trench. Forward Coy HQ in Mustard Quarry M7 B.5.7. 3 Platoons holding isolated posts:- International Post, River Post, Cressy Trench, Barrier post and Mustard Quarry.	
			The left forward Company was disposed as follows – Coy HQ and 1 platoon MAREVAL Trench. Forward Coy HQ in Salt Trench. 3 Platoons holding isolated posts – Salt Trench, Rat Post, Lone Tree post.	
			In the front of the forward post was a wide NO MANS LAND 1000–1500 yards.	
			By day most of the new sectors and the outpost zone was used as a line of Observation. By night the whole of No mans land was actively patrolled. About 4 officers & 80 men were employed each night for this purpose.	

Instructions regarding War Diaries and Intelligence Summaries are contained in F. S. Regs., Part II. and the Staff Manual respectively. Title pages will be prepared in manuscript.

WAR DIARY
or
INTELLIGENCE SUMMARY.
(Erase heading not required.)

Army Form C. 2118.

Place	Date	Hour	Summary of Events and Information	Remarks and references to Appendices
	March 11 1918.		Map BELLENGLISE Special Sheet 1:10,000. The outpost zone was manned in such a way that its garrison could delay and disorganise an enemy attack – the posts being mutually supporting and having good fields of fire. In front of MAREVAL and POINTRU trenches a number of Vickers Guns of the 24th Divl M.G. Battn were in position. The battle zone (Red line) ran through VADENCOURT Chateau defences. Battalion HQ and 2 Companies were in position there, and all the troops had allotted battle positions. The garrison was assisted by 5 Vickers Guns and 2 6" Newton Mortars. Vadencourt was a strong natural position, and the battle positions were in well sited trenches. South of the River OMIGNON the 1st N Staffordshire Regt held ~~a post~~ the other Battalion of the the MAISSEMY post – similar to ours. 72nd Brigade was in Reserve with Brigade HQ at VERMAND. On our left the 17th Brigade was in the line with similar dispositions. The 73rd Brigade was in Divisional Reserve. The Red Line ran in front of MAISSEMY – through VADENCOURT to COOKER Trench. DEAN Trench – BOB Trench in front of LE VERGUIER This was the main battle line to be held to the last.	

Army Form C. 2118.

Instructions regarding War Diaries and Intelligence Summaries are contained in F. S. Regs., Part II. and the Staff Manual respectively. Title pages will be prepared in manuscript.

WAR DIARY
or
~~INTELLIGENCE SUMMARY.~~

(*Erase heading not required.*)

Place	Date March	Hour	Summary of Events and Information	Remarks and references to Appendices
	13		Bombardment by our Artillery from 4 am – 6 am. Lt Col H J WENYON D.S.O to Paris, Short leave. Capt R.P. BAKER in temporary command. Patrols out all night. Enemy attitude very quiet.	RPB
	14.		Poor visibility all day. Usual patrols out all night.	RPB
	15.		Manned battle positions at 12.30 am. Heavy bursts of fire from our own artillery unanswered by enemy. Stood down 7 am. Capt F.C NEEDHAM in temporary command of D Coy.	RPB
	16.		Fine weather continues, Enemy very quiet, no artillery shooting by him.	RPB
	17.		B+D Coys relieved A+C in the outpost line. 2/Lt G.C. TAYLOR joined from 6th Connaught Rangers.	RPB
	18.		Fine weather: great activity by our artillery and aeroplanes.	RPB
	19.		Dull + wet. Patrols out as usual. A + C at work on wire in front of VADENCOURT. Lt Col H J WENYON resumes command.	RPB
	20.		Wet morning A + C continue work on VADENCOURT defences. Capt RPBAKER departed on leave to U.K.	RPB
	21.		Opening of German Offensive. Capt FC NEEDHAM, 2/Lt P.H. TYLER 2/Lt E.C. WEST w/a. 2/Lt CC BARING gassed + died of gas poisoning. Capt C.R.H. ALLWORTH 2/Lt A.B. RICHARDSON, H.W. BEATTIE M.C., D.C.M. OLIVER, J. BOWSKILL, E. LEVEY, C.D. WHITBOURN all missing.	RPB

A7092). Wt. W12839/M1293 750,000. 1/17. D. D & L., Ltd. Forms/C2118/14.

Instructions regarding War Diaries and Intelligence Summaries are contained in F. S. Regs., Part II. and the Staff Manual respectively. Title pages will be prepared in manuscript.

WAR DIARY
or
INTELLIGENCE SUMMARY.
(Erase heading not required.)

Army Form C. 2118.

Place	Date	Hour	Summary of Events and Information	Remarks and references to Appendices
	March 21.		For detailed account of operations for rest of this month see appendix attached (A)	appendix A RPB
	22.		2/Lt J. MALBY w/a	RPB
	25		Capt [struck out], A.E. JONES, 2/Lts J.B. CRYER, B STEPHENS w/a Capt W.J. EWEN K/a. Capt J.H. SELFE took over A Coy.	RPB
	26.		Capt W. KELLOGG, M.O. (USA, R.C) sick	RPB
	27		Lieut E.O. GOULDEN w/a	RPB
	28		2/Lt K. PFEUFFAR, M.C 2/Lt F.J JANAWAY M.C. w/a	RPB
	29 to 31		See appendix A.	appendix A RPB.

RPBaker Capt + Adjt
8th Bn Royal West Kent Regt.

A7092). Wt. W12839/M1293 750,000. 1/17. D. D & L., Ltd. Forms/C2118/14.

Appendix "A". War Diary, March/April 1918.

8TH. (S). BATTN. ROYAL WEST KENT REGT.,

Account of operations from 19th. March 1918 to 5th. April 1918.

Ref. Map Sheet 62.C. (1/40,000).

19th. March 1918. On the 19th. March, the Battalion was in the front line, with Headquarters at Vadencourt Chateau. "B" and "D" Companies were holding the outpost zone in front, extending about 1,500 yards. "A" and "C" Companies and Headquarters were at Vadencourt. On our right, the 1st. North Staffordshire Regt., were in the front line with Headquarters at Maissemy. On our left, the 3rd. Rifle Brigade (17th. Brigade).

20th. March 1918. On the 20th. March, which was very quiet, Captain Baker (Adjutant) went on leave. In the evening, report was received by me from information given by a German prisoner that an enemy attack might take place on the 20th or 21st March. The usual patrolling was carried out on the night of the 20th/21st and no abnormal enemy activity was reported.

21st. March 1918. At 4.30 a.m. on the 21st. March, a general bombardment by the enemy commenced. Vadencourt Chateau was very heavily shelled by gas shells for six hours. There was a dense fog lasting until 11 a.m. through which one could not see more than 15 yards. Immediately the gas shelling commenced, I issued an order to the Companies that all ranks were to put on their gas-masks and wear them continuously until a direct order was given by me for them to be removed. 2/Lieut. C.C. Baring unfortunately got badly gassed by almost the first gas shell thrown over, and has since died of the effects. Apart from this, there has been no known case of a gas casualty in the Battalion. About 10.30 a.m. I gave the order for gas-masks to be removed and a few minutes after this it was reported that the enemy had advanced on our right. Most of my two front companies had been cut off and the enemy was approaching us from the direction of Maissemy and Pointru Trench (R.11.d.). The bridge between Maissemy and Vadencourt was immediately demolished. This was done in the face of the enemy by Lieut. Christonson, R.E., of the 103rd. Field Company. About 11.30 a.m. the fog began to clear and the sun came out. The enemy was seen to be occupying Mareval and Pontru Trench (R.11.d. and R.12.c.) in front of us, and Captain Needham, O.C. "D" Company got back wounded into Vadencourt. He reported that after very heavy shelling, his Company had been surprised in the Right flank and from the rear and very few could have escaped. The general advance of the enemy in large numbers towards Vadencourt and Cookers Quarry now commenced. The swamp and river on our right front formed an obstacle against a direct frontal attack and I did not then know that Maissemy had actually fallen. Vadencourt was subjected to very heavy infilade and direct machine gun fure. The enemy attempted to advance across our front towards Cookers Quarry (R.11.c.8.9.) about 12 noon; he was in close formation about a Battalion strong. Our Vickers Guns, Lewis guns and Rifles did tremendous execution and very few of the enemy got back. During the afternoon the enemy brought up large forces including transport, from the rear. Whole Battalions could be seen advancing in close formation at about 2,000 yards range. We engaged them with Vickers Guns and I send down several messages asking the Artillery to shoot, without success. The enemy's counter-battery and neutralizing fire including his concentrations of gas must have been very effective, as our Artillery fire for the rest of the day was very thin. The enemy had established an observation post on the Tumulus and a group of mounted men remained there all the afternoon. Several times during the afternoon, the enemy renewed his attempts on Vadencourt, but they invariably broke down under our fire.

Our snipers did excellent work all day. Later in the afternoon, some of our guns commenced to shoot but most of the shells were dropping very short into our own positions. In the early evening, the enemy again commenced to shell Vadencourt and its surroundings, but in view of the natural strength of the place, I was confident we could hold the position. During the afternoon, I had recconnoitred our right flank and found that the enemy had captured Maissemy and were in position on our right rear. However, the river formed an effective obstacle and apart from enfilade machine gun fire, we had little to fear from that quarter; provided the troops on our left in Cookers Quarry and Cooker Trench held, we could hold.

At 7.15 p.m. the enemy commenced to advance towards Cooker trench, and unfortunately both Quarry and trench were immediately evacuated, the garrison - some 200 strong - retiring hurriedly in the direction of Vermand. This left me with both flanks hopelessly in the air and the enemy commenced to advance in large numbers up Watling Street and towards the high ground in R.10.b. We engaged him with every available rifle, Lewis Gun and Machine Gun, and considerably delayed his advance. About 8.0 p.m. I finally decided to withdraw to the Brown Line at Bihecourt. The enemy had already got up heavy trench mortars, which commenced to shoot at the cross roads at R.11.c. A strong rearguard was left behind at the Chateau under 2nd.Lieut Pfeuffar, Lieut. Goulden and 2nd.Lieut.Tiley, including 4 Lewis Guns and their teams; 4 Vickers Guns and teams also remained behind under the command of 2nd.Lieut.Peachey, of the 24th.Divisional Machine Gun Battalion. These parties put up a hot fight for nearly an hour, during which time the remainder of the Battn. was enabled to withdraw in orderly fashion to the Brown Line at Bihecourt. Here we reinforced two companies of the 13th. Middlesex Regiment (73rd.Brigade) and the troops were properly organised from the river at R.22.a. through Bihecourt to R.15.b. by midnight. I reported personnaly to the Brigade Headquarters at Vermand and was told there that a message had been sent earlier in the evening that I was to evacuate Vadencourt. Nearly all Officers' and mens' large kit had to be left at the Chateau but most of the Lewis Guns and Vickers Guns, with their belts and magazines were got back to the Brown Line. These were invaluable in the fight which took place their the next day. The greatest credit is due to all who took part in the rearguard left behind at Vadencourt. After the evacuation was ordered, the whole Battalion got back to Bihecourt without a casualty.

22nd.March 1918. I took up quarters at Vermand with the Commanding Officer of the 13th.Middlesex Regiment for the night. In the morning, I was put in command of all troops in the 72nd.Brigadearea North of the River, while Colonel Anderson commanded South of the River. The enemy commenced to advance upon Vermand South of the river about 9.0 a.m. Vermand was heavily shelled for an hour. His attacks were, however, delayed by the Infantry. Thick fog again assisted the enemy. North of the River, the enemy made several attacks on the Brown Line in the course of the morning. Several times he reached the wire, but was stopped there. Our rifles and machine guns did great execution. The troops under my command North of the River consisted of the 8th.Royal West Kent Regiment, + two Companies of the 13th.Middlesex Reg ment. About 1 p.m. the enemy succeeded in driving in our troops at Villecholles, and reached the outskirts of Vermand South of the River. The order was given to withdraw fighting through the 50th.Division who were in the Green Line. North of the river, our troops held out till the last moment and did not retire until 2 p.m. During the withdrawal they were subjected to considerable machine gun fire and had many casualties on the Vermand Road.

The Battalion concentrated on the main road about P.30.d. and at about 7 p.m. marched to Monchy Legache, where we took up a position in trenches in W.7.c. and W.13.a. for the night.

23rd.March 1918. In the morning, it transpired that the green line had been fairly easily forced by the enemy and the Division was ordered to withdraw across the Somme at Falvy. The 72nd.Brigade was ordered to form a rear guard on the eastern bank of the Somme and to allow the rest of the Division to pass through. This was successfully done, and the 8th.Royal West Kent Regt., which now included the remains of the 1st.North. Staffordshire Regiment and the 72nd.Light Trench Mortar Battery crossed the river at about 2.30 p.m. From here, the Brigade concentrated at Licourt. About 6.30 p.m. the Battalion was ordered back to Pargny to reinforce the 8th.Division in the line until the arrival of the 2nd.Rifle Brigade. At this stage, the Officers and men of the Battalion were very exhausted. I went in advance to Pargny; found the 2nd.Rifle Brigade in position; and that we were not therefore required. The Battalion, however had returned to the river, but on arrival at Pargny were told to go back to Licourt, were the men had a good feed and rested for the night. There had been some hitch about demolishing the bridges over the Somme and although our Artillery was now more in evidence than it had been before, the position on the Somme did not seem altogether secure.

24th.March 1918. In the morning, the Battalion marched back to Chaulnes, where we remained during the morning resting. At noon, the 72nd.Brigade was ordered to march to Fonches to take up a position there, as the enemy was reported to have forced a crossing of the Somme at Bethencourt and a gap had been formed between the 8th and 20th. Divisions. We marched to Fonches by companies with strong advanced and flank guards thrown well out. It was very peaceful at Fonches when we arrived and there was no evidence of the enemy within three or four miles of the place. The Brigade was disposed in trenches defending the Hattencourt - Fonches - Fonshette road. The 9th.East Surrey Regiment on the right, the 8th.Rl.West Kent Regiment on the left. The 73rd.Brigade were on our left in front of Punchy and the 17th.Brigade on their left in front of Omiécourt. I got the Battalion's dispositions made and discussed the position with the Battalions on my right and left and took up my Headquarters at Fonches Church. Joint patrols from ourselves and the 7th.Northamptonshire Regiment went out all night under 2nd.Lieut.Pfeuffar, through the wood and valley East of Fonches as far as Curchy.

25th.March 1918. In the morning, it was reported that the 8th.Division and the French were to make an attack in the direction of Morchain and Bethencourt. The 24th.Division was ordered to move up in support of the attack and the 17th. and 73rd.Brigades took up positions on the line Dreslincourt to Pertain. The 72nd. Brigade took up a position in support, astride the railway West of Hyencourt - Le- Pettit. The Royal West Kent Regt., deployed north of the Railway in three lines, "C" Company and the North Staffordshires in front, "A" Company in Support, Headquarters in Reserve. The 17th. and 73rd.Brigades were driven in and at about 1 p.m. the 72nd.Brigade was ordered to return to Fonches and hold the line Hattencourt - Fonchette to the main cross roads 800 yards North-East of Fonchette. After some difficulty, I got the new dispositions made and inspected the flank of our position, I found the 73rd.Brigade had retired and their front was at right angles to ours and running back towards Hallu. I telephoned to the B.G.C. about this and I was ordered to do all I could to re-establish this flank. In any case we were to hold out at Fonches-Fonchette to the last. The 9th.East Surrey's were in position on our right and I left

Major Clark in charge of the garrison while I went to re-adjust the flank. The enemy had advanced considerably opposite the 73rd.Brigade front and appeared to be in Hyencourt-le-petit and in positions South of that village. Considerable machine gun fire was being directed on the area North and West of the cross roads which formed our left flank. After about two hours, I succeeded in getting two Battalions of the 73rd. Brigade forward to the wire running North and South just West of the Fonchette-Omiecourt road. The men were quite game and came forward quite willingly when the case of the people on their flank was put to them. As our flank was now secure I returned to Fonches and I found that my Adjutant, 2nd.Lieut. J.B.Cryer had been wounded, Captain Ewen,commanding "A" Company, killed, and that we had had several other casualties. Fonches was being heavily shelled and being subjected to particularly heavy direct machine gun fire. Our garrison was well disposed to meet attack and the Officers and men were anxious to fight their position to the last. Several sallies by the enemy along the valley running from Curchy to Fonches were stopped dead before dark. All the afternoon, the enemy had been collecting in the large wood South of this valley. Our heavy guns got on to this wood and did excellent work after dark. Shortly after 8.0 p.m. determined efforts were made by the enemy to break through our lines. A party succeeded in getting into a disused trench about 2 0 yards in front of "A" Company. A "cutting out" movement was at once organised and after a stiff fight in which 2nd.Lieut.Stephens was wounded, the enemy retired leaving behind a store of bombs and ammunition We then put a post in this disused trench and established a block there. The night was clear and moonlight, and apart from isolated sallies by the enemy, which were all met by our fire, and dispersed, nothing of note occurred. In one of these sallies, we secured a prisoner. 2nd.Lieut.Cryer had refused to go down to Field Ambulance and behaved with the greatest gallantry, knowing our orders were to fight our position to the last. About 11 p.m. however, we had orders from Brigade to withdraw to positions at Hallu. We moved off at 2 a.m. leaving strong rearguards behind. The withdrawal was made in perfect order without casualties, and we took up positions in front of Hallu by 3.30 a.m.

26th.March 1918. About 5 a.m. I inspected our new line East of Hallu and found a gap between ourselves and the 9th.East Surrey's on our right. This I filled at once with "A" Company. The enemy was just beginning his advance again at this time and had previously put a very heavy bombardment down on the unoccupied village of Fonches. I was ordered to take up my Headquarters at Hallu where there was a direct telephone to Division. By 8 a.m. I received information from Brigade that the enemy had broken through the Entrenching Battalion on the right of the 9th.East Surrey's and if necessary we were to withdraw fighting in echelon from the right. Captain Thompson, who was commanding in our forward trenches, was accordingly ordered to conform with other units. Shortly after this, the left broke also and the 73rd.Brigade withdrew. This left the Royal West Kent Regiment and East Surrey Regt., in line with both flanks in the air. The advanced enemy were within 200 yards of our positions and were advancing in considerable numbers. Captain Thompson informed the East Surrey's that he proposed to withdraw, by platoons, from the left. The enemy was now very near our trenches, but was being well held by our fire. An orderly retirement commenced. Major Clark, with part of the East Surrey's, still hung on to his positions, and their Battn. Headquarters and a considerable proportion of their men were overwhelmed and captured. Their policy appeared to be a mistaken one in the circumstances, but there can be no question of the gallantry of Major Clark and his Officers and men.

After the Battalion left Hallu, they were stopped some half-mile back by Lieut-Colonel Walker, C.R.E, who attempted to form a line in shell holes. It seemed that Colonel Walker had more or less taken leave of his senses and by his action he placed a large body of men in great danger of capture. Captain Thompson finally withdrew and most of the Battalion succeeded in getting back . The Division now concentrated for the defence

Map ref. 66.E. 1/40,000. of Rouvroy. Our men were very done and were kept in Reserve at Warvillers where they got a clean up and a nights rest. The Battalion was re-organised and from now onwards was composed of 8th. Royal West Kents, 9th. East Surrey's, 1st. North Staffordshires. A number of new Lewis Guns were issued to the Battn. on this day.

27th. March 1918. The 72nd. Infantry Brigade now consisted of a composite Battalion under my Command, the 15th. and 19th. Entrenching Battalions and a Battalion formed from the Officers and men of the 18th. Corps School. The battle forRouvroy and 8 trees L.3.b. commenced about 10 a.m. and continued throughout most of the day. "C" Company were disposed in trenches in L.2.d. N.W. of Rouvroy all day; "A" company and the North Staffordshires at about L.7.b. After "ding-dong" fighting all the morning, the enemy took Rouvroy at about 2.0 p.m. The locality about 8 trees in L.3.b. having been forced by the enemy some time earlier. Dispositions were then made for the defence of Warvillers after the North Staffordshire's had made an attempt to re-establish the position in the S.W. part of Rauvroy with the bayonet. A strong line was selected defending the villages of Warvillers, Beaufort and Vrely. In the line were the two Entrenching Battalions and the 18th. Corps School. The composite Battalion was withdrawn into Brigade Reserve in Warvillers. Throughout the evening parties of the enemy frequently attempted to debouch from the S.W. of Rouvroy towards the trenches held by "A" Company and the North Staffordshires. Many casualties were inflicted on the enemy by our fire and any serious attempt to advance was stopped.

28th. March 1918. The new dispositions were completed early in the morning, 72nd. Brigade being in line from K.12.b.0.2 to F.25.c. 3.3. The 73rd. Brigade were on our left and the 17th. Brigade in front of Vrely on their left. The enemy attacked at 8.30 a.m. in large numbers. The line of our Brigade front held firm and great loss was inflicted by rifle and machine gun fire on the enemy. In front of Vrely, however, our troops withdrew and on the right South of Beaufort a break also occurred. We hung on to Warvillers until the last possible moment and when I gave the order to withdraw there were a large number of the enemy established in the village with us doing very good shooting. We had several men sniped at very close quarters, and they, unfortunately, had to be left behind. The Entrenching Battalions and the Corps School had put up a very good fight, ably assisted by the guns of the 24th. Divisional Machine Gun Battalion. It is feared that a number of the front line troops were overwhelmed and cut off. The Company Commander who received my written message to withdraw, did so reluctantly, after manning his parapet and giving the enemy 10 rounds rapid fire. Considerable casualties were inflicted on the enemy. Warvillers was subjected to heavy shelling before and during the attack. From Warvillers the Division moved to the Caix-le-Quesnel line, K.3.a. - E.10.c. which was manned by about 1 p.m. This was a good position and all attempts at frontal attacks by the enemy/frustrated. Our artillery, whose support up to this point had been weak, did excellent work at this line, shooting into woods and open places was obviously concentrating, and inflicting many casualties on him. From a position on the flank and in front of our line, I watched the enemy's movements through glasses for some time. Our machine guns and rifles, as well as the artillery, engaged the enemy in his assembly positions and repeatedly scattered his forces.

/were

The break which had occurred further on the right early in the morning was however the danger point and it had become increasingly evident to me that the enemy was executing an encircling movement some two miles on our right. He was approaching Le Quesnel from the South and was getting well to our rear. There was great danger of a very large force being cut off, and I could not get in touch with Brigade. By chance, I found Lieut-Colonel Whitty and we decided to give the order to withdraw from the right. It seemed that it was none too soon. The whole Division had to get back through a bottle-neck, harrassed all the way by machine guns and artillery fire. The withdrawal was orderly and by good chance rain set in and made observation difficult for the enemy. From here we had a long and weary march to the Bois de Senecat, West of Castal, where the Brigade was concentrated.

29th. March 1918. Here the men got a hot meal about 3 a.m. and laid down in the rain for the night. In the morning we had a short breathing space and the Battalion was re-organised. In the evening, the Division was ordered to take up a position in front of Thezy (Ref. Map 62.D. 1/40,000). From Berteaucourt at C.1.c.2.0 to the Domart - Amiens Road at U.19.c.5.6. 73rd. Brigade on the right, 72nd. Brigade on the left and the 17th. Brigade in Reserve.

30th. March 1918. The Entrenching Battalions took up positions in the line, which consisted of a series of disconnected posts, at 3.30 a.m. We took up a position in support in the Copse at T.23.d. at 5.0 a.m. The whole Battalion proceeded to dig in and by 10 a.m. we had formed a series of posts just in front of the copse on a front of 1,200 yards; the left resting on the Amiens Road at T.24.a. The enemy was reported to have advanced through Mezieres and was proceeding towards Moreuil and Castel. There were a considerable number of troops, French and British, between our positions and the enemy. About 11.0 a.m. the Battn. less the East Surrey's, moved back to Thezy, the East Surrey's remaining in the Copse and manning a few of the posts. We went to good billets in the village and the men were able to get a good feed and some rest.

31st. March 1918. At dawn the Battalion relieved the Entrenching Battalions in the forward posts. Shortly afterwards the B.G.C. came up and decided to leave only one Company up there and have the remainder in the village. "A" Company remained in the line and the rest of the Battalion moved back again to billets in Thezy. In the afternoon considerable activity commenced. The 8th. and 20th. Divisions in front of us appeared to be wavering and we were ordered back to the forward posts. Our dispositions were completed there by 4 p.m. A series of counter-attacks were carried out between four and seven p.m. by the troops in front of us. Cavalry and artillery (the latter was now considerable) co-operated. The position was more than re-established. The village of Hangard was retaken by the 54th. Brigade 18th. Division; and the wood North of Moreuil was entered by our men in face of considerable opposition. The night was quiet and we remained in position in the posts. Our artillery pounded the enemy's positions very severely all night.

1st. April 1918. At dawn we were relieved by two Companies of the Entrenching Battalion and moved back to Thezy. The men rested most of the day and did all they could to clean up. There was plenty of food. The day passed quietly and uneventfully.

2nd. April 1918. We were again at rest in Thezy. I inspected all the Companies during the morning. The men had cleaned up very well and they looked wonderfully fit. The day was quiet. Our Artillery, with which large numbers of French "75's" co-operated, continued to harass the enemy. Clean underclothing and sacks were issued to the men during the day.

3rd. April 1918. At dawn, the East Surrey's and North Staffordshires relieved the two companies of the Entrenching Battalions in the forward posts. "C" Company were detailed for making an advanced Brigade Headquarters and "A" Company was sent 10 at a time to Baths at a Chateau. The situation continued to be quiet. In the afternoon "A" Company carried on the digging and "C" Company proceeded to Baths.

4th. April 1918. At 4.30 a.m. the Battalion left Thezy and marched North across the Amiens Road through Gentelles to the Bois l'abbe (U.1.a.), where the Brigade concentrated. The Depot Battalion, attached 17th. Brigade, relieved the North Staffordshires and East Surrey's in the posts in front of Thezy and the concentration of the Brigade was completed by 6.30 a.m. About 5.0 a.m. an enemy bombardment commenced on a wide front. As we were coming through Gentelles, a shell fell in the road as a platoon of "A" Company was passing and we had 8 casualties. The forward part of Bois l'abbe received attention during the morning, a good deal of gas shell being thrown over. Fairly heavy rain set in however, and the gas did not go far. The bombardment was chiefly directed against our Batteries all along the front. In the course of the day, it transpired that the enemy had attacked opposite Villers-Brettoneaux and Marcelcave and further South. He had made some progress but the ground was very heavy and in places he had been driven back. In the afternoon the 72nd. Brigade which was in support to the Northern half of the 17th. Brigade (Gentelles - Bois l'abbe) moved back about 3,000 yards to the Copse in N.34.c. In the evening, the B.G.C. 72nd. Brigade took command of the Sector from ~~John's Hill~~ GENTELLES to the Northern edge of the Bois l'abbe. Troops in this area, in addition to those of the 72nd. Brigade, were the 8th. Queen's (17th. Brigade), 10th. Essex (18th. Division) and 7th. London (58th. Division). During the night, the 10th. Essex were ordered to move to U.15.b. and our "C" Company took over their line in the Bois l'abbe at dawn.

5th. April 1918. The remainder of the Battalion was disposed during the day as follows :- "A" Company in trenches at T.4.central; East Surrey's in Copse, N.35.c. digging a line of posts from N.35.c. 5.8. to T.5.a.5.5. - the North Staffordshire's in the Western edge of Bois de Blaingy, digging a line of posts from N.35.d.8.4 southwards.

I had a telephone message from the Brigade Major at 1.0 p.m saying that the Division was going out at night. In the afternoon, I went to the Brigade and got what orders there were. The Battalion commenced moving out at 7.45 p.m. and collected at the embussing point T.2.a. After very considerable delay, due to defective staff organization, I left in the tail end bus at 1.30 a.m. and found the Battalion at Salauel, South-west of Amiens. Here we managed to get the men into a laundry for the night. We got a room for the Officers and had, comparitively speaking, a very comfortable night.

6th. April 1918. We proceeded to Saleux Station at 2.30 p.m. and entrained for St.Valerie, on the mouth of the Somme.

.... Lieut-Colonel,

8th. April 1918. Commanding 8th. S. Bn. Rl. West Kent Regiment.

72nd Brigade.

24th Divisioh

8th BATTALION

ROYAL WEST KENT REGIMENT

A P R IL 1 9 1 8

Appendix :-

Operation Order.

Army Form C. 2118.

8th Bn R. W. Kent Regt.

WAR DIARY
or
~~INTELLIGENCE SUMMARY.~~

(*Erase heading not required.*)

Instructions regarding War Diaries and Intelligence Summaries are contained in F. S. Regs., Part II. and the Staff Manual respectively. Title pages will be prepared in manuscript.

Place	Date 1918	Hour	Summary of Events and Information	Remarks and references to Appendices
	April 1. to 6		See Appendix A, attached War diary March 1918	appendix A RPB
	7		Arrived in ST. BLIMONT (SOMME) about 3am in billets with remainder of E. Surreys, 1st N. Staffs and XVII Corps details Draft of 222 OR's arrived in the evening. 2/Lt M. ROUGHLEY reported for duty from 11th Bn R.W.K. Capt R.P. BAKER from leave. Capt A.J PORTER Lt R.A WALKER, 2/Lt E.C ANDREWS rejoined battn The following officers were still left with the Battn after the V Army retirement Lt.Col H.J. WENYON DSO. Capt S.G. THOMPSON, Lt P.A. GEDGE, Lt G.S. BOWEN, a/Capt J.H. SELFE, 2/Lts C.G TILEY, H.G MICHIE, C TRENCHARD-DAVIS, G.C. TAYLOR Casualties were 308 OR's in addition to officers named (See March war diary)	RPB RPB
	8.		Party of 150 OR's arrived from leave, with Capt (+ QM) J R WOOD. Transport arrived by road.	RPB
	9.		Re organization of Coys and platoons. Company commanders:– A Coy a/Capt J.H. SELFE, B Coy 2/Lt H.G. MICHIE, C Capt S.G. THOMPSON, D Capt A J PORTER	RPB
	10.		B.G.C inspected the Battn and addressed them on parade.	RPB
	11.		Training Lewis Gun classes; baths	RPB

A7092). Wt. W12839/M1293. 750,000. 1/17. D. D & L., Ltd. Forms/C2118/14.

Army Form C. 2118.

WAR DIARY
or
~~INTELLIGENCE SUMMARY.~~
(Erase heading not required.)

Instructions regarding War Diaries and Intelligence Summaries are contained in F. S. Regs., Part II. and the Staff Manual respectively. Title pages will be prepared in manuscript.

Ref. Sheet 36 B.

Place	Date	Hour	Summary of Events and Information	Remarks and references to Appendices
	April 12		Draft of 3 officers and 55 OR's. Capt R. G. ROGERS, 2/Lt A. DRUMGOLD D.S.O. 2/Lt C.F.C. MACASKIE. Commanders of Coys:- A Coy A/Capt J H Selfe, B Capt R G Rogers, C Capt S G Thompson, D Capt F. Proctor	RPB.
	13		Training	RPB
	14		Marched to ~~AU~~ AULT on sea coast. Inspection by G.O.C. Had dinners there. Very cold day. CO. left for short leave to England	RPB
	15		Training	RPB
	16.		Paraded 11 pm (less D Coy) marched to FEUQUIERES and entrained. Had to wait 6 hours at station, moved at 7.30 am 17th	appendix B. RPB
	~~17~~		Arrived in BYAS 4.30 pm had teas and marched into OURTON	RPB.
	17		D Coy arrived	
	18 / 19		Intensive training - CO Returned from leave	RPB Rny
	20		marched to PERNES for training on Corps training ground. Range firing. Tactical exercises &c.	
	21.		Church parade and continuation of training	RPB

A7092). Wt. W12839/M1293 750,000. 1/17. D. D & L., Ltd. Forms/C2118/14.

Army Form C. 2118.

Instructions regarding War Diaries and Intelligence Summaries are contained in F. S. Regs., Part II. and the Staff Manual respectively. Title pages will be prepared in manuscript.

WAR DIARY

or

IN~~TELLIGENCE SUMMARY~~. April (ctd.)

(Erase heading not required.)

Place	Date	Hour	Summary of Events and Information	Remarks and references to Appendices
	April 22		Capt H. S. BROWN rejoined and took over 2nd in command	
			18 officers reported for duty	
			2/Lt H. W. TREACHER 2/Lt W. J. GREEN	
			G.A.E. WALLIS N.E. BEYNES	
			D.T. PIGGOTT P E WATTS	
			D.G. GODDEN E.N. WINCH	
			H A QUARTERMAIN W.E.W. THOMAS	
			H. GIBBONS R.C.C.J. BINNEY	
			A.H. JACKSON FCM CHAUNCY	
			Lt D.J. DEAN 2/Lt H. CAMBROOK, 2/Lt E. GIBBS, 2/Lt ~~H CAMBROOK~~ F. C. GOBELL	RPB.
	23		Marched to PERNES for training	RPB
	24 to 26		Intensive training by platoons + sections	RPB
	27.		CO's Parade. Battn Sports arranged by Capt H S BROWN	RPB
	28		Church Parade for Bde at DIEVAL	RPB
	29.		Brigade Rifle meeting at PERNES. The Battalion won most of the prize money	RPB
	30.		Preparing for move.	RPB

RPBaker Capt & Adjt
8th Bn R. W. Kent Regt.

A7092). Wt. W12839/M1293 750,000. 1/17. D. D & L., Ltd. Forms/C2118/14.

Army Form C. 2118.

Instructions regarding War Diaries and Intelligence Summaries are contained in F. S. Regs., Part II. and the Staff Manual respectively. Title pages will be prepared in manuscript.

WAR DIARY
or
INTELLIGENCE SUMMARY.
(Erase heading not required.)

Place	Date	Hour	Summary of Events and Information	Remarks and references to Appendices
			Training &c April 6th - April 30th 1918	

Of the original garrison of the VADENCOURT post ~~at~~ 6 officers and about 150 O.R. got back to ST BLIMONT near the mouth of the Somme when the Division was relieved. At the time when the enemy offensive started over 150 men of the battalion were on ~~at~~ leave in England and on there rejoining us on the 8th April the Battalion consisted of 17 officers and about 380 O.R. (including Transport & Q.M. personnel).

This formed a very excellent nucleus for re-organizing the battalion, and assimilating the new drafts which were sent to us at once, and which raised the battalion up to about 850 strong.

The work of re-organisation of Companies was taken in hand immediately and completed by the 12th April. The remainder of the month was devoted to Intensive Training:- Discipline, Musketry, and Tactical Exercises were the headings under which most training was done.

The training of the Section Commanders and the training of a large number of new Lewis Gunners was also actively carried out.

During the month our Lewis Guns were increased to 24, including 4 for anti-aircraft work.

The battalion was fortunate in its drafts. About 40% were men who had had previous experience in the field - the remainder were men of the A4 class from England - about 19 years of age and very keen

2353 Wt. W2514/1454 700,000 5/15 D. D. & L. A.D.S.S./Forms/C. 2118.

Army Form C. 2118.

WAR DIARY
or
INTELLIGENCE SUMMARY.
(Erase heading not required.)

Instructions regarding War Diaries and Intelligence Summaries are contained in F. S. Regs., Part II. and the Staff Manual respectively. Title pages will be prepared in manuscript.

Place	Date	Hour	Summary of Events and Information	Remarks and references to Appendices
			On the 10th April Brig-General R.W. Morgan D.S.O., 72nd Brigade Commander inspected the whole battalion on parade. He afterwards addressed the battalion, and congratulated very warmly all who had taken part in the recent operations.	
			From April 7th to April 16th while the Battalion remained at ST BLIMONT the work of Re-organising, re-equipping and other matters of interior economy, together with a little general training, and intensive training of new Lewis Gunners occupied all the time.	
			On the 17th April the Battalion was established at OURTON, N.E. of ST POL. ~~where~~ The Division was in G.H.Q Reserve, ready to move at 6 hours notice. Here the battalion had a fortnight's intensive training. Every third day the Canadian School Training Ground at PERNES was at our disposal. Here there was an excellent 30-Target Rifle Range, Bayonet fighting Courses + Drill Grounds. At OURTON we made two rifle ranges. Much valuable musketry training was done.	
			It was decided that for offensive operations in future each section should consist of 1 NCO and 6 men – the remainder being left behind to form a nucleus for re-organisation afterwards, or, if necessary, to form reinforcements during operations. This system was introduced throughout the battalion and the sections ~~were~~ carefully organised accordingly.	

2353 Wt. W2544/1454 700,000 5/15 D. D. & L. A.D.S.S./Forms/C. 2118.

Instructions regarding War Diaries and Intelligence Summaries are contained in F. S. Regs., Part II. and the Staff Manual respectively. Title pages will be prepared in manuscript.

WAR DIARY
or
INTELLIGENCE SUMMARY.
(*Erase heading not required.*)

Army Form C. 2118.

Place	Date	Hour	Summary of Events and Information	Remarks and references to Appendices
			There was very little time for pure Recreation and the Battalion Athletic Sports meeting held on the 27th April did a lot of good, as there was some danger of the men getting stale at the time.	
			A Brigade Rifle meeting was held at PERNES on the 29th April. On the total points scored for Shooting the Battalion was 1st, and on the points scored for Field work particularly Section Commander's control the battalion was very easily 1st. This was a particularly satisfactory feature. Of the total prize money of about 550 francs the Battalion took 385 francs.	
			On the 30th April representatives were sent to reconnoitre the line in front of LENS - the same front on which the Battalion was fighting a year ago when the enemy withdrew after the Battle of VIMY.	
			Final arrangements were made for moving up on the 1st May.	

2353 Wt. W2544/1454 700,000 5/15 D. D. & L. A.D.S.S./Forms/C. 2118.

Appendix B

SECRET

Battalion Operation Order No.1 COPY No. 2....

by

Captain R.P.BAKER,

Commanding 8th.S.Batth Royal West Kent Regiment.

In-the-field, 16th.April 1918.

1. The 72nd.Infantry Brigade will move by train from FEUQUIERES on the 16/17th April to BRYAS - PERNES Area.

2. Transport H.Qs., "A", "B" and "C" Companies will move by train No.5 , dep.FEUQUIERES at 3 a.m. 17th.instant. "D" Company and "D" Company cooker and team move by train No.9 dep.at 9 a.m. 17th.inst.

3. Order of march-

Drums - H.Qs.- "A" - "B" - "C".

Parade in the street opposite Battalion Headquarters with head of column opposite Tailor's Shop at 11.0 p.m. "D" Company and cooker march off at 5.30 a.m.

4. Mess Stores to be dumped at Battalion H.Qs.by 9.30 p.m. 4 men from "A", "B" & "C" to report to Transport Officer at 9.45 p.m. for duty as brakesmen at Transport Lines.

5. Entraining states to be rendered to Battalion Orderly Room by 6.0 p.m.

6. Greatcoats to be worn. Blankets to be carried in the pack.

7. Rations for the 17th. - Details will be issued later.

(Sgd) G.S.B O W E N, Lieut.,

A/Adjutant 8th.S.Bn.R.W.Kent Regt.

Copies to :-

1.File
2.)War Diary.
3.)
4.O.C."A" Coy.
5.O.C."B" Coy.
6.O.C."C" Coy.
7.O.C."D" Coy.
8.H.Q.Mess.
9.R.S.Major.

SECRET.

Army Form C. 2118.

Vol 31

Instructions regarding War Diaries and Intelligence Summaries are contained in F. S. Regs., Part II. and the Staff Manual respectively. Title pages will be prepared in manuscript.

WAR DIARY
or
~~INTELLIGENCE SUMMARY.~~
(Erase heading not required.)

Place	Date	Hour	Summary of Events and Information	Remarks and references to Appendices
			War Diary of 8th S. Bn. R. W. Kent Regt. from 1.5.18 to 31.5.1918 (incl). Volume. -)	

2353 Wt. W2544/1454 700,000 5/15 D. D. & L. A.D.S.S./Forms/C. 2118.

Ref. 36 C. SW 1

WAR DIARY

or

~~INTELLIGENCE SUMMARY.~~

(Erase heading not required.)

8th Bn Royal West Kent Regt.

Army Form C. 2118.

Instructions regarding War Diaries and Intelligence Summaries are contained in F. S. Regs., Part II. and the Staff Manual respectively. Title pages will be prepared in manuscript.

Place	Date	Hour	Summary of Events and Information	Remarks and references to Appendices
	MAY 1		Moved by road from OURTON to MAROC. Halted at SAINS-EN GOHELLE for teas and moved into MAROC at dusk, spent the night in cellars.	Appendix 1 RPB
	2		Moved at dusk to Support billets, St EMILIE Sector in CITE St PIERRE and took over from Cameron Highlanders of Canada. Troops were all accomodated in cellars under the ruined houses	RPB
	3.		Hostile attitude very quiet. About half the men employed on working parties tunnelling, laying pipe lines, RE material etc. Surplus details sent to FOSSE 10 under Capt S.G. THOMPSON	RPB
	4.		Lt. Col WENYON D.S.O. left to join details Capt H.S. BROWN in command. Enemy attitude quiet. Weather fine and warm.	RPB
	5.		Moved up to the line after dark & took over from 1st N. Staffs in the left sub section (Bde O.O no 3) Relief over at 1am on 6th inst. Delay owing to proposed gas projector attack which was cancelled at the last minute. D & B in the line, left & right. A Support and C Reserve. Trench strength 20 Off & 620 OR's, each section being up to establishment of 1 NCO & 6 ORs. 20th Division on our immediate right.	Appendix 2 RPB
	6.		Enemy attitude quiet. 42nd Division, reported to be a "tired" division in the trenches on our front. Occasional Trench mortar activity on B Coy front. Patrols went out nightly and also wiring parties on the front line and BLUE LINE (the main line of resistance)	RPB.

2353 Wt. W2544/1454 700,000 5/15 D. D. & L. A.D.S.S./Forms/C. 2118.

36 C S W 1.

Instructions regarding War Diaries and Intelligence Summaries are contained in F. S. Regs., Part II. and the Staff Manual respectively. Title pages will be prepared in manuscript.

WAR DIARY
or
~~INTELLIGENCE SUMMARY.~~
(Erase heading not required.)

8th Bn R. West Kent Regt

Army Form C. 2118.

Place	MAY Date	Hour	Summary of Events and Information	Remarks and references to Appendices
	6		Rained during the night & made the trenches in very bad condition, the soil being chalky. Wiring parties were found difficult owing to bad weather and small progress made.	RPB.
	8		Capt H. S. BROWN assumes rank of a/major. Enemy attitude quiet. Projector attack by Special RE at 2.20am 8/9th over our front. Went off quite successfully.	RPB.
	9.		This day was spent in completing preparations against expected enemy attack in force on the front LENS – ROBECQ. D & B in the outpost line, 73rd Bde on our left, 1st N Staffs on our right. Lt Col WENYON D.S.O. came up from Transport lines & took over. Weather remained dry and warm. D Coy had a post knocked out 2 killed & 3 w/a. also 1 man killed by our own indirect M.G fire. B 4 men w/a. The expected attack did not come off.	RPB.
	10.		Quiet morning, occasional registration. Wiring & patrolling continued.	RPB.
	11		D relieved by C in front (outpost) line	
	12		Quiet day. B Coy handed over right platoon area to 1st N. Staffs. This was owing to the rearrangement of the Divnl front, making a 3 Brigade frontage	RPB.
	13.		Relief of outpost & Blue line by 1st R. Fusiliers (Bde O O no. 2). Moved out to BULLY GRENAY on relief being complete at 12.40am 13/14th	appendix 3 RPB.
	14 / 15		Baths & interior economy, fitting out etc at BULLY GRENAY, Brigade Reserve Billets by no means clean, or comfortable. A Coy in CITE CALONNE, detached	RPB.

2353 Wt. W2544/1454 700,000 5/15 D. D. & L. A.D.S.S./Forms/C. 2118.

36 C. SW 1

Instructions regarding War Diaries and Intelligence Summaries are contained in F. S. Regs., Part II. and the Staff Manual respectively. Title pages will be prepared in manuscript.

WAR DIARY
or
~~INTELLIGENCE SUMMARY.~~
(Erase heading not required.)

8th Bn Royal West Kent Regt — ~~Army~~ Form C. 2118.

Place	Date (MAY)	Hour	Summary of Events and Information	Remarks and references to Appendices
	16.		Moved up into Support in CITE ST PIERRE & took over from 9th E. Surreys. (Bde OO No 5) 2 Coys having battle positions in Red line, and 2 in Bde support. Relief complete at 11.50 pm.	appendix 4 RPB
	17		Working parties. 2 platoons wiring advanced Blue line, 1 platoon nightly carrying up TM ammunition. and other minor work: fine & warm weather	RPB
	18. to 21		enemy attitude quiet as regards Support area. Only occasional shelling by night of selected spots. No casualties incurred. Occasional shelling with a few gas shells. Work all the time on getting cellars gas proofed, & building latrines etc	RPB
	22		Moved up to front line relieving 9th E. Surreys. (Bde O. O no 7) C & A to front line (outposts) D & B in Blue line. 17th Bde on our left, 20th divn on our right. weather still very fine & warm. Relief complete 11.50 pm	appendix 5 RPB.
	23		Enemy attitude quiet. Occasional minnies over our right Coy front (A.) The two Support Coys engaged in carrying up wire, rations etc and in improving their own Battle positions	RPB
	24. and 25th		Raid conducted by Major H.S. BROWN. This raid was attempted at 11 pm, see appendix 6 but owing to our own barrage and smoke projectors falling short the party got dispersed. The raid was done over again under cover of a gas projector attack at 2 am, by Major H.S BROWN, 2/Lts CAE WALLIS and D.T. PIGGOTT with 1 Section of A Coy, resulting in 3 prisoners.	appendix 6 RPB; appendix 7 RPB
	26 & 27		enemy attitude quiet. very small amount of shell fire, & occasional minnies	RPB; RPB

2353 Wt. W2544/1454 700,000 5/15 D. D. & L. A.D.S.S./Forms/C. 2118.

36 C SW 1

Instructions regarding War Diaries and Intelligence Summaries are contained in F. S. Regs., Part II. and the Staff Manual respectively. Title pages will be prepared in manuscript.

WAR DIARY
or
~~INTELLIGENCE SUMMARY.~~
(Erase heading not required.)

8th Bn Royal West Kent Regt

Army Form C. 2118.

Place	Date MAY	Hour	Summary of Events and Information	Remarks and references to Appendices
	28		Relief by 1st N. Staffs. Move out into Brigade Reserve at BULLY GRENAY with C Coy in CITE CALONNE	Appendix 8 RPB
	29		Interior economy. RSM RANKIN, Sgt GOLDSBURY and 3 ORs killed whilst playing football at BULLY, by aeroplane bomb. 5 OR's wounded at the same time	RPB
	30) 31)		Interior economy, baths. Training under platoon commanders (musketry passing of orders). One working party of 3 shifts of 20 men, for Adv Div Hq.	RPB
			Lt Col H J WENYON DSO in command a/Major H. S. BROWN 2/in " " a/Capt H. J SELFE. O. C A Co Capt R. G. ROGERS " B " " S. G THOMPSON " C " " F. PROCTOR " D "	

R P Baker Capt & Adjt
8th Bn Royal West Kent Regt

2353 Wt. W2544/1454 700,000 5/15 D. D. & L. A.D.S.S./Forms/C. 2118.

Secret Battalion Operation Order No. x Copy. No. 3

by

Lieut-Col. [illegible] D.S.O.

Commanding 6th S. Battn Royal West Kent Regiment.

In the Field. 1st May 1918

appendix 1.

1. The Battalion will move by march route to [illegible] SAILLY-[illegible] AREA on the 1st May 1918.

2. Order of March "A", "B", Drums, H.Qrs., "D", "C".
The Battalion will be formed up with the head of the column at "A" Coy's billet [illegible] 29. d.27 at 10 a.m., with a 100 yard interval between Companies.

3. Companies will halt automatically at 10 minutes to the clock hour and move off again at the hour.

4. Packs and blankets for "B", "C" "D" H.Qrs to be stacked by Companies at the store by 9 a.m. "A" Company's at the side of the road at their billet. Each Company to detail
X. 4 men to load and travel on the lorries. "D" Company to send a loading party of 1 N.C.O. and 20 men to the stores at 8.45 a.m.

5. Dress - fighting order. steel helmets to be carried on the left shoulder.

6. All valises and stores to be at the Q.M. stores by 8.45 a.m. Mess carts will call at Company Messes at 9 a.m.

7. Dinners will be had during the march. Time to be notified later.

(Sgd) R. P. B A K E R Capt.

Adjutant 6th S Bn. R. W. Kent Regt.

Copies to:-

1. File
2. War Diary
3.) do
4. O.C. "A" Coy
5. O.C. "B" Coy.
6. O.C. "C" Coy.
7. O.C. "D" Coy.
8. E. Q. Mess
9. R.S. Major.

Secret

Battalion Operation Orders No 3. Copy No. 2
by
Lieut.Col. H.J.WENYON D.S.O.
In the Field 5th May 1918

Appendix 2

1. The 8th Battalion Royal West Kent Regt. will move on night of 5/6th May into the left Subsection, relieving the Ist North Staffordshire Regt., who will move back into Brigade Support.

2. Order of Relief.

8th R.W.K.	Position.	1 N.Staffs.
"B" Coy.	Right front line	"C" Coy
"D" "	Left " "	"B" "
"A" "	Support	"D" "
"C" "	Reserve	"A" "

3. Guides. "C" Coy will require no guides: relief to commence 9.30 p.m.
Guides for "A" Coy will be at N 7 A 95.50 at 7.30 p.m.
" " "B" " " " " " " " 9 p.m.
" " "D" " " " " " " " 9.45 p.m.

4. Routes. "B" Coy will use COUNTER AND CANTEEN
"D" " " " NASH AND NESTOR
1st North Staffordshire Regt will go out via COSY.

5. O.C. "C" Coy will arrange to push up the rations on trucks from EDDIE DUMP (as soon as they arrive there at 8.45 p.m.) to CATAPULT DUMP for "D","A",& "C" Coys and to DOUGLAS DUMP for "B" Coy & Batt. H.Qrs.
"B" Coy's rations to be carried by "C" Coy from DOUGLAS DUMP to "B" Coy H.Hqs .
Water. "C" Coy to carry for front line Coys under arrangements between Companies concerned.

6. List of Stores takenoever, sketch map of dispositions to be sent into Orderly Room by 5 p.m. 6th inst, together with certificate to the effect that billets have been left clean.

(Sgd. R.P. Baker Capt, & Adjt.
8th S.B.Royal West Kent Regt.

5th May 1918

Ref.
LENS
36.c.S.W.1

Battalion Operation Orders No. 4.
by
Lieut-Col H.J.WENYON, D.S.O.
Commanding 8th S.Bn.R.West Kent Regt.
In the Field 12th May 1918.

Copy No. 3....

Appendix 3

1. The Battalion will be relievd by Two Companies of the 1st Battalion Royal Fusiliers ~~Regiment~~, on the night 13/14th May 1918. On relief the Battalion will proceed to billets in BULLY-GRENAY.

2. GUIDES. Guides to be supplied as under, to report to Lieut P.A. GEDGE at Railway Crossing M.10.C. 70.25 at 8.30 p.m.

8/R.W.K.	To guide in 1st R.F.	Location.
"C" Coy	"D" Coy 14 Platoon	To relieve platoon at junction of NESTOR and NUNS ALLEY.
"C" "	"D" " 15 "	Close Support in NESTOR ALLEY
"A" "	"D" " H.Qrs.	N.7.b.8.9., COSY ALLEY
"A" "	"D" " 13 Platoon	BLUE LINE between COSY and NESTOR
"D" "	"D" " 16 "	BLUE LINE about CATAPULT DUMP
"B" "	"C" " 9 "	Portion of Front Line post just N. of MASON'S HOUSE.
"C" "	"C" " 10 Platoon	COSY and NUNS ALLEY.
"C" "	"C" " H.Qrs	COB TRENCH
"D" "	"C" " 11 Platoon	Right of BLUE LINE, N. of entrance to Tunnel
"D" "	"C" " 12 "	BLUE LINE, S. of COSY

3. Officers Trench bundles, mess stores, and cooking pots, will be collected at 9.30 p.m. at the point where the LENS-Bethune Road is crossed by the Heavy Gauge Tramway. Transport will wait at this spot at 11 p.m. to pick up Lewis Guns and magazines, till all are loaded. Companies will detail loading party and escort.

4. All information to be carefully handed over to the relieving platoons, and every assistance given them in taking up their dispositions. Trench stores and aeroplane photos to be carefully handed over.

5. All Dug outs, latrines, and cookhouses to be inspected after teas.

6. "B" and "C" Companies will move to BULLY-GRENAY, when the Company Commanders are satisfied that their sections have been relieved. "A" and "D" Companies will move on receipt of code Word "RIP" from Battalion Headquarters.

7. Relief complete to be notified to Battn. H.Qrs., and H.Qrs. at BULLY-GRENAY to be notified on arrival of Companies.

(Sgd) R.P.B A K E R. Capt. & Adjt.
8th S.B.Royal West Kent Regiment.

12th May 1918

CopyNo. 1 File.
" 2 War Diary
" 3 do
" 4 O.C. "A" COY
" 5 " "B" "
" 6 " "C" "
" 7 " "D" "
" 8 " 1st Royal Fusiliers ~~Regt~~.
" 9 Transport Officer
" 10 Quartermaster
" 11 H.Qrs Mess

SECRET. 3

Battalion Operation Order No. [illegible]

by

Lieut-Col., [illegible], D.S.O.,
Commanding 8th S.Battn. [illegible] West Kent Regiment.
[illegible] [illegible] 1918.

appendix 4

1. The Battalion will move into SUPPORT on the night 16th/17th M[illegible] relieving the 9th Battn. East Surrey Regiment.

2. Advance parties from [illegible] and "D" Companies [illegible] per Company and 1 N.C.O. per platoon and Sergeant [illegible] will start from the Square, [illegible], at 2.0 p.m. Advance party of "A" Company will proceed direct.

3. Companies will take over as follows:-

8/R.W.Kent Rgt.	9/E.Surrey Regt.
"D" Coy	"B" Coy
"B" Coy	"A" Coy
"C" Coy	"D" Coy
"A" Coy	"C" Coy

4. Order of March:- "D" Company to start from the Square 8.40 p.m. "B" Coy at 8.50 p.m. "C" Company at 9.0 p.m. 100 yards between platoons after passing [illegible]. "A" Company not to move out of CITE CALONNE before 9.40 p.m. Dress:- Fighting order - Great coats rolled.

5. Blankets, packs and valises for the Stores to be stacked outside Company billets by 12 noon. Blankets and valises for Detail Camp to be stacked at No.18 [illegible] by 2.0 p.m. Orderly Room Stores, Trench bundles, Lewis Guns, cooking pots, [illegible] to be outside Company billets by 7.30 p.m. Mess carts will call at Company messes at 3.30 p.m.

6. "Details" for Detail Camp at [illegible] 10 to parade in the Square at 5.30 p.m. - Marching Order.

7. "A" Company's valises and "A" Company's "Details" valises and blankets will be stacked for collection by 2.0 p.m. at their billets. One limber will report at 9.30 p.m. for their Lewis Guns and trench bundles and proceed with the Company.

8. Rations:- Ration limbers will proceed with the Companies.

9. Companies will render to Battn. Orderly Room by 7.30 p.m. tomorrow 16th. instant, a statement that their billets have been left clean. Arrival in CITE St.PIERRE to be notified in the usual manner to Battalion Headquarters.

(Sgd.) [illegible] P. [illegible], Capt.

Adjutant, 8th.S.Battn. Royal West Kent Regt.

Copies to:-

1. File.
2. Ward Diary.
3. War Diary.
4. O.C. "A" Company.
5. O.C. "B" Company.
6. O.C. "C" Company.
7. O.C. "D" Company.
8. Transport Officer.
9. Quartermaster.
10. Headquarters Mess.
11. R. S. Major.
12. O.C., 1st.[illegible]th. Staffordshire Regt.,
13. O.C., 9th.Bn. East Surrey Regt.,

SECRET Battalion Operation Order No.7 Copy No.3...

by

Lieut-Col., H.J.WENYON D.S.O.

Commanding 8th.S.Battn.Royal West Kent Regt.

In-the-field 21st.May1918

appendix 5

1. The Battalion will move into the front line St.EMILE Sector on the night of the 22/23 rd.inst., in relief of the 9th.East Surrey Regt. The billets in CITE St.PIERRE to be handed over to the 1st.North Stafford Regt.

2. Dispositions will be as follows :-

Front Line	"C" Company	Left	"A" Company	Right.
Support	"D" Company	Left	"B" Company	Right.

"C" Coy.8th.R.W.Kent Regt.takes over from			"C" Coy.9th.E.Surrey Rgt.	
"A" "	-do-	-do-	"D" "	-do-
"D" "	-do-	-do-	"B" "	-do-
"B" "	-do-	-do-	"A" "	-do-

3. Order of relief and routes;-

"D" Coy moves off at 9.30 p.m. via COUNTER ALLEY

"B" " " " " 9.30 p.m. via COW ALLEY

"A" " " " " 9.40 p.m. via COW ALLEY

"B" " " " " 9.50 p.m. via COUNTER ALLEY

4. Company cooks' stores and trench bundles to be carried under Company arrangements. No Transport will be available.

5. The Support Companies to provide ration andwater carrying parties for the corresponding Front Line Coys,under arrangements to be made by the Coys concerned.

6. Usual advance parties for taking over to be sent up in the afternoon.

7. Certificates to the effect that the dug-outs and cellars have been left scrupulously clean to be rendered to Battalion Orderly Room by 8.0 p.m. 22nd.inst.

8. Disposition maps and trench distribution states to be sent to Battalion Orderly Room by 1.0 p.m. 23rd.inst.,together with the list of stores taken over.

9. Relief complete to be notified as usual.

(Sgd) R. P. B A K E R Captain,

Adjutant 8th.S.Bn.Royal West Kent Regiment.

Copies to :-

1. File
2.)War Diary
3.)
4. O.C."A"Company
5. O.C."B"Company
6. O.C."C"Company
7. O.C."D"Company
8. Sergeant PRESTON
9. Headquarters Mess
10. Transport Mess
11. O.C.1st.North Staffordshire Regt.
12. O.C.9th.East Surrey Regt.

SECRET.

COPY No. 3

Battalion Operation Order No.6,
by
Lieut-Col., H.E.WENYON, D.S.O.,
Commanding 8th.S.Battn. Royal West Kent Regiment.
In-the-field, 21st. May 1918.
-@-@-@-@-@-@-@-@-@-@-@-@-

Appendix 6

Ref.Sheet 36.C.S.W. 1/10,000.

1. A Raid will be carried out on the Enemy Trenches between N.14.a.70.35
and N.14.~~a~~b.03.68., on the night of the ~~23rd/24th~~ 24/25. May.

2. Object of Raid to capture prisoners and generally inflict
casualties on the enemy.

3. Strength of Raiding Party- 2 Officers and one platoon plus one
section.
These will be divided into 3 groups :-

(1). Parapet Group- 2/Lieut.WALLIS, Platoon Headquarters and
Lewis Gun Section.
(2). Left Group- 2/Lieut.TREACHER and two sections.
(3). Right Group- Sergeant GRAY and two sections.

4. The party will assemble at N.14.a.78.92.

5. Artillery arrangements, etc., 18-pdr. Barrage will open on enemy
wire at 'Zero' minus 6 minutes. At 'Zero' minus 3 minutes it will
lift on to enemy trench. At 'Zero' it will lift clear on to houses
in rear of enemy line and remain there.
4.5 and 6 inch Howitzers and 6 inch Newtons and Stokes Mortars
will fire on selected targets on the flanks of and in rear of the
enemy positions. At 'Zero' minus 4 minutes a gas Projector attack
will take place. Should the wind prove favourable a real attack
will take place. Should it not be favourable, projectors filled
with smoke only will be fired. The party will leave 'P' bombs
burning in the enemy trenches on withdrawal to cover movement across
'No Man's Land.'

6. At 'Zero' minus 6 minutes the Raiding Party will leave the Assembly
Position and move up under the Barrage to a point opposite the point
of entry at N.14.a.55.55 in the centre of the areas to be raided.
At 'Zero' all three groups will enter enemy trenches simultaneously
moving in file in three parallel lines, the parapet group in the
centre. 2/Lieut.WALLIS will establish Raid Headquarters at the
point of entry.

7. The signal for withdrawal will be a Green Very Light fired low in
the direction of the enemy Support line. The Left and Right Groups
will withdraw to the point of entry. Each Section Commander will
report his Section present to 2/Lieut.WALLIS and will not leave the
trench with his section until so ordered.

8. A tape will be carried across from point of assembly to point of
entry in enemy trenches and Prisoners and Casalties will be evacuated
down the tape. A relay of Battalion Runners will be posted along
this to transmit messages and prisoners.

9. Medical arrangements and advanced Battalion H.Qs will be notified
later.

10. Watches will be syncronised at Battn.H.Qs at 8.0 p.m.

11. 'Zero' Hour will be 11.0 p.m.

(Sgd). R. P. B A K E R, Captain,
Adjutant, 8th.S.Battn. ROYAL WEST KENT REGIMENT.

Copies to:-

1. File	2 & 3. War Diary.
4. 72nd.Inf.Brigade.	5. Right Group R.F.A.
6. O.C. "A" Company	7. O.C. "B" Company.
8. O.C. "C" Company.	9. O.C. "D" Company.
10. Comdg.Officer.	11. 2nd.-in-command.
12. Headquarters.	13. Spare.

appendix 7.

8th Royal West Kent Regt.

The raid on the enemy trenches N.14.a.70.35. - N.14.b.03.68. took place last night.

The whole party was assembled in the sap at N.14.a.78.92 and in correct order by 10.50 p.m. and the end of the tape secured ready to move out.

The party left the assembly position on commencement of the barrage at 10.54 and moved on a compass bearing of 153°. At 10.56 the Gas Projector attack took place. A number of the cylinders fell in No Mans Land among the raiders, and, although they probably contained smoke only, they had a suffocating effect on the men and the whole party got badly disorganised. 2nd Lieut. THEACHER reached the enemy's wire with one or two men only. He found that it was possible to get through the enemy wire, but as he was practically alone he decided to come back. The party was back in our trenches at 11.15 p.m.

I did not hear of the situation till 11.20 as the telephone wires forward of advanced Battalion H.Q. had been cut.

At 11.25 Major BROWN came to advanced Headquarters and reported that the raiders had failed to enter the enemy trenches and were back in our line. The artillery barrage had been stopped.

I decided that the raid should be done again with half the party at 2 a.m. when another gas projector attack was ~~done~~. due.

A new barrage was arranged for 2 a.m. to remain on the enemy front line for 1 minute then lift on to his support line. I saw the Officers of the raiding party, and the O.C. 6" Newton Battery. The men of the raiding party had been sent back to their posts in our trenches and collecting them took a long time.

Major BROWN with a runner went out at about 1.40 from assembly position and laid the tape to a point within 30 yards of the enemy wire. On his return he found 2nd Lieut. WALLIS and 2nd Lieut. PIGGOTT with one section ready in the assembly position.

The projector attack which had been put forward 10 minutes and took place at 1.50 called ~~further~~ some retaliation on our front line and hampered the assembly considerably.

The party proceeded at once down the tape and successfully got through the loose wire and entered the enemy's trenches. No opposition was encountered in entering the trench, and only one M.G. from the left was firing while the party was crossing No Mans Land - and that very widly and without effect. On entering the trench 2nd Lieut. PIGGOTT worked to the left with 4 men, and 2nd Lieut WALLIS to the right with the remainder of the party. Major BROWN and a runner took up a position at the point of entry as Raid Headquarters. As 2nd Lieut WALLIS started down the trench with his party 2 of the enemy appeared round a traverse. They were at once fired on and 2nd Lieut. WALLIS threw a bomb into the next Fire Bay. The Huns gave a loud yell and retired at the double followed by 2nd Lieut WALLIS and his party. About 40 yards down the trench 2nd Lieut WALLIS came to a dug-out entrance. He called down but got no response, he then threw a Mills bomb down and, following shrieks from the bottom of the steps, One man emerged. No signs of anyone else being inside could be found, so after doing as much damage as possible to the dug-out and throwing more bombs down, 2nd Lieut WALLIS returned with the prisoner to the point of entry

2nd Lieut PIGGOTT had meantime worked down about 50 yards to the left and was having trouble at a dug-out with some fractious Bosche. Hearing the noise Major BROWN sent his runner to investigate and assist. On arriving at the dug-out entrance 2nd Lieut. PIGGOTT had shouted down and some guttural response had been given but no inclination to come up. He then fired his revolver through the gas curtains, which were down and the gas curtains were then raised. A Hun appeared on the steps and was evidently enquiring what was the matter. 2nd Lieut PIGGOTT then threatened him with his revolver. The Hun emitted a piercing shriek and came forward with his hands up. Another Bosche came to the bottom of the steps and was extracted in a similar ~~position~~ fashion. No more response could he get from this dug-out although Mills Bombs were thrown down. 2nd Lieut. PIGGOTT then returned with his prisoners to the point of entry, 2nd Lieut. WALLIS fired the Green Light the signal for withdrawal. The whole party then returned to our line. They had been in the enemy trenches 12 minutes. No trouble from enemy M.Gs. or Rifle fire was experienced while the party was crossing No Mans Land. Major BROWN and 2nd Lieut. WALLIS got back most of the tape from No Mans Land when they returned.

The party which entered the enemy trench consisted of the following :-

Major H.S. BROWN.
2nd Lieut. G.A.E. WALLIS.
2nd Lieut. D.P. PIGGOTT.
L/Cpl. WARFORD.
Pte. BAKER.
Pte. TILBY.
Pte. SMYTH.
Pte. BONNEY.
Pte. HARGIN.
Pte. BOWES.

I wish to mention particularly the work of the following :-

Major H.S. BROWN who carried out the preliminary arrangements for the raid. When the second attempt was ordered he went out in advance and laid the tape. He then returned and after the party had gone over he followed them and took up a position on the enemy's parapet throughout the proceedings.

2nd Lieut. G.A.E. WALLIS who took part in both attempts. In the first attempt he made great efforts to collect the parties in No Mans Land after they had been scattered by the Smoke Cylinders.
On the second attempt he led the party, dealt with one dug-out himself and remained in the enemy trench until all the rest had got back.

2nd Lieut. PIGGOTT who volunteered at a moments notice to go over with the second attempt. Although he had no details of the scheme, he led the left fighting party with great success and secured 2 Prisoners.

L/Cpl. Warford who took part in both attempts. He reached the enemy wire on the first attempt and on the second he accompanied 2nd Lieut PIGGOTT. and rendered invaluable assistance.

Pte. Baker who went with 2nd Lieut WALLIS on both attempts and rendered great assistance.

(Sd) H.J. KENYON.

Lieut.-Col.

25th May 1918.

SECRET Battalion Operation Orders No.8 Copy No. 3

by
Lieut-Col., H" J. Wenyon D.S.O.
Commanding 8th. S. Battn. Royal West Kent Regiment.
In-the-field 27th. May 1918.

Appendix 8

1. The Bat talion will be relieved in the Front Line on the night of the 28/29th. instant by the 1st. Battn. North Staffordshire Regt on relief the Bat talion will move into Brigade Reserve at BULLY GRENAY, with one Company in CITECALONNE.

2. Advance parties of 1 Officer per Coy. and 1 N.C.O. per platoon will proceed after dinners to reconoitre the Battle positions:-

"B" Coy.	RAILWAY POST and COUGAR POST.
"A" Coy.	FOSSE POST to N. Bde Boundary M.10.b.55
"D" Coy	EDGWARE POST
"C" Coy.	CALONNE Defences between M.15.c.0.0. and M.15.a.4.9.
Bat tn. H.Qs.	M.9.d.5.5.

Advance partieswill rendezvous with the Quartermaster in the square BULLY GRENAY at5.0 p.m. for taking over billets.

3. Trench stores, dispositions and work in hand to be carefully handed over. Certificates that the billets have been left clean to reach Battalon Oredrly Roo m by noon 29th. instant.

4. Lewis guns and stores to be dumped for collection by Transport on the LENS-BETHUNE Road where heavy guage trench tramway crosses it.
Companies are responsible for seeing that all their stores are loaded and for providing escort. They will detail a responsible N.C.O. for this purpose who will report to Transport Sergeant when all his Company stores are loaded.

5. Completion of relief and notification of arrival of Companies to be forwarded as usual.

(Sgd) R. P. B A K E R. Captain,

Adjutant 8th. S. Bn. Royal West Kent Regt.

Copies to :-

1. File.
2.) War Diary.
3.)
4. O.C. "A" Company
5. O.C. "B" Company
6. O.C. "C" COmpany
7. O.C. "D" Company
8. Transport Mess.
9. Headquarters Mess.
10. O.C. 1st. North Staffordshire Regt.
11. O.C. 9th. East Surrey Regt.

Army Form C. 2118.

Instructions regarding War Diaries and Intelligence Summaries are contained in F. S. Regs., Part II. and the Staff Manual respectively. Title pages will be prepared in manuscript.

WAR DIARY
or
INTELLIGENCE SUMMARY.
(Erase heading not required.)

Vol 32

Place	Date	Hour	Summary of Events and Information	Remarks and references to Appendices
			War Diary (1st - 30th June 1918). 8th S Bn Royal West Kent Regt. (Vol)	

2353 Wt. W2544/1454 700,000 5/15 D. D. & L. A.D.S.S./Forms/C. 2118.

Instructions regarding War Diaries and Intelligence Summaries are contained in F. S. Regs., Part II. and the Staff Manual respectively. Title pages will be prepared in manuscript.

Ref Trench map LENS 44a (36 C) SW.1 1/10000

WAR DIARY
or
~~INTELLIGENCE SUMMARY.~~
(Erase heading not required.)

8th Bn Royal West Kent Regt. June 1918.

Army Form C. 2118.

Place	Date	Hour	Summary of Events and Information	Remarks and references to Appendices
BULLY-GRENAY	1-6-18		Training. 3 Coys. at BULLY-GRENAY. C Coy. at CALONNE	
do	2-6-18		Church parades.	
do	3-6-18		Batt^n moved into Support, relieving the 9th E. Surreys in Cité St PIERRE. Billets in cellars.	Appendix A
St PIERRE	4-6-18		In support. Batt^n finding working parties of approximately half its strength. Major H.S. Brown in command. C.O. at Transport lines.	
do	5-6-18		In support. Weather fine. Working parties as usual.	
do	6-6-18		Sgt HALL and 4 O.R. of 'D' Coy hit by H.E. Working parties as usual - wiring support lines, carrying T.M. shells, clearing dugouts etc.	
do	7-6-18 / 8-6-18		Working parties as usual. Coys. are able to obtain baths at St PIERRE, but no clean changes available.	
do	9-6-18		Relieved 9th E. Surrey Regt. in the front line. Major Brown left for details. C.O. arrived. 'A' Coy right front, 'B' Coy in support. 'C' Coy left front, 'D' Coy in support.	Appendix B
Forward line	10-6-18		Enemy party approached a post of 'C' Coy but were driven off without loss to us. Enemy's loss could not be ascertained in the dark.	
do	11-6-18		MASON'S HOUSE post held by 'C' Coy heavily shelled by T.M. Our T.M. retaliated and enemy fire ceased. Two deserters of the enemy 42nd Division gave themselves up to 'C' Coy. At dawn an enemy party approached a post of 'C' Coy, probably looking for the two deserters. The party was hailed by 2Lt BEYNES and invited to surrender but fired in reply. They were then driven off by our fire. Deserters state a raid would take place on our line on night of 11th/12th.	
do	12-6-18		Dispositions made to meet the enemy raid on night 11th/12th. No raid took place, but enemy T.M. active on front line.	Appendix C and D
do	13-6-18		First appearance of epidemic pyrexia. 3 officers and 12 men of 'C' Coy ill. Raid by 'B' Coy on night of 12th/13th. Quiet day. Some men of 'D' Coy down with pyrexia. Steps taken to disinfect all dugouts, especially CANTEEN TUNNEL, where disease first made its appearance.	
do	14-6-18		Quiet, warm day. More cases of pyrexia. Batt^n was relieved by the 1st N. Staffordshire Regt and moved into Reserve billets.	Appendix E

2353 Wt. W2544/1454 700,000 5/15 D. D. & L. A.D.S.S./Forms/C. 2118.

Army Form C. 2118.

Instructions regarding War Diaries and Intelligence Summaries are contained in F. S. Regs., Part II. and the Staff Manual respectively. Title pages will be prepared in manuscript.

Ref Trench map LENS 44a (36 C) SW1 1/10000

WAR DIARY

or

~~INTELLIGENCE SUMMARY.~~

(Erase heading not required.)

Place	Date	Hour	Summary of Events and Information	Remarks and references to Appendices
BULLY-GRENAY	15-6-18		In Reserve. A, B and D Coys at BULLY GRENAY. B Coy at CALONNE. Baths and clothing parades. Major BROWN evacuated suffering from pyrexia. Working parties as usual.	
do	16-6-18		Col WENYON evacuated suffering from pyrexia. Capt. BAKER assumes command of the Battalion. Evacuations now amount to 5 officers, 108 o.r.	
do	17-6-18		Heavy thunderstorm. Usual working parties. Training much interfered with by shortage of men.	
do	18-6-18		Regimental tour of Reserve battle positions. A further 3 officers and 110 other ranks evacuated in the last 48 hours.	
do	19-6-18		Cloudy, rain in morning. Col. WENYON returned and resumed command.	
do	20-6-18		Further evacuations on 19th and 20th 2 officers 180 OR. Battn relieved 9th E Surrey Regt in support. B and D Coy taking over new positions in CRASSIER SWITCH, and new billets in West of St PIERRE. A, C and H.Q. in same positions as before. Enemy shelling not marked.	Appendix F.
St PIERRE	21-6-18		Cold. Raining slightly. Whole Battn on working parties. Reduced numbers make it impossible to find all working parties required.	
do	22-6-18		Cold but fine. Working parties as usual. Evacuations 21st 22nd 1 officer 35 OR. Enemy artillery quiet.	
do	23-6-18 } 24-6-18 }		Cold spell continues. Evacuations only 7 OR. It appears that the epidemic is dying out. Col. WENYON proceeds on leave. Capt. BAKER in command.	
do	25-6-18		Warmer weather. 2 men evacuated. Working parties as usual.	
do.	26-6-18		Battn relieved 9th E. Surrey Regt in forward line. Owing to shortage of men A and B Coy were amalgamated under Capt. ROGERS and C and D under Capt. PORTER. Capt BAKER to Transport suffering from pyrexia. Capt. PROCTOR in command. A and B Coy on right sector, C and D on left.	Appendix G
Forward line	27-6-18		Quiet day. Slightly warmer. Patrols as usual. One man slightly wounded. Enemy appears to hold line more strongly and to be more alert than formerly.	
do	28-6-18		Quiet warm day. Major ESDAILE, 8th R.W. Surrey Regt arrived and assumed command	
do	29-6-18		Morning dull and cloudy. Enemy very quiet. 2 men of A Coy wounded by enemy T.M.	
do.	30-6-18		Quiet day, but heavy enemy shelling of rear areas at night. Forward area did not receive much attention. Battn carried out change of dispositions. C and D Coy remaining in the forward zone, A and B withdrawing to the Black line positions.	

R P Baker Capt & Adjt
8th Bn R. W. Kent Regt

2353 Wt. W2544/1454 700,000 5/15 D. D. & L. A.D.S.S./Forms/C. 2118.

SECRET. Battalion Operation Order No.9 COPY No... A

by

Lieut-Col., H.J.WENYON, D.S.O.,

Commanding 8th.S.Battn.Royal West Kent Regiment. Field,

3rd.June 18

-@--@-@-@-@-@-@-@-@-@-@-@--@-

1. The Battalion will move into SUPPORT on the night 3rd/4th June, relieving the 9th.Battn. East Surrey Regiment.

2. Advance parties from "A", "B" and "D" Companies of 1 Officer per Company and 1 N.C.O. per platoon and Sergeant PRESTON (Headquarters') will start from the Square, BULLY GRENAY at 2.30 p.m. Advance party of "C" Company will proceed direct.

3. Companies will take over same accomodation as before.

4. Order of march- "D" Company to start from the Square 9.30 p.m. - "B" Coy at 9.40 p.m. "A" Coy at 9.50 p.m. 100 yards between platoons after passing FOSSE 11. "C" Coy not to move out of CITE CALONNE before 10.30 p.m. Dress- Fighting order - Great coats rolled.

5. Packs and valises for the Stores to be stacked outside Company billets by 12 noon. Valises for Details to be stacked at No.18 Rue de la Mine by 2.0 p.m.

Trench bundles, Lewis Guns, cooking pots, Orderly Room Stores to be outside Company billets by 8.0 p.m. Mess carts will call at Company messes at 8.30 p.m.

6. "Details" to parade in the Square at 5.30 p.m. - Marching Order.

7. "C" Coy's valises and "C" Coy's "Detail's" valises will be stacked for collection by 9.0 p.m. at their billet. One limber will report at 10.0 p.m. for their Lewis Guns and trench bundles and proceed with the Company.

Battalion Operation Order No.9 conts., Sheet -2-

8. Rations- Ration limbers will proceed with the Companies.

9. Companies will render to Battn.Orderly Room by 12 noon tomorrow 4th. instant, a statement that their billets have been left clean. Arrival in CITE St.PIERRE to be notified in the usual manner to Battalion Headquarters.

(Sd) R C Burke
.... Capt. & Adjt.
8th (S) Battn. Royal West Kent Regt.

Copies to:-

1. File.
2. War Diary.
3. " "
4. O.C. "A" Company.
5. O.C. "B" Company.
6. O.C. "C" Company.
7. O.C. "D" Company.
8. Transport Officer.
9. Quartermaster.
10. Headquarters' Mess.
11. A/R.S.Major.
12. O.C., 9th.Bn.East Surrey Regiment.

B

SECRET. Battalion Operation Order No.10 **COPY No. 3....**
by
Lieut-Col., H.J.WENYON,D.S.O.
Commanding 8th.S.Battn.Royal West Kent Regt.
In-the-Field, 8th June 1918.
@@

1. The Battalion will move into the front line ST.EMILE Sector, on the night of 9/10th inst., in relief of the 9th East Surrey Rgt. Billets in CITE ST. PIERRE to be handed over to the 1st North Staffordshire Regiment.

2. __Dispositions__.

Front Line	"C"	Coy	Left.
	"A"	"	Right.
Support	"D"	"	Left.
	"B"	"	Right.

3. __Order of Relief & Routes__.

"D"	Coy	moves off	at	10.30 p.m.	via		COUNTER ALLEY
"B"	"	"	"	" 10.15	"	"	COW ALLEY
"A"	"	"	"	" 10.0	"	"	COW ALLEY
"C"	"	"	"	" 10,0	"	"	COUNTER ALLEY

4. Cooks stores and trench bundles to be carried under Company arrangements.

5. Advance parties for taking over as usual.

6. Trench states, list of stores taken over, to be rendered by noon 10th inst. Anti-gas appliances to be rendered on separate list.

7 Completion of relief to be notified as usual.

(Sgd) R. P. B A K E R, Captn.
....

Adjutant, 8th.S.B.Royal West Kent Rgt.

Copies to:-

1. File
2. War Diary
3. War Diary
4. O.C. "A" Coy
5. O.C. "B" Coy
6. O.C. "C" Coy
7. O.C. "D" Coy
8. Tansport Officer
9. Quartermaster
10. Headquarters' Mess
11. O.C. 1st North Staffordshire Regt.
12. O.C. 9th East Surrey Regt.

E

SECRET

BATTALION OPERATION ORDERS NO. 11 COPY No. 2

by

Lieut-Col. H.J.WENYON, D.S.O.

Commanding 8th S.Battn.Royal West Kent Regiment.

In-the-field. 13th June 1918.

1. The Battalion will be relieved in the Front Line on the night of 14/15th June 1918, by the 1st North Staffordshire Regt.

2. On Relief the Battalion will move into Reserve ; H.Q.,"A", "C", and "D" Coys., at BULLY GRENAY, "B" Coy at CITE CALONNE.

3. Advance parties will be detailed as follows:-

"C" Coy - 1 Officer and 1 N.COO per platoon.
"B" " - 1 Officer and 1 N.C.O. per platoon.
"A" " - 1 N.CMO.
"D" " - 1 N.C.O.

Advance parties will report at Battn. H.Qs. at 2.30 p.m. 14th June 1918, and will meet the Quartermaster in the square at BULLY GRENAY at 5 p.m., for taking over billets.

4. Lewis Guns and stores to be dumped at junction of STAFFORD ST. and COW ALLEY, M.12.c.60.95. by 12 midnight.
Companies are responsible for seeing that all their stores are loaded, and for providing escort. They will detail a responsible N.C.O. for this purpose who will report to Transport Sergeant when all his Company stores are loaded.

5. Trench Stores, dispositions, and work in hand, to be carefully handed over. Certificates that the billets have been left clean to reach Battalion Orderly Room by noon 15th June 1918.

6. Completion of relief and notification of arrival of Companies to be forwarded as usual.

7. ACKNOWLEDGE.

(Sgd) C.F.C.MACASKIE, 2/Lieut,
for Capt. & Adjt.
8th S.Battn.Royal WestKent Regt.

Copies to:-
1. File.
2. War Diary
3. War Diary
4. O.C. "A" Coy
5. O.C. "B" Coy
6. O.C. "C" Coy
7. O.C. "D" Coy
8. Transport Mess
9. Headquarters Mess
10. O.C. 1st North Staffordshire Regiment.
11. O.C. 9th East Surrey Regiment.

2 F

Secret. BATTALION OPERATION ORDERS NO.12. COPY NO.

by

Lieut-Col. H.J.WENYON,D.S.O.

Commanding 8th.S.Battn.Royal West Kent Regiment.

In the Field. 19th June 1918.

1. The Battalion will move up into Support in CITE ST. PIERRE on the night of 20/21st, in relief of 9th East Surrey Regt. Company Areas and Battle Positions as already notified.

2. Advance Parties for taking over stores, to proceed in small parties at 6 p.m. Companies to make their own arrangements for meeting and guiding in their Platoons.

3. Order of March and times of start from the Square:-

"A" Coy - 9.30.p.m.
"C" Coy - 9.40.p.m.
"D" Coy - 9.50.p.m.
"B" Company from CITE CALONNE. - 9.45.p.m.

Dress. Fighting Order. Greatcoats rolled.

4. Packs and Officers valises for the stores to be stacked outside Compay billets by 12 noon.

5. Trench bundles, Lewis guns & Magazines,& Orderly Room Stores for the Line, to be outside Company billets by 8 p.m. Mess carts will call at Company messes at 8,30 p.m.

6. Men recommended for Transport Lines, to parade in the Square a 6 p.m., Sgt Bateman to march them down. No details will be sent toDivisional Reception Camp.

7. Ration Limbers will proceed with Companies. Transport Officer to arrange to collect "B" Coy's valises and pcks for the stores, as soon as dark, and also to send Transport for their Lewis Guns and Trench Bundles. "B" Company to provide gyide.

8. Companies to report arrival to Battalion Headquarters.

(Sgd) R.P. BAKER, Capt. & Adjt.

8th S.Battn.Royal West Kent Regiment,

Copies to:-

1. File
2. War Diary
3. War Diary
4. O.C."A" Coy
5. O.C."B" Coy
6. O.C."C" Coy
7. O.C."D" Coy
8. Transport Mess
9. Headquarters Mes.
10. 10. O.C. 1st North Staffordshire Regiment.
11. O.C. 9th East Surrey Regiment.

9

SECRET. BATTALION OPERATION ORDER NO.13. COPY NO. 3...

by

CAPTAIN R.P.BAKER,M.C.

COMMANDING 8TH.BATTN.ROYAL WEST KENT REGT.

IN-THE-FIELD. 26TH JUNE 1918.

1. The Battalion will move into the front line ST.EMILE Sector, on the night of 26/27th inst., in relief of the 9th East Surrey Regt. Billets in CITE ST.PIERRE to be handed over to the 1st North Staffordshire Regiment.

2. DISPOSITIONS.

"A" & "B" Coys. will relieve the Companies holding the Right Sector.
"C" & "D" Coys. will relieve the Companies holding the Left Sector.

3. ORDER OF RELIEF & ROUTES.

"C" & "D" Coys. will move off at 10 p.m. via COUNTER ALLEY.
"A" & "B" Coys. will move off at 10.30 p.m. via COW ALLEY.

4. Cook stores and trench bundles to be carried under Company arrangements.

5. Advance parties for taking over as usual. Parties will move up after tea by Trench and not by Road.

6. Trench States, list of Stores taken over, to be rendered by noon 27th inst. Anti-gas appliances to be rendered on separate list.

7. Completion of relief to be notified as usual.

(Sgd) C.F.C.M A C A S K I E, 2/Lieut.,
A/Adjutant, 8th S.B.Royal West Kent Regiment.

Copies to :-

1. File.
2. War Diary.
3. War Diary.
4. O.C. "A" Coy.
5. O.C. "B" Coy.
6. O.C. "C" Coy.
7. O.C. "D" Coy.
8. Transport Mess.
9. Headquarters Mess.
10. O.C.1st North Staffordshire Regt.
11. O.C. 9th East Surrey Regt.

C

ORDERSFOR RAID BY 2 OFFICERS & 3 SECTIONS.

A Raid on Enemy Trenches at N.14.b.12.93 will be carried out on night of 12/13th June 1918.

TAPE laid on bearing 102 Magnetic from 2nd loop in CONDUCTOR SAP by 11.45 p.m.

ASSEMBLY. At N.14.a.87.95. Completed by 11.45 p.m.

ORDER OF ADVANCE along TAPE.

2nd Lt.BINNEY) On Tape
Bangalore Party)
and 1 Section)

Sgt CATER)
and 1 Section)

followed by:-

2nd Lt. MICHIE, 2 Runners,
2 S.Bs., 4 Bn.Runners (left along the tape on the advance)

TRENCH MORTARS. 6" NEWTONS.

11.45 p.m. Commence firing on N.8.d.27.25.
N.14.b.13.68.
at rate of 1 round per minute on each target.

ON TORPEDO EXPLODING & RED LIGHT fired parallel to our trenches or backtowards our Support Line:-

Fire on above 2 Targetsand also on N.8.d.4.0

RATE OF FIRE.

5 minutes. 3 per minute per Target
after 5 " 2 " " " "
Till ceasefire be given.

STOKES on CINNABAR TRENCH (4 targets) comencing when RED LIGHT Signal is given.

TRENCH PARTIES.

Left party (2nd Lt.BINNEY) will work to C.T. N.8.d.18.00 and establish a temporary block there.

Right party (Sgt. CATER) will work to about N.14.b.1.8.

O.C. Raid (2nd Lt.MICHIE, 2 Runners, and 2 S.Bs.) on Enemy's parapet at POINT OF ENTRY.

"NOMAN'S LAND"PARTY.

3 Runners ar intervals along Tape, to remain till all TRENCH parties have have returned. They will work in relays for taking messages or prisoners.

CONDUCTOR SAP. S.Bs. party.

RETURN. On reaching objective in enemy's Trench . O.C. Right & Left Parties (respectively) will send message back to O.C.RAID "TRENCH CLEARED".
O.C.RAID will then fire GREEN Very Light towards Enemy Support Line.
Parties will then withdraw by original Point Of Entry.
O.C. RAID will count the parties as they leave andwill return after all have passed him, taking up the Tape and taking in the Runners with him.

After all TRENCH parties have returned to our line, a coloured STAR ROCKET will be fired which will be the Signal for T.Ms. tocease fire and L.G. Sections in "NO MAN's LAND" to return.

EQUIPMENT. Clean fatigue dress. 1 Bandolier. Rifle and Bayonet. 2 Bombs.

STOKES SHELLS. 2 with each party.

(Sgd) H.J.WENYON" Lieut-Colonel,
Commanding 8th S.B.Royal West Kent Regiment.

12th June 1918

D

REPORT ON PATROL.

A figh ting Patrol of 2 Officers and 2 Sections enetererd the Enemy Trenches at N.14.b.12.93 last night.
The tape laying party (2nd Lieut. Michie & 2 O.Rs.) left our trench at 11 p.m. Proceeding beyond our wire by CONDUCTOR SAP an Enemy patrol of abou t 16 was seen advancing on MASONS HOUSE. Ourtrenches were being trench Mortared atthe time. Our Raiding party was temporarily got into position to repel this raid, and our 2 Officerswent forward again into "No Mans Land" to reconnoitre. On being approached the Enemy dispersed and made his way hurriedly to his own line. The Enemy was using gas in T.Ms. and it was decided that our men should wear box respirators. After this, 2nd Lieut. Michie went out and laid the tape successfully, from CONDUCTOR SAp to the enemy wire. A covering party (with L.Guns) was then placed in positi on in "No Man's Land", and the 2 Sections and the Bangalore Torpedo party advanced to the end of the tape on the Enemy's wire.
The Torpedo was exploded successfully at 110 a.m. and 2nd Lieut Binney led half the party through the gap into the Enemy's Trenches.
Immediately the Bangalore Torpedo exploded the enemy put up 2 GREENLights and within a few seconds he opened up with T.Ms. on "No Man's Land" and his own wire. Several T.Ms. fell almost in the gap made by the torpedo and divided our patrol into two parts inflicting 2 casualties onthe rear section. 2nd LieuttBinney with the leading section remained in the enemy Trenches for some minutes and thoroughly investigated it.
The Trench still looks quite new but is only about 3 feet deep, and there are no dug-outs in this vicinity. About 1.23 a.m. the order was given to return to our lines. This was done successfully without further casualties, although T.Ms. were bursting freely in "No Man's Land".
From the speed and accuracy with which the Enemy's barrage was brought down it would appear that the exact locality of the raid had been discovered. Probably the tape laying and Bangalore parties had been spotted.
2nd Lieut. Michie did good work in organising his party to counter the enemy's raid at a moments notice, and afterwards in laying the tape right on to t he enemy's wire, and getting the party out to the tape.
The Sappers from the 103rd R.E. Coy took great trouble with the torpedo and a perfect gap was cut.

D

2nd Lieut. Binney led his section with great dash into the enemy's trenches and did all he could to find some enemy, kill orcapture, but the trench was deserted and there were no dug-outs.
The wire is not very thick and is very sketchy in places.
2nd Lieut Binney returned from a point in the enemy trenches some distance from the point of entry, and he got through the wire without difficulty.
The Light Signals were sent up by the enemy from CINNABAR TRENCH.

....................Lieut.-Colonel,

13th June 1918. Commanding 8th S.Battn.Royal West Kent Regt.

ORDERLY ROOM
No. A/ 988
AUG 1 1918
8th (Service) Bn. Queen's Own
Royal West Kent Regiment.

VR 33

SECRET.

War Diary

of

8th S. Battn. Royal West Kent Regt.,

from 1st July to 31st July 1918.
(Volume.-).

To:- D.A.G.,
3rd ECHELON.
(thro' H.Qs. 72nd I.B.).

R.V. Baker Capt. A/Lt.Col. ....Lt-Col.,
Cmdg. 8th (S) Battn. Royal West Kent Regt.

8th S Bn Royal West Kent Regt

Instructions regarding War Diaries and Intelligence Summaries are contained in F. S. Regs., Part II. and the Staff Manual respectively. Title pages will be prepared in manuscript.

WAR DIARY
or
INTELLIGENCE SUMMARY.
(Erase heading not required.)

Army Form C. 2118.

Place	Date	Hour	Summary of Events and Information	Remarks and references to Appendices
Front Line	1-7-18		Warm quiet day. Heavy enemy shelling of back areas started at 9.30 PM and continued for some hours	OH
St EMILE, LENS.			Front line and forward sector not affected. Capt. PROCTOR left for Senior Officers Course in England	
			Capt. PORTER took over command of D Coy. No evacuations for pyrexia. Sick begin to return from Hospl.	OH
do.	2-7-18		Quiet day. Batn moved into Reserve on relief by 1st N. Staff Regt. D Coy to CALONNE, remainder	Appendix A
			to BULLY-GRENAY	OH
BULLY-	3-7-18		In Reserve. Inspection of billets by D A Q M G Corps. Many working parties on battle positions	
GRENAY			and Bde Battle H Q. 2 Platoons nightly wiring FOSSE POIT. Re-organization of companies commenced.	OH Appendix B
do.	4-7-18		Working parties as usual. Lt J. C ORCHARDSON from England - to D Coy. Work on cookhouses and Kitchens.	OH
do.	5-7-18		Working parties as usual. Training and re-organization.	OH
do	6-7-18		Major BROWN returned from hospital. Working parties as usual. Lewis gun classes and general training.	OH
do	7-7-18		Usual working parties. Many pyrexia cases rejoined. In some cases men have been re-posted to other	
			battalions and men of other battalions sent to us. The matter has been taken up.	OH
do.	8-7-18		Major ESPAILE, temporarily in command, left the Batn. Batn moved up into Support. 16 officers, 531 OR	OH Appendix C
St PIERRE	9-7-18		Working parties about 60 men per Coy daily on defences, emplacements etc. Test man battle stations during	
			the night. A and C Coy in St PIERRE SWITCH. D and B Coy in VILLAGE LINE	OH
do.	10-7-18		Work as usual. Lt Col. WENYON resumed command. 2 Lt F. CARVILLE from England - to D Coy.	OH

(A9175) Wt W2535/P360 600,000 12/17 D. D. & L. Sch. 52a. Forms/C2118/15.

8th S. Bn Royal West Kent Regt

Instructions regarding War Diaries and Intelligence Summaries are contained in F. S. Regs., Part II. and the Staff Manual respectively. Title pages will be prepared in manuscript.

WAR DIARY
or
INTELLIGENCE SUMMARY.
(*Erase heading not required.*)

Army Form C. 2118.

Place	Date	Hour	Summary of Events and Information	Remarks and references to Appendices
St PIERRE.	11-7-18		Showery weather. Usual working parties.	CH
do.	12-7-18		Capt. PORTER on leave to England. Lt ORCHARDSON took over command of D Coy. Usual working parties.	CH
do	13-7-18		Area round OPERA HOUSE heavily shelled by 5.9 calibre guns. Sgt PRESTON of H.Q. wounded. Usual work.	CH
do	14-7-18		Batn relieved 9th E. Surrey Regt in the front line. Rain made relief unpleasant. Batn H.Q. moved	Appendix D
			back since last tour in front line.	CH
Front Line	15-7-18		Quiet. Patrol on night 14/15 examining wire only.	CH
St EMILE	16-7-18		Quiet by day. St PIERRE shelled with gas shells in evening. Test man battle positions carried out.	
SECTOR,			Patrols on night 15/16 2Lt WATTS and 5 OR found enemy wiring party at N8D6797, and dispersed	
LENS area.			them with bombs. Enemy party was re-inforced and advanced to attack. Our patrol bombed them again and	
			withdrew.	CH
do	17-7-18		2Lt PIGGOTT and 3 OR. examined FOSSE 1 on night 16/17. No sign of enemy occupation. Enemy M.G. at	
			N14 c39. opened fire on them. Quiet day	CH
do	18-7-18		Quiet day occasional thunderstorms. Patrol on night 17/18 2Lt BINNEY and 5 OR examined CONDUCTOR	
			SAP. No sign of enemy found.	CH
do	19-7-18		Quiet day. Patrols on night 18/19 under 2Lt WATTS and 2Lt TAYLOR examined enemy's wire.	CH
do.	20-7-18		Corps Commander Sir A. HUNTER-WESTON visited the line. Enemy heavily shelled COIN and COUNTER trenches.	CH

(A9475) Wt W2358/P360 600,000 12/17 D. D. & L. Sch. 52a. Forms/C2118/15.

Instructions regarding War Diaries and Intelligence Summaries are contained in F. S. Regs., Part II. and the Staff Manual respectively. Title pages will be prepared in manuscript.

8th S. Bn Royal West Kent Regt

WAR DIARY
or
INTELLIGENCE SUMMARY.
(Erase heading not required.)

Army Form C. 2118.

Place	Date	Hour	Summary of Events and Information	Remarks and references to Appendices
Front Line	20-7-18		Some 600 shells round these trenches during the course of the day. No casualties. Patrols on night of 19/20	
			working in bright moonlight. Post in CONDUCTOR sap was found to be occupied by enemy. Batn was	
			relieved by 1st N. Staff. Regt, and moved to Reserve. B Coy at CALONNE, remainder at BULLY-GRENAY.	CH Appendix E
BULLY-GRENAY	21-7-18		In Reserve. Baths, clothing parades etc. Few working parties. 1 Platoon daily at Bde H.Q.	CH
do	22-7-18		clothing and inspection parades etc. Training	CH
do	23-7-18		Training - chiefly Lewis gun instruction.	CH
do	24-7-18		Treated today as Sunday. Church parades. Cricket matches, shooting competition.	CH
do	25-7-18		Batn marched out to MARQUEFFLES FARM for range firing and training. B. Coy. did a successful	
			field firing scheme in co-operation with a contact aeroplane.	CH
do	26-7-18		Batn relieved the 9th E Surrey Regt in Support. Rainy weather	CH Appendix F
St PIERRE	27-7-18		In support. Many working parties. Enemy quiet	CH
do	28-7-18		Enemy quiet. Usual working parties. Draft of 35 O.R. arrived.	CH
do	29-7-18		Col Wenyon left on short course. Major Brown in command. Captain Baker to Transport lines. Capt. Porter returned	
			from leave and resumed command of D. Coy. Misty afternoon.	CH
do.	30-7-18		Shelling at night by enemy, probably retaliation for 20th Div. raids. Usual working parties.	CH
do.	31-7-18		Very warm, quiet day. Aerial activity considerable. Usual working parties.	CH

(A9175) Wt W2352/P560 600,000 12/17 D. D. & L. Sch. 52a. Forms/C2118/15.

Map of Dispositions attached Appendix G.

CH [illegible] 2Lt
a/adjt

[illegible] 7th [illegible] Bn Royal West Kent Regt [illegible] 3

A.

[illegible]

1. The [illegible] will be relieved [illegible] the front line [illegible] night of 2nd/3rd July 1918 [illegible]

2. On relief the Battalion will [illegible] [illegible] Coys at [illegible] D Coy at [illegible]

3. Advance parties will be detailed as follows:

[illegible] Coy [illegible] 1 N.C.O. per platoon

[illegible] Coy 1 N.C.O.

[illegible] Coy 1 N.C.O.

[illegible] Coy 1 N.C.O.

Advance parties will report at [illegible] H.Q. at 2 p.m. 2nd July 1918 [illegible] the Quartermaster [illegible] at 5 p.m. [illegible]

4. [illegible]

5. Trench stores [illegible]

6. Completion of relief [illegible] to be forwarded [illegible]

7. Acknowledge.

8. 1st July 1918

Issued at 5. p.m. 1-7-18

Sgd [illegible] Capt & Adjt

7th Bn Royal West Kent Regt

Copies to

1. [illegible] 7. [illegible]
2. [illegible] 8. [illegible]
3. [illegible] 9. [illegible]
4. [illegible] 10. [illegible]
5. [illegible] 11. [illegible]
6. [illegible] 12. [illegible]

C

S E C R E T   Battalion Operation Orders No.15   Copy No.3..

by

Major P.C.ESDAILE

Commanding 8th.S.Battn.Royal West Kent Regiment.

In-the-field.,7th.July 1918.

1. The Battalion will move into Support in CITE St.PIERRE on the night of the 8/9th.July, in relief of the 9th.East Surrey Regt. Company Areas and BATTLE Positions will be taken over as before.

2. Advance parties for taking over Stores etc.,(on no account more than 2 per Company) to proceed not before 6 p.m.

3. The order of march and times of start from the Square are shown below.

"A" Company	...9.20 p.m.
"B" Company	...9.30 p.m.
"C" Company	...9.40 p.m.
"D" Company (from CITE CALONNE) ...	...9.30 p.m.

4. Packs, Officer's valises and stores for Transport Lines to be stacked outside Company billets by 3 p.m.

5. Trench Bundles , Lewis Guns and magazines, cooks utensils to be outside Company billets by 8 p.m.
Mess Cart will call at Company Messes at 8.30 p.m., for Mess stores.

6. Any men recommended for Transport Lines, to parade in the Square at 6 p.m. to be marched down by Sgt.Philp.

7. Ration limbers will proceed in rear of Companies.

8. Transport Officer will arrange transport for "D" Company as soon as dusk.

9. Report on sanitary conditions of billets taken over, to be rendered on reporting arrival. List of stores taken over , trench states and list of anti-gas appliances taken over, together with the certificate that billets vacated have been left clean, to be sent into Orderly Room by noon 9th.instant.

(Sgd) R. P. B A K E R Captain,

Adjutant 8th.S.Bn.ROYAL WEST KENT REGT.

Copies to:-

1.File
2.)
3.) War Diary
4. O.C."A" Company
5.O.C."B" Company
6.O.C."C" Company
7.O.C."D" Company
8.Headquarters Mess
9.Transport Mess
10.O.C.9th.East Surrey Regt.
11.O.C.1st.North Staffordshire Regt.
12.A/R.S.Major.

B

TABLE "A".

BATTALION TEMPORARILY REDUCED TO LOWER ESTABLISHMENT
(900 OTHER RANKS).

Battalion H.Q:	Fighting Portion............	72		
	Sergeant Instructors........	6 (a)		
	A.A.Lewis Gun Section........	13 (b)		
	Administrative...............	61		
			152	
4 Company H.Q:	Fighting Portion @ 23.......	92		
	Administrative @ 4............	16		
			108	
16 Platoon H.Q @ 4.......................			64	
			324	324
(c) 32 Rifle Sections; minimum 7, maximum 11.... (d)		224	224	352
16 Lewis Gun Sections; minimum 11, maximum 14 (d)			176	224
			724	900

Battalion H.Q.

Fighting Portion:

Sergeant Major.......	1
Orderly Room Clerks..	1
Sergeant Drummer.....	1
Prov.Sergt.& Police..	5
Scout Sgt. & Corpl....	2
Signallers............	25
Stretcher bearers....	9
Pioneers..............	11
M.O. Orderly..........	1
Sergt.Cook & Cooks....	3
Sanitary..............	1
Runners...............	5
Batmen................	7
	72

Administrative:

Q.M.S. & storemen.....	3
Orderly Room Clerks...	2
Cooks.................	2
M.O. Orderly..........	1
Transport Estblmt....	28
C.O's groom...........	1
Grooms for 8 mounted Officers.....	4
Water duties.........	5
Sanitary..............	2
Shoemakers............	5
Tailors...............	3
Butcher...............	1
Postman...............	1
Batmen................	3
	61

Company H.Q.

Fighting Portion:

C.S.M.............	1
Signallers.......	7
Stretcher beareres	4
Gas..............	1
Cooks............	2
Runners (e)......	4
Drummers (f).....	2
Batmen (f).......	2
	23

Administrative:

C.Q.M.S..........	1
Groom............	1
Sanitary.........	2
	4

Platoon H.Q.

Scout............	1
Platoon Sergeant.	1
Runner...........	1
Batman (f).......	1
	4

(a) 1 Musketry, 1 P.& B.T., 1 Bombing, 2 Lewis Guns, 1 Gas.
(b) Separate provision made as a temporary measure only until Battalions can be raised to higher establishment.
(c) When circumstances admit of raising Battalions to higher Estblmt it is proposed to add a third rifle section to each platoon, making 48 rifle sections in all.

(P.T.O.).

D

SECRET. 8th S.Bn.Royal West Kent Regiment. Copy No. 2

Order No.16.

In-the-Field. 13th July 1918.

1. The Battalion will take over the OUTPOST ZONE on the night of 14/15th July, relieving the 9th East Surrey Regiment.

2. DISPOSITIONS.

"A" Coy.	OBSERVATION LINE	
"B" "	BLACK LINE	(RIGHT)
"C" "	" "	(CENTRE)
"D" "	" "	(LEFT)

3. ADVANCE PARTIES of 1 Officer and 1 N.C.O. for taking over Stores will proceed during th e afternoon.

4. TIMES OF START.

"A" Coy	9.30 p.m.
"B" "	9.30 p.m.
"C" "	9.45 p.m.
"D" "	9.45 p.m.

5. Lists of Trench Stores taken over, Anti-Gas Appliances, and Trench States, to be rendered to Orderly Room by noon 15th inst. Report on Senityary conditions of billets and dugouts taken over, to be rendered as soon as pos sible after arrival, with certificate that billets vacated have been left clean.

6 Completion of Relief to be notified to Battalion Headquarters.

R M Baker ....Captain & Adjutant,

8th S.B.Royal West Kent Regiment.

Issued at 6 pm

Copies to;-

1. File
2. War Diary
3. War Diary
4. O.C. "A" Coy
5. " "B" "
6. " "C" "
7. " "D" "
8. Headquarters Mess
9. C.S.M. Greenaway
10. O.C. 9th East Surrey Regiment
11. O.C. 1st North Staffoedshire Regiment.
12. Transport Mess.

<u>SECRET</u> 6th.S.Bn.Royal West Kent Regt. Copy No. 3. E

Order No.17.
In-the-field.,19th.July 1918.

---

1. The Battalion will be relieved in the St.EMILE Sector on the night of the 20th/21st instant by the 1st.North Staffordshire Regt, and on relief will move into Reserve at Bully Grenay ("B" Company to CALONNE).

2. <u>Advance Parties.</u> No parties to be sent down to Bully during daylight. The Quartermaster will arrange to take over billets fromthe 9th.East Surrey Regt. O.C."B" Company will detail 1 Officer and 1 N.C.O to take over work and dispositions at Calonne during the afternoon.

3. Limbers for cooking utensils, Lewis Gun and Officers trench bundles will collect at the following points:-

"A" Company	HODSON'S HOUSE.
"B" Company) "C" Company) "D" Company)	Junction of COW ALLEY with STAFFORD STREET.
Headquarters	Battalion Headquarters.

4. Each Company will detail a responsible N.C.O. to report to theTransport Sergeant when all his Company stores are loaded.

4. Stores,dispositions work in hand to be carefully handed over . Certificates thatbillets and dug outs have been left clean to reach Battalion Orderly Room by noon 21st.instant.

5. Completion of relief and notification of arrival (with certificate ref.inspection of arms)to be rendered as usual.

6. Acknowledge.

(Sgd) R.P.BAKER Captain,
....
Adjutant 6th.S.Bn.Royal West Kent Regt.

Copies to:-
1. File
2.)War Diary.
3.)
4. O.C"A" Company
5.O.C."B" Company
6.O.C."C" Company
7.O.C."D" Company
8.Transport Mess.
9.Headquarter's Mess.
10.O.C.1st.North Staffordshire Regt.
11.O.C.9th.EastSurrey Regt.
12.A/Regimental Sergeant Major.

SECRET. 8th. S. Battn. R. W. Kent Regiment. **Copy No. 5**

F

Order No., 18.

In-the-field, 25th. July 1918.

-----

1. The Battalion will move into Support in CITE St.PIERRE on the evening of 26th. instant in relief of the 9th. East Surrey Regiment. Company Areas and Battle Positions will be taken over as before.

2. Advance parties for taking over of 2 per Company to proceed at 6.0 p.m.

3. Order of March and times of moving off-

"A" Company.......................... 9.15 p.m.
"B" Company (from CALONNE)........ 9.15 p.m.
"C" Company.......................... 9.25 p.m.
"D" Company.......................... 9.35 p.m.
Headquarters......................... 9.40 p.m.

4. Packs, valises, etc., for Transport Lines to be ready by 3.0 p.m.

5. Trench bundles, Lewis Guns, cooks' utensils, to be ready by 8.0 p.m. Mess Carts will call at 8.30 p.m. at Company messes.

6. Personnel for Transport Lines parade in Square under Sgt. PHILP at 6.0 p.m.

7. Report on Sanitary condition of billets, stores taken over, Trench states, list of anti-gas appliances, etc., to be rendered by Noon, ~~[illegible]~~. 27th. instant.

COPIES AS USUAL.

(Sgd). R. P. B A K E R, Capt.,
....
Adjutant, 8th. S. Battn. Royal West Kent Regiment.

SECRET. 8th.S.Battn. Royal West Kent Regt., Copy No.

Order No.

19.

In-the-field, 31st.July 18.

-0-0-0-0-0-0-0-0-0-0-0-0-0-0-0-0-0-0-0-0-

1. The Battalion will take over the Outpost Zone on the night of 1st/2nd.August, relieving the 9th.East Surrey Regiment.

2. DISPOSITIONS.

"C" Company........ OBSERVATION LINE.
"B" Company........ BLACK LINE (RIGHT).
"A" Company........ BLACK LINE (CENTRE).
"D" Company........ BLACK LINE (LEFT).

3. ADVANCE PARTIES of 1 Officer and 1 N.C.O. for taking over Stores will proceed during the afternoon.

4. TIMES OF START.

"C" Company........ 9.0 p.m.
"B" Company........ 9.0 p.m.
"A" Company........ [illegible] p.m.
"D" Company........ [illegible] p.m.

5. Lists of Trench Stores taken over, Anti Gas Appliances and Trench States, to be rendered to Orderly Room by Noon, 2nd.prox. Report on Sanitary conditions of Billets and dug-outs taken over, to be rendered as soon as possible after arrival, with certificate that billets vacated have been left clean.

6. Completion of relief to be notified to Battalion Headquarters.

(Sgd.) C.F.C. MACASKIE, 2nd.Lieut.,

A/Adjutant, 8th.S.Battn.Royal West Kent Regt.,

ISSUED AT.........p.m.

Copies to:-

1. File.
2. War Diary.
3. War Diary.
4. O.C. "A" Company.
5. O.C. "B" Company.
6. O.C. "C" Company.
7. O.C. "D" Company.
8. Headquarters' Mess.
9. 9th.East Surrey Regiment.
10. 1st.North Staffordshire Regiment.
11. Transport Officer.
12. Quartermaster.
13. A/Regimental Sergeant Major.

SECRET. 8th.S.Battn. Royal West Kent Regt., Copy No. 2.

Order No.

19.

In-the-field, 31st.July 18.

-0-0-0-0-0-0-0-0-0-0-0-0-0-0-0-0-0-0-0-0-0-

1. The Battalion will take over the Outpost Zone on the night of 1st/2nd.August, relieving the 9th.East Surrey Regiment.

2. DISPOSITIONS-

"C" Company.......... OBSERVATION LINE.
"B" Company.......... BLACK LINE (RIGHT).
"A" Company.......... BLACK LINE (CENTRE).
"D" Company.......... BLACK LINE (LEFT).

3. ADVANCE PARTIES of 1 Officer and 1 N.C.O. for taking over Stores will proceed during the afternoon.

4. TIMES OF START-

"C" Company.......... 9.0 p.m.
"B" Company.......... [illegible] p.m.
"A" Company.......... [illegible] p.m.
"D" Company.......... [illegible] p.m.

5. Lists of Trench Stores taken over, Anti Gas Appliances and Trench States, to be rendered to Orderly Room by noon, 2nd.prox. Report on Sanitary conditions of billets and dug-outs taken over, to be rendered as soon as possible after arrival, with certificate that billets vacated have been left clean.

6. Completion of relief to be notified to Battalion Headquarters.

(Sgd.) C.D.C.MACASKIE, 2nd.Lieut.,

ISSUED AT [illegible] p.m. A/Adjutant, 8th.S.Battn.Royal West Kent Regt.,

Copies to:-

1. File.
2. Qr. Duty.
3. War Diary.
4. O.C. "A" Company.
5. O.C. "B" Company.
6. O.C. "C" Company.
7. O.C. "D" Company.
8. Headquarters' Mess.
9. 9th.East Surrey Regiment.
10. 1st.North Staffordshire Regiment.
11. Transport Officer.
12. Quartermaster.
13. A/Regimental Sergeant Major.

I

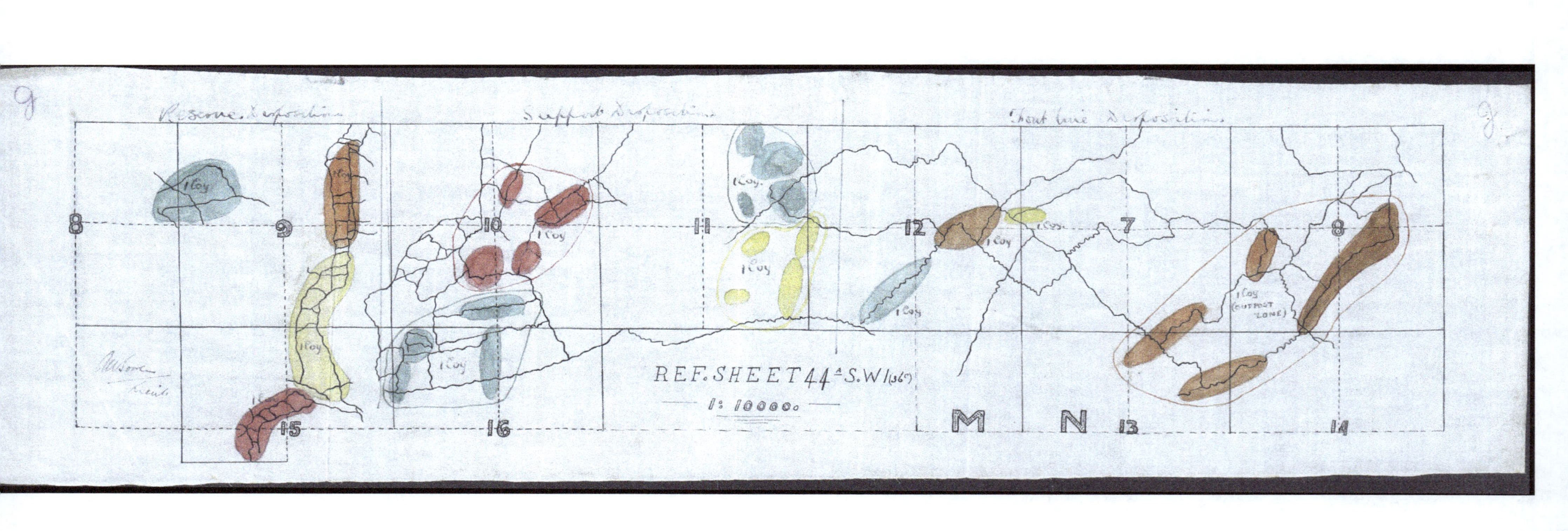

Reserve Disposition
Support Disposition
Front line Disposition
1 Coy
1 Coy
1 Coy
1 Coy
1 Coy
1 Coy
1 Coy
1 Coy
1 Coy
1 Coy
1 Coy
(OUTPOST ZONE)
8
9
10
11
12
7
8
15
16
M
N
13
14
REF. SHEET 44A S.W.1
1: 10000.

Vol 3/4 4

ORDERLY ROOM
No. N. 6299
5 9 1918
8th (Service) Bn. Queen's Own
Royal West Kent Regiment.

72/24

SECRET.

War Diary

of

8th S. Battn. Royal West Kent Regt.,

from 1.8.1918 to 31.8.1918.

(Volume ..).

To:-

D.A.G., 3rd Echelon
(thro' H.Qs 72nd I.B.).

Ref Map LENS 44a SW1 1/10000 (Ed 11a)

Instructions regarding War Diaries and Intelligence Summaries are contained in F. S. Regs., Part II. and the Staff Manual respectively. Title pages will be prepared in manuscript.

WAR DIARY or ~~INTELLIGENCE SUMMARY.~~

(Erase heading not required.)

8th S Battn Royal West Kent Regt

Army Form C. 2118.

Place	Date	Hour	Summary of Events and Information	Remarks and references to Appendices
	August 1		In Support in CITE St PIERRE. Moved up to front line and relieved 9th E. Surreys. Relief over at 12.5 am 1st/2nd. C Coy in front line, remainder in Black Line, right to left B A D	appendix 1 RPB.
	2		misty drizzling weather. Notice received that enemy were contemplating a raid on our front between 1 am and 2 am night 2/3 Precautions taken and C Coy were pushed out in front of usual posts.	RPB
	3		All quiet: no raid came off. Test "Prepare for actions and test "man battle stations received at 8.48 pm and 9 pm. Coys all in position by 10 pm. C Coy and 3 Sections of D not affected	RPB
	4		Projector attack by our RE at 11.30 pm. D relieved C in front line Hq was shelled with HE and Blue Cross mixed.	RPB
	5		Some enemy shelling around Hq. Probably searching for the Opera House Guns. Slightly more enemy activity in forward area. 3 Casualties by shell.	RPB

(A9475) Wt W2335/P360 600,000 12/17 D. D. & L. Sch. 52a. Forms/C2118/15.

LENS 44 a SW1 (11a) 1/10000

Instructions regarding War Diaries and Intelligence Summaries are contained in F. S. Regs., Part II. and the Staff Manual respectively. Title pages will be prepared in manuscript.

WAR DIARY
or
INTELLIGENCE SUMMARY.
(Erase heading not required.)

Army Form C. 2118.

Place	Date	Hour	Summary of Events and Information	Remarks and references to Appendices
	5		Quiet night, Patrol under 2/Lt W J GREEN went out to house at N14 a 16 40 from there just E of LA BASSEE Rd. No movement observed. Enemy sending up very lights from his support lines 11 OR on patrol left 11.20 pm returned 2.40	RPB
	6		Patrol by 2/Lt N.E. BEYNES and 10 OR from N 8 C 65, 06 out 150 yds no signs of enemy.	RPB
	7		quiet day. Bn was relieved by 1st N Staffs & moved to BULLY	appendix II RPB
	8		In reserve at BULLY (B Coy in CALONNE). Interior economy and cricket match (Officers v. Battn.)	RPB
	9.		Divnl Horse Show. 2nd Prize in Transport Turnout and officers' chargers	RPB
	10.		Training outfitting and reorganization (10th, 11th, 12th)	RPB
	13		Moved into support in CITE ST PIERRE (8 off and 80 OR's to Divnl Recept Camp) Lt H. R. SMITH joined for duty. Visit of Corps Commander	appendix III RPB
	14		Quiet day. Working parties daily on BLACK LINE Pill boxes	

(A9175) Wt W2355/P360 600,000 12/17 D. D. & L. Sch. 52a. Forms/C2118/15.

LENS 44 a SW1
1/10000 (10a)

Instructions regarding War Diaries and Intelligence Summaries are contained in F. S. Regs., Part II. and the Staff Manual respectively. Title pages will be prepared in manuscript.

WAR DIARY
or
INTELLIGENCE SUMMARY.
(Erase heading not required.)

Army Form C. 2118.

Place	Date	Hour	Summary of Events and Information	Remarks and references to Appendices
	15		quiet day; usual working parties on defences	RPB
	16		Same	RPB
	17		notified of contemplated extension of Brigade front.	RPB
	19		Relieved 9th E. Surreys in front line. A Coy in outpost zone. Relief complete 10.15 pm	appendix IV RPB
	20		Gas bombardment by our RE on right Battn front. Patrols.	RPB
	21		Enemy attempted raid on CONDUCTOR SAP. Repulsed	RPB
	22		Bombardment by enemy on OPERA HOUSE 9.30 – 12.30 pm, otherwise quiet. B relieved A in outpost zone. Capt ROGERS arrd from Course and assumed command of B. Transport lines at FOSSE 10 Shelled. One man killed there	RPB
	23		Area of Transport lines Shelled and T.O's mess demolished	RPB
	24		Reconnoitred Rt Bn front recently taken over by 72nd Bde from the 20th Divn. Enemy attempted raid on COUNTER POST 10.30 pm. No Cas. Test of SOS arrangements at 10.20 & 10.40 2 Patrols out at dark. VIII Corps Horse Show	RPB

(A9173) Wt W2358/P360 600,000 12/17 D. D. & L. Sch. 52a. Forms/C2118/15.

LENS 44a SW1 (10a) 1/10000

Instructions regarding War Diaries and Intelligence Summaries are contained in F. S. Regs., Part II. and the Staff Manual respectively. Title pages will be prepared in manuscript.

WAR DIARY
or
~~INTELLIGENCE SUMMARY.~~

(Erase heading not required.)

Army Form C. 2118.

Place	Date	Hour	Summary of Events and Information	Remarks and references to Appendices
	24		Transport lines shifted to AIX-NOULETTE owing to constant long range shelling of FOSSE 10	RPB
	25		Relieved in the line by 9th E. Surreys 1am complete	appendix V RPB
	26.		At BULLY-GRENAY. Interior economy. B Coy at CALONNE	RPB
	27		moved into the line in relief of 12th Kings (20th Div) on the right of Bde front for 1 night. C Coy to outpost line. A Coy in Reserve in LIEVIN were shelled with yellow x and had 6 cas.	RPB
	28.		QM Stores shifted to AIX NOULETTE. The Battn returned to BULLY on relief by 9th R Sussex, 73rd Bde. 2 Lt H.A. GREEN joined for duty	RPB.
	29		BULLY shelled by long range 4.2 during the night. 1 OR w/a Special performance by Bde concert party in aid of Regtl P of W fund	RPB
	30		Bn marched over to MARQUEFFLES range. Fired section and L. Gun Competitions. Sergeants mess concert in Commemoration of 3rd year that Bn had completed on the Front	RPB

(A9175) Wt W2355/P560 600,000 12/17 D. D. & L. Sch. 52a. Forms/C2118/15.

LENS 44a SW1 1/10000 (10a)

Instructions regarding War Diaries and Intelligence Summaries are contained in F. S. Regs., Part II. and the Staff Manual respectively. Title pages will be prepared in manuscript.

WAR DIARY
or
~~INTELLIGENCE SUMMARY.~~
(*Erase heading not required.*)

Army Form C. 2118.

Place	Date	Hour	Summary of Events and Information	Remarks and references to Appendices
	31		Moved up to front line (Right Bn), the 9th E. Surreys being in on our left and 9th R Sussex on our Right. C Coy took over the outpost zone. During the early part of the night before relief the 1st N. Staffs pushed out patrols to ascertain whether the enemy shewed any signs of retirement foreshadowed by the Intelligence. He was found to be holding his normal dispositions. C Coy went out on patrol before dawn and found the same	appendix VI RPB
			Battn Dispositions	appendix VII RPB
			Organization, Battn Hq + Coy Officers + NCO's	VIII RPB
			R P Baker Capt + Adjt 8th (S) Bn Royal West Kent Regt.	

(A9173) Wt W2355/P360 600,000 12/17 D. D. & L. Sch. 52a. Forms/C2118/13.

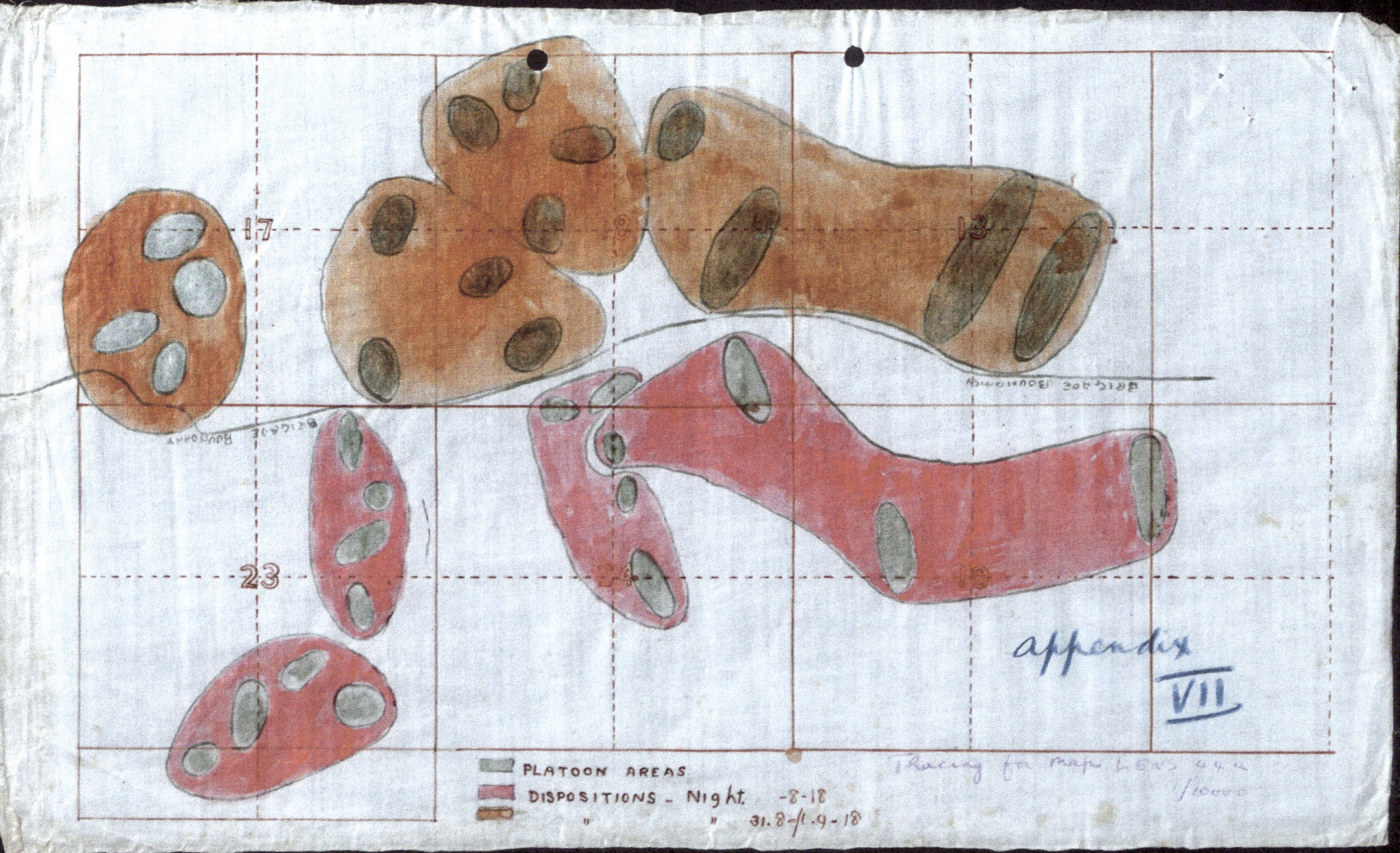
17
13
23
BRIGADE BOUNDARY
BRIGADE BOUNDARY
Appendix
VII
PLATOON AREAS
DISPOSITIONS - Night -8-18
" " 31.8-/1.9-18
Tracing for map LENS 44a
1/10000

Battalion Organization- 10/8/1918-

Headquarters-

	Commanding Officer-	Lt.Col., H.J.WENYON, D.S.O.,
	Second-in-Command-	Major H.S.BROWN, M.C.,
	Adjutant-	Captain R.P.BAKER, M.C.,
	Assistant Adjutant-	2/Lieut.C.F.C.MACASKIE.
	Intelligence Officer-	Lieut.G.S.BOWEN, M.C.,
Transport-	Transport Officer-	Captain J.N.ARNAUD.
	Asstnt. Transport Officer-	2/Lieut.H.E.OUTRAM.
	Transport Sergeant-	1369 Sgt G.Sheppard.
Q.M.Stores-	Quartermaster-	Capt. & Q.M. J.R.WOOD.
	R.Q.M.Sergeant-	3818 A/R.Q.M.Sgt W.Dunk, DCM. D.C.M,
Staff W.Os & N.C.Os-	Regtl.Sgt.Major-	2530 A/R.S.M. F.Greenaway,
	O.R.Clerk-	1886 Sgt W.C.Carr.
	Sgt.Cook-	6114 Sgt J.Luckhurst.
	Sgt.Drummer-	203657 Sgt J.Catherwood.
Battn.Instructors-	Musketry-	200162 Sgt.W.Charles.
	Lewis Gun-	1366 Sgt.E.Bateman.
		4232 L/Sgt A.Cook, D.C.M.,
	Gas-	7280 L/Sgt W.Hillman.

Companies- "A" Company-

	Company Commander-	Captain J.H.SELFE.
	Second-in-Command-	2/Lieut.C.G.TILEY.
	Compy.Sgt.Major-	3713 C.S.Major G.Buck, M.M.,
	Coy.Qr.Mr.Sergt-	203552 A/CQMSgt D.Gray.
No.1 Pltn.	Platoon Commander-	2/Lieut.G.A.E.WALLIS, M.C.,
	Platoon Sergeant-	2761 Sgt A.Sharpe.
No.1 Sectn.	Section Commander-	2696 Cpl H.Frewer, M.M.,
	Sectn.2-i/Command-	19685 Pte B.Sparrow.
No.2 Sectn.	Section Commander-	3667 Cpl W.Jasper, M.M.,
	Sectn.2-i/Command-	19675 L/Cpl.H.Richardson.
No.3 Sectn.	Section Commander-	1406 Sgt E.Cunningham.
	Sectn.2-i/Command-	19643 L/Cpl E.Eley.
No.2 Pltn.	Platoon Commander-	2/Lieut.D.G.GODDEN.
	Platoon Sergeant-	6541 Sgt E.Bailey.
No.4 Sectn.	Section Commander-	2540 Cpl W.Ready.
	Sectn.2-i/Command-	6179 L/Cpl W.List.
No.5 Sectn.	Section Commander-	18710 L/Cpl A.Slatter.
	Sectn.2-i/Command-	5425 Pte W.Boorm
No.6 Sectn.	Section Commander-	200078 Sgt H.Underdown.
	Sectn.2-i/Command-	20339 L/Cpl L.Foreman.
No.3 Pltn.	Platoon Commander-	2/Lieut.C.G.TAYLOR.
	Platoon Sergeant-	378 Sgt A.Ashdown.
No.7 Sectn.	Section Commander-	201079 Cpl E.Ponting.
	Sectn.2-i/Command-	8054 Pte C.Datlen.
No.8 Sectn.	Section Commander-	9142 L/Sgt S.Brown, M.M.,
	Sectn.2-i/Command-	6131 Cpl H.Bell.
No.9 Sectn.	Section Commander-	10702 Cpl H.Warford, M.M.,
	Sectn.2-i/Command-	24893 L/Cpl E.Harding.

"A" Company-Contd.,

No.4 Pltn. Platoon Commander- 2/Lieut.D.T.PIGGOTT, M.C.,
Platoon Sergeant- 200969 Sgt H.Leggett.

No.10 Sectn. Section Commander-20629 L/Sgt A.Hodge.
Sectn.2-i/Command-9442 A/Cpl L.Slade.

No.11 Sectn. Section Commander-5296 L/Cpl W.Thompson.
Sectn.2-i/Command-203849 L/Cpl A.Barratt.

No.12 Section. Sectn.Commander-2506 Cpl A.Smith, D.C.M.,
Sectn.2-i/Command-28934 L/Cpl A.Smith.

"B" Company-

Company Commander- Captain R.G.ROGERS.
Second-in-Command- 2/Lieut.H.G.MICHIE.
Compy.Sgt.Major- 1324 C.S.Major J.Gutteridge.
Coy.Qr.Mr.Sergt- 1892 A/CQMSgt E.J.Cooper.

No.5 Pltn. Platoon Commander- 2/Lieut.C.P.H.MANLEY.
Platoon Sergeant- 265215 Sgt H.Cater.

No.1 Sectn. Section Commander-20944 L/Cpl T.Booth.
Sectn.2-i/Command-205697 Pte A.Pearse.

No.2 Sectn. Section Commander-4248 Cpl E.Easey.
Sectn.2-i/Command-20882 L/Cpl T.Payne.

No.3 Sectn. Section Commander-8913 Cpl T.Harrild.
Sectn.2-i/Command-20902 Pte J.Banham.

No.6 Pltn. Platoon Commander- 2/Lieut.P.E.WATTS.
Platoon Sergeant- 205305 Sgt B.Osborne.

No.4 Sectn. Section Commander-4213 Cpl F.Smith.
Sectn.2-i/Command-20896 Pte S.Johnson.

No.5 Sectn. Section Commander-4792 A/Cpl F.Winder.
Sectn.2-i/Command-10622 Pte F.Apps.

No.6 Sectn. Section Commander-20919 L/Cpl H.King.
Sectn.2-i/Command-20907 Pte A.Everidge.

No.7 Pltn. Platoon Commander- Lieut.R.C.C.J.BINNEY.
Platoon Sergeant- 3993 Sgt F.Crow.

No.7 Sectn. Section Commander-6778 Cpl J.Marshall.
Sectn.2-i/Command-18989 Pte P.Smith.

No.8 Sectn. Section Commander-7371 L/Cpl C.Philpott.
Sectn.2-i/Command-20939 L/Cpl C.Block.

No.9 Sectn. Section Commander-30753 L/Cpl C.Grix.
Sectn.2-i/Command-9733 Pte T.Kennard.

No.8 Pltn. Platoon Commander- 2/Lieut.E.N.WINCH.
Platoon Sergeant- 200476 Sgt F.Hodge.

No.10 Sectn. Section Commander-6006 Cpl P.Vile.
Sectn.2-i/Command-2306 L/Cpl B.Nunn.

No.11 Sectn. Section Commander-4741 L/Cpl G.Cook.
Sectn.2-i/Command-205113 L/Cpl J.Fawkes.

No.12 Sectn. Section Commander-202352 L/Cpl A.Jones.
Sectn.2-i/Command-20727 Pte J.Vozza.

"C" Company-

Company Commander- Captain S.G.THOMPSON, M.C.,
Second-in-Command- Lieut.A.DRUMGOLD, D.S.O.,
Compy.Sgt.Major- 2956 A/C.S.Major E.Philp.
Coy.Qr.Mr.Sergt- 1884 C.Q.M.Sgt A.E.Judd.

No.9 Pltn. Platoon Commander- 2/Lieut.C.TRENCHARD-DAVIS.
Pltn.2-i/Command- 2/Lieut.N.E.BEYNES.
Platoon Sergeant- 1374 Sgt.W.Mitchell, D.C.M.,
2nd.Platoon Sergeant- 3819 Sgt.A.Westbury.

No.1 Sectn. Section Commander-10516 L/Cpl E.Gollop.
Sectn.2-i/Command-240384 Pte R.Morriss.

No.2 Sectn. Section Commander-214 Cpl H.Webb.
Sectn.2-i/Command-19668 L/Cpl W.Palfrey.

No.3 Sectn. Section Commander-24841 L/Cpl R.Moore.
Sectn.2-i/Command-204030 L/Cpl J.Day.

No.10 Pltn. Platoon Commander- 2/Lieut.F.C.M.CHAUNCY.
Platoon Sergeant- 9279 Sgt C.Williams, M.M.,

No.4 Sectn. Section Commander-8093 L/Cpl P.Mullins.
Sectn.2-i/Command-6745 Pte H.Tabrett.

No.5 Sectn. Section Commander-242927 L/Cpl T.McCarty.
Sectn.2-i/Command-20928 Pte J.Connell.

No.6 Secn. Section Commander-108 Cpl D.Jarrett.
Sectn.2-i/Command-20877 Pte C.Smith.

No.11 Pltn. Platoon Commander- 2/Lieut.W.J.GREEN.
Platoon Sergeant- 10608 Sgt A.Cox.

No.7 Sectn. Section Commander-18187 L/Cpl H.Binks.
Sectn.2-i/Command-11915 Pte E.Friend.

No.8 Sectn. Section Commander-20883 L/Cpl A.Webber.
Sectn.2-i/Command-203000 L/Cpl G.Newman.

No.9 Sectn. Section Commander-266204 Cpl C.Hurdman.
Sectn.2-i/Command-7622 L/Cpl R.Taylor.

No.12 Pltn. Platoon Commander- 2/Lieut.R.N.KILLICK,D.C.M.,
Platoon Sergeant- 11022 Sgt.T.Bromfield.

No.10 Sectn. Section Commander-20884 L/Cpl T.Johns.
Sectn.2-i/Command-23199 Pte T.Sage.

No.11 Sectn. Section Commander-202321 Cpl H.Bunce.
Sectn.2-i/Command-20943 Pte C.Bailey.

No.12 Sectn. Section Commander-240961 L/Cpl C.Payliss.
Sectn.2-i/Command-10538 Pte R.Collins.

"D" Company- Commander of Company- Captain A.J.PORTER.
Second-in-Command- Lieut.J.C.ORCHARDSON.
Actg.Coy Sgt.Major-. 2578 Sgt.E.Kirby.
Coy.Qr.Mr.Sergeant- 3473 C.Q.M.Sgt W.Dunk.

No.13 Pltn. Platoon Commander- 2/Lieut.F.CARVILLE, M.C.,
Platoon Sergeant- 19121 Sgt.E.Vanner, D.C.M.,

No.1 Sectn. Section Commander-7377 Cpl J.Puttick.
Sectn.2-i/Command-4822 L/Cpl E.Baker.

No.2 Sectn. Section Commander-10535 Cpl E.Boylan, M.M.,
Sectn.2-i/Command-11781 L/Cpl E.Sheepwash.

No.3 Sectn. Section Commander-10781 Cpl E.Read.
Sectn.2-i/Command-1613 Pte E.Varty.

"D" Company-contd.,

No.14 Pltn. Platoon Commander- 2/Lieut.P.C.BRUNGER.
Platoon Sergeant- 7687 Sgt J.C.Orme.

No.4 Sectn. Section Commander-8267 Cpl A.Pink.
Sectn.2-i/Command-13485 L/Cpl F.Hale.

No.5 Sectn. Section Commander-7539 L/Cpl H.Clark.
Sectn.2-i/Command-203589 L/Cpl C.Allen.

No.6 Sectn. Section Commander-498 L/Cpl P.Newman.
Sectn.2-i/Command-23144 Pte W.Ware.

No.15 Pltn. Platoon Commander- 2/Lieut.H.CAMBROOK.
Platoon Sergeant- 12712 L/Sgt R.Alderman.

No.7 Sectn. Section Commander-20910 Cpl H.Marshall.
Sectn.2-i/Command-18467 L/Cpl H.Mills.

No.8 Sectn. Section Commander-6862 L/Cpl T.Rowswell.
Sectn.2-i/Command-10774 Pte W.Chapman.

No.9 Sectn. Section Commander-20948 L/Cpl G.Bulled.
Sectn.2-i/Command-7748 L/Cpl E.Molineaux.

No.16 Pltn. Platoon Commander- Lieut.D.J.DEAN.
Platoon Sergeant- 201103 Sgt J.Skipper.

No.10 Sectn. Section Commander-240745 Sgt G.Heath.
Sectn.2-i/Command-11247 L/Cpl R.Wissenden.

No.11 Sectn. Section Commander-201117 Cpl J.Eversfield.
Sectn.2-i/Command-20916 L/Cpl S.Jackson.

No.12 Sectn. Section Commander-240904 L/Cpl W.Goodwin.
Sectn.2-i/Command-2572 L/Cpl H.Spender.

-o-o-o-o-o-o-o-o-o-o-o-o-o-o-o-o-o-o-o-o-

R.P.Baker
Captain,
12th.August 1918. Adjutant, 8th.S.Battn.Rl.West Kent Regt.,

IX

SECRET

8th.S.Bn.Royal West Kent Regt.
Order No.20
IN-the-field.,6th.August 1918.

Copy No..2.

1. The Battalion will be relieved in the St.EMILE Sector on the n ight of the 7th/8th.August by the 1st,Bn. North Staffordshire Regt.,and on relief will proceed to Reserve at BULLY GRENAY ("B"Company to CALONNE)

2. Advanced Parties. No parties to be sent down to BULLY during daylight . The Quartermaster will arrange to take over the billets from the 9th.East Surrey Regt. O.C."B" Company will detail 1 Officer and 1 N.C.O. to take over the work anddispositions at CALONNE dur ing the aft ernoon.

3. Limbers for Lewis Guns,cooking utensiles and Officers trench bundles will collect at the following points.

"B"Company	HODSON'S HOUSE
"A"Company) "C"Company) "D"Company)	Junction of COW ALLEY and Stafford Street.
Headquarters	Battalion Headquarters.

Each Company will detail a res ponsible N.C.O. to report to the T ransport Sergeant when all his Company stores are loaded.

4. Stores, dispositions and work in hand to be carefully hande d over, Certificates that billets and dugouts have bee n left clean toreach Battalion Orderly Room by noon 8th.inst ant.

5. Completion of relief and notification of arrival (with certificates eref.inspection of arms) tobe rendered as us ual.

6. Acknowledge.

(Sgd) C.F.C.MACASKIE 2nd.Lieut.,
....
A/Adjutant 8th.S.Bn.Royal West Kent Regiment.

Copies to:-

1. File
2.)
3.) War Diary.
4. O.C."A"Company
5. O.C."B"Company
6. O.C."C"Company
7. O.C."D"Company
8. Headquarters Mess.
9. T ransport Mess.
10. O.C.1st.Bn .North Staffordshire Regt.
11. O.C.9th.East Surrey Regt.
12. A/R.S.Major.

[illegible] 8th.S.Battn.R.W.Kent Regt. COPY NO. 2

Order No. [illegible]

[illegible], 12th.Aug.16.

-:-:-:-

1. The Battalion will [illegible] SUPPORT in [illegible] ST.PIERRE in relief of the 9th.[illegible] Surrey Regiment on the night of 13/14th. inst.

2. Order of March and times of starting:-

"A" Company.................. 8.40 p.m.
"B" Company. (from [illegible]).. 8.40 p.m.
"C" Company.................. ~~xxxxxx~~, 8.50 p.m.
"D" Company.................. 9.0 p.m.
Head Quarters................ 9.10 p.m.

3. Advance parties as usual.

4. Details Parade Orders will be issued later.

5. Packs and stores for Transport Lines to be ready by 5.0 p.m. Mess carts will call at 5.30 p.m.

6. Trench bundles, etc., for the line, 8.0 p.m.

7. Report on Sanitary condition of billets, list of stores, trench stores, anti-gas appliances, etc., taken over, to be rendered by noon, 14th. instant.

E. P. [illegible] Capt.
Adjutant, 8th.S.Battn.Royal West Kent R[illegible]

Copies to:-

1. File
2. War Diary
3. War Diary.
4. O.C. "A" Company.
5. O.C. "B" Company.
6. O.C. "C" Company.
7. O.C. "D" Company.
8. Headquarters [illegible]
9. Transport Officer.
10. Quartermaster.
11. O.C., 1/Nth. Staffs Regt.
12. O.C., 9/East Surrey Regt.
13. Actg.Regtl.Sergeant Major.

SECRET. 8th.S.BN.ROYAL WEST KENT REGIMENT. Copy No. 3

ORDER No. 22.

IN-THE-FIELD. 18TH.AUGUST 1918.

1. The Battalion will take over the OUTPOST ZONE on the night of 19th/20th August, relieving the 9th East Surrey Regiment.

2. DISPOSITIONS.

"A" Coy..........OBSERVATION LINE.
"B" " ....BLACK LINE. (Right)
"D" " ....BLACK LINE. (Left)
"C" " ....RESERVE

3. ADVANCE PARTIES of 1 Officer and 1 N.C.O. for taking over Stores will proceed during the afternoon.

4. TIMES OF START.

"A" Coy..........8.30 p.m.
"B" Coy..........8.45 p.m.
"D" Coy..........8.45 p.m.
"C" Coy..........8.30 p.m.

5. Lists of Trench Stores taken over, Anti-Gas Appliances and Trench States, to be rendered to Orderly Room by Noon, 20th. inst. Report on Sanitary conditions of billets and dug-outs taken over, to be rendered as soon as possible after arrival, with certificate that billets vacated have been left clean.

6. Completion of Relief to be notified to Battalion Headquarters.

(Sgd) C.F.C.MACASKIE, 2nd.Lieut.,

ISSUED at.......p.m. A/Adjutant, 8th.S.Battn.Royal West Kent Regt.

Copies to:-

1. File.
2. War Diary.
3. War Diary.
4. O.C. "A" Company.
5. O.C. "B" Company.
6. O.C. "C" Company.
7. O.C. "D" Company.
8. Headquarters' Mess.
9. O.C. 9th East Surrey Regiment.
10. O.C. 1st North Staffordshire Regiment.
11. Transport Mess.
12. Sgt. Bateman.

SECRET

8TH.S.Bn.ROYAL WEST KENT REGT.
ORDER No. 23.
IN-THE-FIELD.,24th AUGUST 1918.

Copy No.......

1. The Battalion will be relieved in the ST.EMILE Sector on the night of the 25/26th August 1918, by the 9th East Surrey Regt., and on relief will proceed to billets at BULLY GRENAY, "B" Company to CALONNE.

2. No advance parties will be required .
Quartermaster will arrange to take over billets.

3. Lewis Guns and Stores to be dumped for collection by the Transport :-

"B" Coy.	Junction of COW ALLEY & Stafford Street.
"A" "	" " " " " "
"D" "	" " " " " "
"C" "	HODSON'S HOUSE.
H.Qrs.	Battalion Headquarters.

Each Company will detail a responsible N.C.O. to report to the Transport Officer when all his Company's Stores are loaded.

4. Stores, dispositions, and work in hand to be carefully handed over. Certificates that billets and dugouts have been left clean, to reach Battalion Orderly Room by noon 26th. inst.

5. Completion of relief and notification of arrival (with certificate ref. inspection of area) to be rendered as usual.

6. Acknowledge.

(Sgd) R.P.BAKER, Captain,

Adjutant,8th.S.B.Royal West Kent Rgt.

Copies to:-
1. File.
2. War Diary.
3. War Diary.
4. O.C. "A" Coy.
5. O.C. "B" "
6. O.C. "C" "
7. O.C. "D" "
8. Headquaters' Mess.
9. Transport Mess.
10. O.C.9th.East Surrey Regiment.
11. Sgt. Bateman.

SECRET. 8TH.BN.ROYAL WEST KENT REGT. COPY NO. 2.

ORDER NO.24.

IN-THE-FIELD.,30TH AUGUST 1918.

1. The Battalion will relieve the 1st North Staffordshire Regt. in the Right Sub-Sector/ No guides will be required./ on night of 31st Aug/1st Sept.

2. ORDER OF RELIEF.

"C" Coy. OUTPOST LINE. Move off 7.30 p.m.
"A" " BLACK LINE (Left) Move off 7.40 p.m.
"D" " BLACK LINE (Right) Move off 7.50 p.m.
"B" " RESERVE Move off 7.40 p.m.

3. Limbers with rations and Lewis Guns etc. will move off with Companies.

4. Mess Cart will call round at 7 p.m.

5. Usual advance parties to proceed after teas.

6. Valises and packs for the Stores will be collected at 4 p.m. Orderly Room Stores and Headquarters' Mess Stores will be collected at 8.30 p.m.

7. DETAILS. Parade in the SQUARE at 4.30 p.m. Transport Officer to provide transport for packs and valises, and rations for 1st September. Parade States to be rendered by noon, so that quartermaster may deduct necessary rations for the party.

8. Usual certificates to be rendered as usual.

9. Relief complete to be notified.

(Sd) R.P.B A K E R. Captain,

Adjutant, 8th.S.Bn.Royal West Kent Regiment.

Copies to:-
1. File.
2. War Diary.
3. War Diary.
4. O.C. "A" Coy.
5. " "B" "
6. " "C" "
7. " "D" "
8. Headquarters' Mess.
9. Transport Mess.
10. O.C. 1st North Staffordshire Regt.
11. O.C. 9th East Surrey Regt.
12. A/R.S.M.

SECRET.

9

ORDERLY ROOM
No. V 6346
3 OCT 1918
8th (Service) Bn. Queen's Own Royal West Kent Regiment

35

WAR DIARY

of

8th S. Battn. Royal West Kent Rgt.

from 1.9.18 to 30.9.18.

(Volume. -)

To:- D.A.G.
3rd Echelon, B.E.F.
(through H.Qs
72nd Inf. Bde).

8th S.B. Royal West Kent Regt.

WAR DIARY
or
INTELLIGENCE SUMMARY.
(Erase heading not required.)

Army Form C. 2118.

Instructions regarding War Diaries and Intelligence Summaries are contained in F. S. Regs., Part II. and the Staff Manual respectively. Title pages will be prepared in manuscript.

Place	Date	Hour	Summary of Events and Information	Remarks and references to Appendices
Front Line	1-9-18		'C' Coy pushed patrols out into outskirts of LENS in view of an anticipated withdrawal by enemy. 2Lt KILLICK's platoon got into touch with the enemy at 6 P.M. We took up a line from Ry Junction at N20a48 to fork road N.14c4.8 (Operation Order No 25)	Appendix A. CWH
"	2-9-18		'D' Coy relieved the two forward platoons of 'C' Coy. Quiet day. Work started on Great Peter Street.	CWH
"	3-9-18		9th E. Surrey posts on our left were attacked and driven in, but afterwards re-established. 2Lt CARVILLE M.C. wounded while going to assistance of a post attacked on our left. Dumps formed in forward positions.	CWH
"	4-9-18		Much work on consolidation. 'C' Coy in outpost line. Signal communication established with forward positions.	CWH
"	5-9-18		9th E. Surrey again attacked, but positions restored. A Coy relieved the forward platoons of 'B' Coy. Heavy enemy harassing fire. 6 men of 'B' Coy gassed by shell gas.	CWH
"	6-9-18		'A' Coy in front line. Enemy quiet. Occasional shelling of our posts	CWH
"	7-9-18		Heavy rain. Enemy quiet. 2 platoons of 'D' Coy relieved 2 platoons of 'A'.	CWH
"	8-9-18		Enemy quiet. Wet weather. Bombardment of selected points by our 9.2", 6" NEWTONS and Stokes.	CWH
"	9-9-18		'B' Coy relieved 'A' Coy in front line. Enemy quiet. More heavy rain.	CWH
"	10-9-18		Quiet day. Much work done on roads and general consolidation.	CWH
"	11-9-18		Quiet day. Work proceeded. Forward dumps formed. Hard work for all ranks under bad weather conditions.	CWH

(A9175) Wt W2358/P360 600,000 12/17 D. D. & L. Sch. 52a. Forms/C2118/15.

8th S B Royal West Kent Regt

Army Form C. 2118.

2.

WAR DIARY
or
INTELLIGENCE SUMMARY.
(*Erase heading not required.*)

Instructions regarding War Diaries and Intelligence Summaries are contained in F. S. Regs., Part II. and the Staff Manual respectively. Title pages will be prepared in manuscript.

Place	Date	Hour	Summary of Events and Information	Remarks and references to Appendices
Front Line	12-9-18		Usual working parties by day. Relief at night by the 9th E. Surreys. Relief complete at 10.45 P.M.	Appendix B
			Bn moved to Reserve at BULLY-GRENAY. 'B' Coy at CALONNE.	CMH
BULLY-GRENAY	13-9-18 }		Coy. training. Baths, refitting, etc. N.C.O's class started. Class for training observers and scouts	
"	14-9-18 }		started.	CMH
"	15-9-18		Staff Ride. Bn marched to MARQUEFFLES to see a Tank demonstration. BULLY shelled at night.	CMH
"	16-9-18		Bn Tactical Scheme - Advanced Guards practised on MARQUEFFLES area. Guns, M.G. and	
			Stokes co-operated.	CMH
"	17-9-18		Coy. Training	CMH
"	18-9-18		Preparing to move into the line. Relieved 9th E Surrey Regt. in Right Sector. 'A' and 'C' Coy in front line.	Appendix C
			'B' and 'D' in support. Quiet night. C.O. at transport. Major Brown in command.	CMH
Front Line	19-9-18		Quiet day. Few R.E. working parties but much work on posts done.	CMH
"	20-9-18		C.O. came up. 'C' Coy had 1 OR killed, 2 wounded by M.G. fire. Our patrols active.	CMH
"	21-9-18		Quiet day. Bn H.Q. shelled by small calibre guns at long range. Active patrolling at night.	CMH
"	22-9-18		Some shelling. 'C' Coy had 1 OR killed 2 wounded.	CMH
"	23-9-18 }		Our patrols established in forward posts on night 23rd/24th. At dawn enemy raided one of our new	CMH
"	24-9-18 }		posts held by 2nd Lt ~~[illegible]~~ DAVIS' platoon. They occupied one post and captured 1 N.C.O. and 5 men. 2nd Lt DAVIS	

Instructions regarding War Diaries and Intelligence Summaries are contained in F. S. Regs., Part II. and the Staff Manual respectively. Title pages will be prepared in manuscript.

WAR DIARY
or
INTELLIGENCE SUMMARY.
(Erase heading not required.)

Army Form C. 2118.

3.

Place	Date	Hour	Summary of Events and Information	Remarks and references to Appendices
Front Line.	23/24-9-18		and BEYNES immediately organized a counter-attack and drove the enemy out. During the counter attack the	Appendix D.
			N.C.O. L/c BINKS and one other man turned on their escort and brought him in with another wounded German.	
			For details of action and location of posts see appendix D. Capt. BAKER M.C. evacuated sick.	CM
"	25-9-18		Front line heavily shelled. 'D' Coy relieved 'C' Coy night of 24th/25th. Enemy made no attempt to approach.	CM
"	26-9-18		Lt DEAN'S post attacked twice during the night, but attacks driven off. In morning enemy again attacked. some	
			50 strong. The post was temporarily withdrawn but an immediate attack by Lt DEAN drove them out again with	
			many casualties. Sec. Lt CAMBROOK led a party out to cut off enemy retreat and inflicted several casualties, and	
			was himself severely wounded. at 3 P.M. 2Lt KILLICK and DAVIS and a party of 4 sections raided the	
			enemy lines. An enemy M.G. was captured and an officer killed while gallantly trying to get his gun	Appendix E
			into action. The remainder of the gun team took refuge in a sap and refused to come out. The sap was	
			blown in by a mobile charge. Sec. Lt KILLICK was severely wounded. Several valuable papers and a	
			disposition map were ~~obtained~~ found on the enemy officer, whose body was brought in. Our casualties	Appendix F
			Sec. Lt KILLICK and 1 OR. wounded. In hostile bombardment before the raid 2 OR killed and 7 wounded.	CM
	27-9-18		'B' Coy heavily shelled in morning. Much work on consolidation done. At midnight 'B' Coy raided. 2Lt MANLEY	
			severely wounded while handling the L.G. of the post. Enemy was driven off leaving several rifles and 5	
			mobile charges.	CM

4
3

Army Form C. 2118.

Instructions regarding War Diaries and Intelligence Summaries are contained in F. S. Regs., Part II. and the Staff Manual respectively. Title pages will be prepared in manuscript.

WAR DIARY
or
INTELLIGENCE SUMMARY.
(Erase heading not required.)

Place	Date	Hour	Summary of Events and Information	Remarks and references to Appendices
Front Line	28-9-18		'B' Coy again heavily shelled in morning. Advance parties of 2/24th London Regt arrived 58th Division.	
			Quiet night very little enemy shelling. 2Lt CHAUNCEY evacuated sick	CWL
"	29-9-18		Preparing for handing over. Very quiet day. Relieved by 2/24th London Regt. Relief very smooth, all	Appendix G
			over by 11.30 p.m. Bn embussed at BULLY-GRENAY for COUPIGNY HUTS. All in by 3.30 AM	CWL
	30-9-18		Bn entrained at HERSIN for DOULLENS and detrained BOUQUEMAISON and marched to SUS-St-LEGERE	Appendix H
			all in by 10.P.M. Raining heavily.	CWL

[illegible]
Capt. & Adjt.
8th (S) Battn. Royal West Kent [illegible]

(A9475) Wt W2358/P360 600,000 12/17 D. D. & L. Sch. 52a. Forms/C2118/15.

A

SECRET.

8th. S. Bn. Rl. West Kent Regt., COPY No. 9.

Operation Order No. 25. 1st. Septr. 1918.

1. "C" Company are pushing out patrols this afternoon to reach the following objectives :-

1st. Objective.	2nd. Objective.	3rd. Objective.
N.13.d.68.27	N.13.d.98.35.	N.14.c.40.15
N.13.d.78.55	N.13.d.99.55.	N.14.c.40.30.
N.13.d.75.85	N.14.c.03.73.	N.14.c.40.80.

2. When these objectives have been reached, the patrols will be reinforced and the positions held.

3. On the 3rd. Objective being reached and held, "C" Company will probably be disposed from our present front line forwards, and "D" Company will be prepared to go up and hold the positions at present held by "C", on receipt of the code word- "BUCK".

4. Companies will ensure at once that all men are fully equipped, water bottles full and iron rations complete.

(Sgd). R.P.Baker, Captain,
Adjutant, 8th. S. Bn. Rl. West Kent Regiment.

Issued at 5.25 p.m.

Copies to :-

1. "A" Company.
2. "B" Company.
3. "C" Company.
4. "D" Company.
5. Headquarters' Mess.
6. O.C., 9/East Surrey Regt.,
7. O.C., 9/Rl. Sussex Regt.,
8.) War
9.) Diaries.
10. File.

2 B

[illegible] 8th Battn. Royal West Kent Regiment. COPY No. [illegible]

Operation Order No.2[illegible]. 11th September [illegible]

RESERVE [illegible]

1. The Battalion will be relieved on the night of 12/13th by the 9th East Surrey Regiment, and on relief will proceed to [illegible] ("C" Company to [illegible]).

2. [illegible] will [illegible] as under :-

H.Qs.	9.[illegible] p.m.	from Bat'n. H.Qs.
"A" Company	10.15 p.m.	M.18.c.68.95.
"B" Company	10.30 p.m.	Crater on Ct.[illegible] F.15.c.10.62.
"C" Company	9.30 p.m.	"C" Coy's H.Qs.
"D" Company	10.15 p.m.	M.18.c.65.95.

3. Trench stores, dispositions, work in hand, defence schemes, to be carefully handed over.

4. The usual returns to be rendered on arrival in Reserve.

5. Completion of relief to be wired as under :-

"A" Company........ "JEHU".
"B" Company........ "JUDAS".
"C" Company........ By runner.
"D" Company........ "JEROBOAM".

R. P. B A K E R, Captain,
Adjutant, 8th S. Batt'n. Royal West Kent Regiment.

Issued at p.m.

Copies to:-

1. File.
2.)
3.) War Diaries.
4. O.C. "A" Company.
5. O.C. "B" Company.
6. O.C. "C" Company.
7. O.C. "D" Company.
8. Headquarters' Mess.
9. Transport Mess.
10. T/Sgt. COOK, D.C.M., (H.Qs).
11. O.C., Batt'n. Details.
12. O.C., 9th E.Surrey Regt.)
13. O.C., 1st.N.Staffords Regt.) [illegible]

SECRET. 8TH.S.BN.ROYAL WEST KENT REGT. COPY NO....2

ORDER NO.27.

IN-THE-FIELD., 18TH.SEPTEMBER 1918.

1. The Battalion will relieve the 9th East Surrey Regiment in the Right Sub-Sector, on the night of 18/19th September 1918.

2. ORDER OF RELIEF.

"A" Company - Right Front Company.
Guides at Company Headquarters - MINNIE HOUSE (N.13.B.Central)

"B" Company - BLACK LINE.
Guides at COmpany Headquarters - HODSON'S HOUSE.

"C" COMpany - Left Front Company.
Guides at N.7.C.70.05. - (former Company Headquarters).

"D" Company - in Reserve.
Guides at HODSON'S HOUSE.

"A" Company will move off at 7. p.m.
"B" " " " " " 7.15 p.m.
"C" " " " " " 7.10 p.m.
"D" " " " " " 7.20 p.m.

3. Limbers with Lewis Guns and Rations etc will move off with Coys.

4. Mess Cart will call round at 6.30 p.m.

5. 1 Officer per Company to proceed after lunch.
Usual advance parties after teas.

6. Valises and packs to Stores, will be collected at 3.30 p.m.
Orderly Room and Headquarter Mess Stores at 8 p.m.

7. DETAILS. Parade at 3 p.m. in the SQUARE.
Transport Officer to provide transport for packs and valises and rations for the 19th September. Par ade States to be rendered by noon, so that Quartermaster may deduct necessary rations for the party.

8. Certificates to be rendered as usual.

9. Relief complete to be notified.

(Sd) C.F.C.MACASKIE, 2/Lieut.,

A/Adjutant, 8th.S.Bn.Royal West Kent Regt.

Copies to :-

1. File
2. War Diary
3. War Diary
4. O.C. "A" Coy.
5. " "B" "
6. " "C" "
7. " "D" "
8. Headquarters' Mess
9. Transport Officer
10. Quartermaster.
11. O.C. 1st North Staffordshire Regt.
12. O.C. 9th East Surrey Regt.
13. A/R.S.M.

8th S. Battn. Royal West Kent Regiment.
In-the-field. 2[illegible]th September 1918.

[illegible]

<u>SPECIAL BATTALION ORDER.</u>

During the past few days the Battalion has passed through experiences which have tested the soldierlike qualities of all ranks to the utmost degree.

You have stood the test in the finest possible way and the fact that our line still remains intact and stronger than ever, and that very heavy casualties have been inflicted on a brave and resolute enemy, redounds very greatly to the credit of all concerned.

I wish to mention the magnificent defence put up by "D" Company during two days of very great stress and difficulty.

Five times a determined enemy, supported by all means at his disposal, has attempted to drive in our posts and five times he has been thrown back with heavy losses.

I also wish to mention the very excellent work done by all ranks of "C" Company, first, in capturing the positions from the enemy which we now hold, secondly, for reestablishing our post when a strong attack by the enemy had temporarily driven it in, and lastly, for the very gallant manner in which the successful raid was carried out by them in co-operation with "D" Company on the afternoon of the [illegible] September.

All the Companies have done a tremendous amount of work in consolidating the new positions, and in daring patrol work.

"A" and "B" Companies on the right have been subjected to the trial of heavy shelling in their posts on several occasions. I know that the Officers Commanding and all ranks of "A" and "B" Companies will be the first to join me in congratulating "D" and "C" Companies for their magnificent work.

With the certain knowledge that soldierlike qualities of the highest order exist throughout all the Companies, we can look forward confidently to the future.

Whatever tasks lie in front of you, will be carried out to the utmost of your powers.

The fine work of the past few days is worthy of the very best traditions of our magnificent Regiment, and the Queen's Own will always be proud of the Officers, N.C.Os. and Men- many of whom have laid down their lives- who have done such sterling work during this week of stress.

[illegible]

Battn. H.Qs. Lieut.-Colonel,

[illegible] Commanding 8th S. Battn. ROYAL WEST KENT [illegible]

9

SECRET. 8th.(S) BN. ROYAL WEST KENT REGT., COPY No.. 2

ORDER No. 28.

In-the-field, 28th. September 1918.

1. The Battalion will be relieved in the Line by the 2/24th. LONDON REGIMENT on the night of the 29th/30th. Septr. 1918.

2. Companies will send one guide per platoon to report to Sec.Lieut. QUARTERMAIN in the Square, BULLY GRENAY, at 8.30 p.m. to guide relieving opposite number into the line.

3. Limbers for Lewis Guns etc. will be at the following points:-

for "A" & "C" Companies [illegible] HOUSE.
for Bn.H.Q. "B" & "D" Companies [illegible] CASTLE.

Mess Cart will collect Mess stores etc. for Battn. H.Qs. "B" and "D" Companies at [illegible] CASTLE at 9 p.m. and for "A" and "C" Companies at St. PIERRE CHURCH at 9.30 p.m.

4. Trench Stores, Maps, Aeroplane photos, dispositions work in-hand, defence schemes to be carefully handed over and receipts obtained.

5. [illegible] and usual returns to be rendered on arrival in billets.

6. Completion of relief will be notified in the usual manner.

7. After relief, the Battalion will move to COUPIGNY HUTS by bus. Embussing point will be [illegible] 10 - BULLY GRENAY ROAD, head of column at R.S.c.7.8. On arrival at embussing point, Officers in Charge of Companies and Platoons will report to Major E.S.[illegible], M.C., who will superintend the embussing.

8. Battalion Transport will move by road to COUPIGNY HUTS.

C.E.C.Mackie, 2nd.Lieut.,
ISSUED AT .... p.m. A/Adjutant 8th S.Bn. R. West Kent Regt.

Copies to:-

1. File.
2.) War
3.) Diaries.
4. O.C. "A" Company.
5. O.C. "B" Company.
6. O.C. "C" Company.
7. O.C. "D" Company.
8. Headquarters' Mess.
9. Transport Mess.
10. Sergeant PRESTON.
11. O.C., Battn. Details.

[illegible] No. 28.
[illegible], [illegible] 1918.

1. [illegible] 30th.Sept. for [illegible] of [illegible].

2. [illegible] stores will be stacked at [illegible] Station [illegible] to be made [illegible]. A Guard will be provided [illegible] arrangements (Major [illegible]) [illegible] details.

3. [illegible] will be [illegible] and [illegible] tonight.

4. [illegible] will travel by road under separate [illegible] will be carried on the [illegible].

5. [illegible] HALL, [illegible] party of the Drums, [illegible] at 8.0 a.m. 30th.Sept.1918.

6. [illegible], Officers' mess stores, and [illegible] Stores, will be [illegible] at 8.30 a.m. for transport by lorry to [illegible] Station.
[illegible] of [illegible] under 2nd.Lieut.[illegible], [illegible] will load the [illegible] and will report to [illegible] Station at 10.[illegible] a.m. [illegible] will be in possession of a [illegible] of the Battalion.
[illegible] Commanders will render to Orderly Room a [illegible] of their Companies by 9.30 a.m. on the 30th. [illegible]

7. [illegible] the 30th. will be issued before the Battalion moves [illegible] and will be carried on the man.
[illegible] for the 1st. [illegible] will be delivered at the [illegible] area by lorry.

8. [illegible] party, under Captain A.[illegible], D.S.O., will proceed [illegible] arrangements already notified.

10. The Battalion [illegible] will proceed to [illegible] by bicycle under [illegible], under arrangements already notified.

11. The Battalion will parade in the [illegible] at [illegible] in full marching order, ready to move off at 10.15 a.m. on 30th.instant.
Order of March:- Drums.
Headquarters.
"A" Company.
"B" Company.
"C" Company.
"D" Company.
100 yards interval between Companies.

12. The strictest [illegible] will be observed. [illegible] the carriages except [illegible] dressed [illegible]. [illegible] will be responsible for notifying authorised [illegible] to all [illegible].

[illegible], Captain,
[illegible]

3. War Diary.
4. O.C. "A" Company.
[illegible] Company. 6. O.C. "C" Company.
[illegible] "D" Company. 8. [illegible]
[illegible], M.O. 10. Quartermaster.
[illegible] Transport Officer. 12. [illegible]
13. Sergeant [illegible]. 14. [illegible]
15. Headquarters Mess. 16. [illegible]

D

Ref. Map HETTY ROAD.

REPORT ON HOSTILE RAID ON POST AT N.8.D.3.5.

During the night 23/24th the enemy was ejected from this post and we occupied it.

At the same time Posts were established in CANARY Trench Southwards. A patrol also worked up to junction of CINNABAR and CLAUD, where a block was found, and enemy rifle fire and bombing prevented it being captured. Another Post was ~~established~~ therefore established in CLAUD and a block commenced East of it.

The consolidation of all these Posts were carried on vigorously, and by 6.30 a.m. considerable improvement had been made in the positions. The Post at N.8.d.3.5. which was an organised enemy post required more work than the others to make it into a strong defensive position for ourselves.

At 6.15 a.m., 2/Lt.C.TRENCHARD DAVIS went over to MASON'S HOUSE to get in touch with the post of the 9th East Surrey Regt there, and to get a position for a Post between their post and ours. He returned to his Platoon Headquarters at junction of CLARA and CANARY about 6.35, to take a section out to an intermediate post.

About 6.40 a.m. the enemy commenced to shoot up CHICORY and our old C.T's with 5.9s, and at 6.45 2/lt DAVIS and 2/Lt BEYNES heard the noise of heavy bombing from the direction of the post N.8.d.3.5. The enemy (reported to number about 40) had entered CANARY where TWISTER ALLEY crosses it.

The garrison of the Post (1 N.C.O. and 10 men) appeared to have been captured with the exception of 3 men who were in shell holes about 40 yards South of the post.

A counter Raid was immediateley organised.

Rifle grenadiers commenced a very effective shoot from about N.8.d.2.3. and further under 2/Lt.DAVIS and 2/Lt BEYNES worked up CANARY and either side of it.

The enemy were ejected again, and retreated hurriedly up CANARY and across the open. They were followed with rifle fire from our counter raid party and from 2 Lewis Guns in COUNTER SAP.

One German was killed just beyond the Post, and two were captured (1 wounded who has since died). Some of the men of the Post were ~~found~~ then found to have taken up a position down CLAUD and they joined in following the enemy with fire.

A lance corporal and 1 man who were captured were left with the wounded German under an escort, while two other Germans went to get a stretcher. When our counter raid commenced, the escort turned round and the Lance Corporal seized his rifle, and brought the escort and wounded man back as prisoners. A number of our men under an Officer went forward over the open after the retreating enemy, but they were heavily fired on by M.Gs and could not get far. It seems very probable that several more casualties were inflicted on the enemy in his disorderly retirement.

The position was completely restored by 7.30 a.m. and the two sections which formed the garrison were found to be short of 4 men.

CASUALTIES.:-

Ours. 4. Missing
2. Wounded (slightly)

Enemy. 1 Killed
2 Prisoners (1 since died of wounds).

2/lt TRENCHARD DAVIS and 2/Lt.BEYNES acted fearlessly and with great resource, in organising and launching a counter raid immediateley.

L/c Binks displayed very great presence of mind and determination in turning the tables on his escorts, and bringing them in as prisoners.

We now hold CANARY up to CLAUD inclusive with one Post in CLAUD.

CINNABAR up to N.8.d.5.2.

The position at Junction of CINNABAR and CLAUD is not quite clear.

Sd H.J. WENYON.

Lieut.-Col.,

24.9.18 Commanding 8th.S.Battn.Royal West Kent Regiment.

appear that the enemy worked S.E. along CANARY as far as about N 8 Δ 58. Splitting at this point a small party worked across the open to about N 8 Δ 36 covered from view of the Western embankment of Twisted Alley. The remainder of the party probably worked down to N 8 Δ 41 splitting into two again, and under cover from bombs thrown by the party in the open, attacked the post (1) By advancing straight down CANARY (2) By entering CLAUD where it crosses Twisted alley. The other party from about N 8 Δ 36 entered almost at the same time.

E

1. FIGHTING PATROL to clear up situation at Junction of [illegible]

[illegible] and CLAUD.
[illegible] and [illegible]

[illegible] Company.

[illegible] and Mobile charges.

(1) [illegible] Section [illegible] up CIL ABAR as far as the block [illegible] open into the enemy post.

(2) [illegible] Officer and 1 Section advance down CLAUD as far as the block, [illegible] over open into enemy post.

(3) [illegible] Section ("D" Company) advance down CLAUD with Sappers and Bangalore and wire cutters. Sappers with Mobile Charges.

(4) [illegible] Section ("D" Company) advance up CIL ABAR with Sappers and Bangalores.

4. TIME-TABLE

Zero [illegible] Stokes fire 1 minute rapid.
Zero plus 1 to Zero) Silent while parties (1) and (2)
plus 3 mins.) rush enemy post.
Zero plus 3 till firing of RED LIGHT [illegible] H.Q. signifying "All clear" - T.M. & M.G. firing according to programme below

PROGRAMME FOR T.M's and M.G's. -

Stokes- Zero to Zero plus 1 min. 10 rounds rapid into Junction of CLAUD and CIL ABAR. 10 rounds rapid into Junction of CUTHBERT & CIL ABAR.
Zero plus 1 to Zero plus 3. Silent.
Zero plus 3 till RED LIGHT - fire on
N.S.D. [illegible]
N.S.D. [illegible]

[illegible]S- Zero plus 3 till RED LIGHT [illegible]

(1) Junction of [illegible] and [illegible]
(2) [illegible]
(3) [illegible]

5 rounds a minute for 1 minute, then 1 round a minute.

[illegible] [illegible]

[illegible]

6. [illegible] [illegible] Party and will [illegible] destroy [illegible] [illegible] and [illegible] CIL ABAR [illegible] CLAUD and CUTHBERT.

7. TRENCH GARRISON-

(overleaf)-

E2

[illegible] for 25th Septr 1918 Contd. Sheet 2-

TRENCH GARRISON- will stand by ready to assist with fire in any way possible.

Posts in CINNABAR will be provided with Smoke Rifle Grenades to put a smoke screen on the AUGUST CITY Road only if enemy opens heavy Machine Gun Fire.

A party in our post at N.8.D.30.55 will engage trench junction at N.8.D.60.32 with No.36 Rifle Grenades from Zero plus 3 minutes.

8. HEADQUARTERS-

Raid H.Q. at Junction of CLARA and CANARY.

9. "ZERO" TIME- 3 a.m.

10. WATCHES- Watches will be synchronised by all concerned at Battalion Headquarters, CAMERON CASTLE, at 10.30 p.m.

(Sd) H.J. Wenyon Lieut Colonel,

Septr. 25th.1918. Commanding 8th S. Battn. R. West Kent Regiment.

Copies to:-

72nd. Infantry Brigade Headquarters.
O.C. "A" Company.
O.C. "B" Company.
O.C. "C" Company.
O.C. "D" Company.
1st. North Staffordshire Regiment.
"A" Company, 24th. Battn. Machine Gun Corps.
"[illegible]" Battery, 6" Howitzers.
72nd. Light Trench Mortar Battery.
10[illegible] (Field) Company, R.E.
Commanding Officer.
File.
War Diaries. (2).

SECRET

14

7/24

VR 36

War Diary

of

8th S. Battn. Royal West Kent Regt.

from

1st Oct. 1918

to

31st October 1918

(Volume. -   ).

To:- D.A.G. 3rd Echl.
B.E.F.
(through 72nd I.B.H.Qs)

October 1918
8th Bn Royal West Kent Regt

Instructions regarding War Diaries and Intelligence Summaries are contained in F. S. Regs., Part II. and the Staff Manual respectively. Title pages will be prepared in manuscript.

WAR DIARY or INTELLIGENCE SUMMARY.

(Erase heading not required.)

Army Form C. 2118.

Place	Date	Hour	Summary of Events and Information	Remarks and references to Appendices
SUS ST LEGER	Oct 1st		Battn at rest Interior economy Capt Proctor rejoined appointed L.G.O.	CML
do	2		Address to Battn by B.G.C. on general situation	CML
			Tactical ride during afternoon Capt Wheeler & 2/Lt Thomas rejoined	CML
do	3		Tactical scheme All day field day	CML
do	4		All day on Range, shooting for musketry & Lewis gun cup	CML
do	5		No parades, preparation for move "B" echelon left by road	CML
do	6		Battn marched from SUS ST LEGER to MONTICOURT entrained there	Appendix A
			detrained at RIBICOURT & marched thro' GRAINCOURT bivouacked	
			there in a field about one mile east of GRAINCOURT Enemy planes	
			dropped several bombs in the vicinity	CML
GRAINCOURT	7		Front line E of RUMILLY reconnoitred Battn moved into CANTAING	
			Tr (S.W. of CANTAING) & stayed there the night	CML
	8		Battn moved into RUMILLY support trench & were shelled for ½ hour	
			Buried about 12 men of the Hampshire regt. Moved forward at	
			4.30 PM to E of RUMILLY Battn Hqrs about 1 mile W of NIERGNIES	
			coys ½ mile behind, casualties from gas & H.E. shells. Assembly trench	

(A9173) Wt W2358/P360 600,000 12/17 D. D. & L. Sch. 52a. Forms/C2118/15

forw[illegible]

October, 1918 — 2

8th Bn Royal West Kent Regt

Instructions regarding War Diaries and Intelligence Summaries are contained in F. S. Regs., Part II. and the Staff Manual respectively. Title pages will be prepared in manuscript.

WAR DIARY
or
INTELLIGENCE SUMMARY.
(*Erase heading not required.*)

Army Form C. 2118.

Place	Date	Hour	Summary of Events and Information	Remarks and references to Appendices
	Oct 8		south of NIERGNIES reconnoitred	ell
	" 9		Attacked at 5.30 am. Canadians worked round CAMBRAI on the left Coldstream Guards on the right. Objective AWOINGT & 500x South along railway embankment. Several casualties from our own barrage thro' two of our guns firing short. Little opposition met with. Hqrs established in AWOINGT	
			Prisoners 29	
			Tanks 3	
			Guns 2	
			2/Lts Winch & Green killed. 9 OR killed 48 OR wounded	ell
	" 10		Advance continued 72nd Bgde in reserve. Billeted in CAGNONCLES 2/Lts Laskey, Bain, Cornford, Holman joined the Battn for duty. Capt Porter returned from course.	ell
	" 11		Advance continued at 5.30 AM. 72 Inf Bde still in support. Bn dug in across CAMBRAI–St VAAST road 2 miles East of RIEUX. Some shelling. Lt DEAN wounded.	ell

(A9175) Wt W2353/P360 600,000 12/17 D. D. & L. Sch. 52a. Forms/C2118/15

October, 1918 3

8th Bn Royal West Kent Regt

Instructions regarding War Diaries and Intelligence Summaries are contained in F. S. Regs., Part II. and the Staff Manual respectively. Title pages will be prepared in manuscript.

WAR DIARY
or
INTELLIGENCE SUMMARY.
(Erase heading not required.)

Army Form C. 2118.

Place	Date	Hour	Summary of Events and Information	Remarks and references to Appendices
	Oct 12		Bn moved into billets in AVESNES. Good billets – houses in disorder but not greatly damaged.	[initials]
	" 13		Bn moved out at 0300 hrs and relieved 3rd Bn Rifle Bde at positions West of HAUSSY. Considerable H.E. and gas shelling all day.	[initials]
	" 14		'A' Coy pushed patrols into HAUSSY. 3 prisoners taken. 1 section under Sgt BROWN went East of SELLE river and was there heavily attacked. Sgt BROWN and 1 OR missing. Lt PIGGOTT and Sgt ASHDOWN killed by shell fire in HAUSSY. Many civilians in HAUSSY. Great welcome to our men	[initials]
	" 15		Wet day. Usual heavy harassing fire by enemy. Some 200 civilians evacuated from HAUSSY.	[initials]
	" 16		72nd Bde attacked to secure a crossing over the SELLE. 1st N. Staff. Regt on left, we in centre, 9th E. Surrey Regt on right. Attack started at 5.10 AM. 2Lt WALLIS crossed SELLE at 0300 hrs with his platoon and advanced to ... to cover assembly. D Coy on right – 'B' Coy on left, 'C' in support, 'A' in Reserve. All objectives and about 200 prisoners taken by the Bn. 1st N. Staff Regt failed to assemble owing to counter-barrage and 'B' Coy was caught by enfilade M.G. fire and had many casualties. In afternoon we had to retire to 1st Objective as Bn on the right was counter-attacked and driven to West side of river. 2Lt LASKEY, BAIN and HOLMAN killed. Capt PORTER and 2Lt WALLIS, CSM GUTTERIDGE and DYER wounded. In evening the 7th North Hants Regt relieved the Bn. Bn proceeded to AVESNES. Total casualties before HAUSSY 4 officers 12 OR killed 2 officers 76 OR wounded.	[initials]

(A9175) Wt. W4553/P560 600,000 11/17 D. D. & L. Sch. 52a. Forms/C2118/13.

October 1918

4

8th Bn Royal West Kent Regt

Army Form C. 2118.

Instructions regarding War Diaries and Intelligence Summaries are contained in F. S. Regs., Part II. and the Staff Manual respectively. Title pages will be prepared in manuscript.

WAR DIARY
or
INTELLIGENCE SUMMARY.

(Erase heading not required.)

Place	Date	Hour	Summary of Events and Information	Remarks and references to Appendices
CAMBRAI	Oct 17		Bn moved to CAMBRAI to billets	[illegible] Appendix B
"	" 18, 19, 20		Cleaning up, clothing parades, interior economy etc.	[illegible]
"	" 21, 22		Coy Training	[illegible]
"	" 23		Bn Training	[illegible]
"	" 24		Coy Training	[illegible]
"	" 25		Bde Field Day	[illegible]
"	" 26		Bn marched to AVESNES and billetted there	[illegible]
	27–31		Coy and Bn Training	[illegible]

[illegible] 2/Lt
for O.C. 8th Bn R.W. Kent Regt

In the field 10-11-18

(A9475) Wt W2358/P360 600,000 12/17 D. D. & L. Sch. 52a. Forms/C2118/15.

SECRET. 8TH.(S) BATTN. RL. WEST KENT REGT., COPY No..

ORDER No. 30-

In-the-field, 5th. October 1918.

-:-:-:-:-:-:-:-:-:-:-:-:-:-:-:-:-:-:-

1. On the 6th.Octr.1918, the Battalion will entrain at MONDICOURT at 1106 hours and proceed by tactical train to RIBECOURT.

2. The Battalion will parade in marching order, ready to move off, at 0755 hours on the road facing S.E. outside "C" Company's Officers' Mess.

3. ORDER OF MARCH-

Drums-
"D" Company-
"B" Company-
"C" Company-
Headquarters-
"A" Company.

4. Blankets, Mess Stores, Officers' valises, etc., will be stacked by 0745 hours outside Battalion Headquarters Mess.
Headquarters will detail a loading party to remain behind and load the above stores on the lorries.

5. Rations for the 6th. instant will be carried on the men.

6. Lewis Gun limbers, Cookers, etc., will move by separate route under 2nd.Lieut.M.E.OUTRAM.

7. All Billets are to be left clean. Usual certificates will be rendered by noon, 7th.Octr.

8. Sick parade will be at 0630 hours.

9. The strictest train discipline will be maintained.

ISSUED at 2300 hours. G.F.C.Macaskie, 2nd.Lieut.
A/Adjutant, 8th.S.Battn.Rl.West Kent Regt.,

Copies to:-

1. File. 2. War Diary.
3. War Diary. 4. O.C. "A" Company.
5. O.C. "B" Company. 6. O.C. "C" Company.
7. O.C. "D" Company. 8. Quartermaster.
9. Transport Officer. 10. Major H.S.BROWN, M.C.,
11. Medical Officer. 12. Headquarters' Mess.
13. R.S.Major.

Secret

Copy No. 2

B

57 A.B. Ref 27 B. 1/14.00

8th Royal West Kent Regiment.
Operation Orders

17/10/18

1. The Battalion will move into rest billets in Cambrai at A16 Area

2. Order of March

Headquarters
"A" Coy
"B" Coy
"C" Coy
"D" Coy
"A" Echelon

Starting Point

Head of column facing S.W. U.28.a.6.4

Time
1500 hours

5. Dress
Marching Order with Steel Helmets.

6. Officers Mess Stores will be collected by mess cart at 1430 hours.

7. "B" Echelon will join the column at B1.c7.8. at 1530 hours.

(Sd) F. Procter Captain
a/Adj 8th Royal West Kent Regiment

Copies to:—
1 File
2 War Diary
3
4 OC "A" Coy
5 " B "
6 " C "
7 " D
8 "A" Echelon
9 Headquarter Mess.

SECRET.

WR 37

WAR DIARY

of

8th S Battn. Royal West Kent Regt.

from 1st Novr 1918

to 30th Novr 1918

(Volume.-).

To:

D.A.G. 3rd Ech.

(thro' H.Qs.

72nd I.B.)

Per Registered Post

ORDERLY ROOM

No.A/ 2200

5 DEC 1918

8th (Service) Bn. Queen's Own Royal West Kent Regiment.

Instructions regarding War Diaries and Intelligence Summaries are contained in F. S. Regs., Part II. and the Staff Manual respectively. Title pages will be prepared in manuscript.

November, 1918.

8th S. Bn Royal WAR DIARY West Kent Regt. or INTELLIGENCE SUMMARY.

(Erase heading not required.)

Army Form C. 2118.

Place	Date	Hour	Summary of Events and Information	Remarks and references to Appendices
AVESNES	1 Nov.		Interior economy and general preparations	
"	2	"	Marched to HAUSSY and occupied billets in the village.	Appendix A
HAUSSY	3	"	At HAUSSY under one hours notice to move forward	
SEPTMERIES	4	"	Marched to SEPTMERIES and occupied billets in the village. Very close billetting.	Appendix B
WARGNIES	5	"	Marched to WARGNIES LE GRAND through MARECHIES. Very wet. Bad billets.	
LE GRAND	6	"	Changed H.Q. billet with Divisional H.Q. Some shelling of the village Sec Lt JORDAN and 4 OR wounded. 3 horses wounded.	
	7	"	Advanced in support of the 17th Bde through St WAAST, and passing through, became front line of attack. Lt HR SMITH and 2Lt H.T. EVERSON and 3 OR killed. 8 OR wounded. We dug in 1500 yds East of BAVAY, meeting some M.G. fire. Captures for the day - 50 boxes M.G. belts filled.	
	8	"	Advanced to West of FIEGNIES and met determined M.G. opposition. Patrols pressed on under cover of darkness and advanced 1000 yds during the night. Sec Lt BARNES wounded.	
	9	"	Resumed the advance at dawn and made the line of the 1st objective - MONS - MAUBERGE Railway - without opposition. We occupied FIEGNIES and the	

Sheet 2.

Army Form C. 2118.

Instructions regarding War Diaries and Intelligence Summaries are contained in F. S. Regs., Part II. and the Staff Manual respectively. Title pages will be prepared in manuscript.

November, 1918

8th S.B. Royal **WAR DIARY** West Kent Regt

or

INTELLIGENCE SUMMARY.

(Erase heading not required.)

Place	Date	Hour	Summary of Events and Information	Remarks and references to Appendices
	9th Nov.		9th E. Surrey Regt passed through. Excellent billets in the town. Many civilians who gave us an enthusiastic welcome. Very little damage had been done to the town, except the Railway buildings. We captured at FIEGNIES a complete factory, used for making T.M. shells. Major ROGERS in command.	CWH
FIEGNIES	10 "		Spent day resting and cleaning up. Lt Col. WENYON and Capt. ARNAUD left on leave.	
PISSOTIAU	11 "		Marched out at 0500 hrs to PISSOTIAU. Wretched billets, the worst we had had for many weeks. At 1325 hrs received news of cessation of hostilities.	Appendix C CWH
"	12 "		We are able to extend our billets and secure habitable quarters for the men. Accommodation still of poor quality. Cleaning up generally.	CWH
"	13 "		Training, football, local baths. Clean clothing obtained. Very cold weather.	CWH
"	14 "		Thanksgiving Service. Football and interior economy	CWH
"	15 "		Training and football. Cold spell continued.	CWH
"	16 "		Church Service. Whole holiday	CWH
SEPTMERIES	17 "		Marched from PISSOTIAU to SEPTMERIES. Poor billets and very cold.	CWH Appendix D
LOURCHES	18 "		Marched on to LOURCHES. Good billets. Left 0730 hrs, arrived 14.00 hrs, a tiring march.	Appendix E CWH
BRUILLE	19 "		Marched from LOURCHES to BRUILLE. Some trouble to find accommodation but	Appendix F

(A9175) Wt W2335/P360 600,000 12/17 D. D. & L. **Sch. 53a.** Forms/C2118/15.

Sheet 3

Army Form C. 2118.

Instructions regarding War Diaries and Intelligence Summaries are contained in F. S. Regs., Part II. and the Staff Manual respectively. Title pages will be prepared in manuscript.

November, 1918

8th S.B. Royal **WAR DIARY** West Kent Regt.
or
INTELLIGENCE SUMMARY.
(Erase heading not required.)

Place	Date	Hour	Summary of Events and Information	Remarks and references to Appendices
			all fairly satisfactorily placed.	CL
BRUILLE	20th Nov		At BRUILLE, resting and cleaning up. Major BROWN returned from leave and took command.	CL
MASNY	21	"	Moved to MASNY about 3 kilometres away. Good billets.	CL Appendix G
"	22	"	Training. Football. Major ROGERS sick to hospital.	CL
"	23	"	Training. Lecture by Educational Officer of Division on Demobilization. Football	CL
"	24	"	Church Service. Lorries to LENS for 75 of all ranks. Football	CL
LANDAS	25	"	Marched to LANDAS. Fair accommodation.	CL Appendix H
NOMAIN	26		Marched to NOMAIN. Fair accommodation, but some of the men's billets very dismal. No fuel up.	Appendix I CL
"	27		At NOMAIN. Interior economy, training etc. Capt. ARNAUD returned from leave.	CL
"	28		C.O. inspected C and D Coys. on parade, wet weather. Football.	CL
"	29		C.O. inspected A and B Coys. A lorry took 30 of all ranks to LENS.	CL
"	30		Route march. Lt Col. WENYON returned from leave and resumed command. Football in afternoon	CL

C L Lacey [illegible] Capt & Adjt.
8th (S) Battn. Royal West Kent Regt.
4-12-18

(A9173) Wt W2350/P360 600,000 12/17 D. D. & L. Sch. 52a. Forms/C2118/15.

Appendix A

SECRET

8th. S. Bn. Royal West Kent Regiment
Order No. 35
In-the-field , 1st November 1918

COPY NO. 3

1. The Battalion will move by Route March to MAUSSY tomorrow 2nd. November 1918.

2. Order of March.

Drums , H.Qs., "C" , "D", "A" ,"B", Transport.

The Battalion will form up ready to move off with the head of the column opposite "D" Company Headquarters facing North at 13.30 hours.

3. Dress. Marching Order , with jerkins neatly folded under the flap of the pack.

4. Advance Parties. Details will be notified later.

5. Lorries for Blankets. Time of arrival will be notified, (probably in the afternoon).

6. Officers ' valises , Orderly Room and Medical Stores and Blankets will be dumped in the entrance to Headquarters Mess by 12.00 hours, Mess cart will collect Mess stores at 12.45hrs

7. Surplus Stores. Any surplus stores will be sent to the Brigade Store No 112 Rue de l'ERCLIN (Map ref. Sheet 51a. U.21.b.55.05.) where they will be in charge of the Brigade Concert Party.

8. All latrines , Urinals etc., will be filled in.
All refuse to be buried and billets left clean and tidy.

(Sgd). F. P R O C T O R Captain,

A/Adjutant 8th. S. Bn. Royal West Kent Regiment

Copied to:-

1. File.
2. War Diary.
3. War Diary.
4. O.C. "A" Company.
5. O.C. "B" Company.
6. O.C. "C" Company.
7. O.C. "D" Company.
8. Headquarters Mess.
9. Transport Officer.
10. Quartermaster.
11. A/R.S. Major.

Appendix B

SECRET. 8th. S. Battn. Royal West Kent Regiment COPY No. 1
Order No. 34.,
In-the-field, 3rd. Novr. 1918.

1. The Battalion will move to Assembly Positions N.W. of BERMERAIN between the BERMERAIN - FAMARS and the BERMERAIN - VENDEGIES Roads tomorrow, November 4th. 1918.

2. Order of March- Drums, "A", "C", "D", "B", Bn. H. Qs, & "A" Echelon.

Companies and Headquarters will move by Platoons at 50 yards interval. Lewis Gun Limbers will move behind their respective Companies.

Head of Column facing S.W. on Pathway by the Battn. Orderly Room, ready to move off, at 07.00 hrs.

3. Dress- Fighting Order. Shrapnel helmets will be worn. Greatcoats will be carried in the Packs.

4. Blankets and Haversacks will be dumped at the Brigade Store, V.11.d.7.3. by 06.00 hours.

5. Officers' valises, Orderly Room Stores, will be dumped at the Q.M. Stores by 06.00 hours.

6. The mess cart will collect mess Stores at 06.30 hours.

7. Sick parade will be at 05.30 hours.

8. All latrines, urinals (other than permanent ones) will be filled in. All billets will be left clean and tidy.

9. All first line transport will move off with units, and on arrival at BERMERAIN will be 'parked' in a convenient field or space off the road.

F. P R O C T O R, Captain,
Actg. Adjutant, 8th. S. Battn. Royal West Kent Regiment.

ISSUED AT 22.40 hrs.

Copies to:-

1. File.
2. War Diary.
3. War Diary.
4. O.C. "A" Company.
5. O.C. "B" Company.
6. O.C. "C" Company.
7. O.C. "D" Company.
8. Headquarters' Mess.
9. Transport Officer.
10. Quartermaster.
11. A/R. S. Major.

Appendix C

SECRET. 8TH.S.BN.ROYAL WEST KENT REGT. COPY NO. 2.
ORDER NO.[illegible]
[illegible], 10th NOVR.1918.
[illegible]

1. The Battalion will move by march route tomorrow 11.11.18 to Billets in Squares [illegible] 29, C8, and 30.

2. The Battalion will parade ready to march off at [illegible] hours, [illegible] facing West, head of column on road outside "C" Company Officers' Mess.

Order of March.

"A" Company
"C" Company
Drums
Headquarters.
"D" Company
"B" Company.

Dress.

Full Marching Order. Shrapnel Helmets to be worn.

3. Transport, including cookers and Company L.G. Limbers will march in rear of Battalion.

4. Lewis Guns will be carried on Lewis Gun Limbers.

5. Mess Cart will call for Officers Mess Stores at Coy.H.Qrs. at 0430 hours.

6. An advance party, under Captain S.C.THOMPSON M.C., of 1 N.C.O. per Coy will report to the Adjutant at 0500 hours at the starting point.

7. Particular// attention will be paid to march discipline.

C.H.O.MACKENZIE, 2/Lt.,
A/Adjt. 8th.S.Bn.Royal West Kent Regt.

ISSUED at 2230 hours.

Copies to :-

1. File
2. War Diary
3. War Diary
4. O.C. "A" Company.
5. O.C. "B" Company.
6. O.C. "C" Company.
7. O.C. "D" Company.
8. Headquarters Mess.
9. Transport Officer
10. Quartermaster.
11. A/R.S.Major.

appendix D

SECRET.

8TH. S. BN. ROYAL WEST KENT REGT.
ORDER NO. 36.
IN-THE-FIELD. 16th. NOVR. 1918.
[illegible]

COPY NO. 2

1. The Battalion will move by route march to SEPMERIES tomorrow 17th November 1918.

2. The Battalion will parade facing N.E., head of column opposite "A" Company Officers' Mess at 0730 hours ready to move off.
ORDER OF MARCH.
Headquarters.
"A" Company
"B" Company
"DRUMS"
"C" Company
"D" Company
All Transport will follow the Battalion.
Full Marching order. Soft caps and jerkins will be worn, steel hats on packs.
Special attention must be paid to smart turnout and the proper fitting of packs and equipment.

3. Reveille at 0530 hours.
Breakfast at 0600 hours.
Mess cart will call for Officers' Mess kit at 0645.
Officers valises, Drums packs, and Blankets to be at Q.M. Stores at 0645 hours.
Valises and Mess kit must be ready punctually at hours stated.

4. Strict attention must be paid to march discipline.

5. On arrival at SEPMERIES all S.A.A. above 50 rounds per man will be collected and stacked at Company Headquarters.
A limber will collect same to take to A.R.P.

6. A loading party of one man per Company to report to the Quartermaster at 0630 hours for loading duties. These men will ride in the blanket lorries.

C.F.[illegible], 2/Lieut.,

A/Adjt. 8th.S.Bn.Royal West Kent Regiment.

ISSUED at 2200 hours.

Copies to :-
1. File
2. War Diary
3. War Diary
4. O.C. "A" Company
5. O.C. "B" Company
6. O.C. "C" Company
7. O.C. "D" Company
8. Headquarters Mess
9. Transport Officer
10. Quartermaster.
11. A/R.S.Major.

Appendix G

2

SECRET. 8th.S.Battn.Rl.West Kent Regt., COPY No....
Order No. 87
In-the-field, 20th.November 1918.
-:-:-:-:-:-:-:-:-:-:-:-:-:-:-:-:-

1. The Battalion will move to HASNY tomorrow 21-11-1918.

2. The Battalion will parade at 10.30 hours facing WEST, on the [illegible] - [illegible] Road, head of column opposite Battalion H.Qs Mess.

Order of March :-

Drums.
Headquarters.
"D" Company.
"C" Company.
"B" Company.
"A" Company.

Dress-

As for 19th. instant.

Valises, Company Stores and Blankets to be at the Q.M's Store at 09.30 hours. Mess Cart for Officers' Mess Stores will collect Stores at 09.00 hours and will proceed direct to HASNY. Servants and Cooks may be sent with mess cart to HASNY if desired. Cookers will prepare dinners en route.

3. An advance Party of 1 N.C.O. per Platoon will report to Sec.Lieut. A.E.JACKSON at Battalion Orderly Room at 07.30 hours. Party will report to Lieut.ROYAL at [illegible], HASNY at 08.30 hours. An Officer for each Company may be sent also if desired.

C.E.D.Mackenzie, 2nd.Lieut.,
Actg.Adjutant, 8th.S.Bn.Royal West Kent Regt.,

ISSUED AT
2015 hours.

Copies to :-

1. [illegible]
2. War Diary.
3. War Diary.
4. O.C. "A" Company.
5. O.C. "B" Company.
6. O.C. "C" Company.
7. O.C. "D" Company.
8. Headquarters [illegible]
9. Transport Officer.
10. Quartermaster.
11. Regtl. Sergeant Major.
12. [illegible]

Appendix 'H' 2

SECRET.

8th.(Service) Bn. ROYAL WEST KENT REGT.
Order No. [illegible]
[illegible], [illegible] Nov. 1918.

1. The Battalion will move by Route March to the [illegible] Area tomorrow, 25th. November 1918.
   Route:- ECAILLON - BRUILLE - VILLERS CAMPEAU - [illegible] - X Roads 200 yards N.W. of first 'L' in Les 3 [illegible] - BEUVRY - LANDAS.

2. Order of March:-

   Drums.
   Headquarters.
   "A" Company.
   "B" Company.
   "C" Company.
   "D" Company.

3. Dress:- Marching Order. Jerkins will be worn.

4. The Battalion will parade, Head of Column facing South at Road Junction North of Church, ready to move off at 06.30 hours.

5. Officers' valises, Blankets, Orderly Room Stores, etc. to be at the Quartermaster's Store at 05.30 hours.

6. Mess Carts will collect Officers' Mess Stores at 06.00 hours.

7. All Billets are to be left clean and tidy. All latrines, urinals, etc., other than permanent ones, are to be filled in.

8. Guides will meet the Battalion at the Railway Crossing by LANDAS Station on the BEUVRY - LANDAS Road.

9. Breakfasts tomorrow, 25th instant, at 05.15 hours.

G. [illegible] C. [illegible], 2nd.Lieut.,
Actg.Adjutant, 8th.S.Bn.Rl.West Kent Rgt.,

Issued at 19.[illegible] hours.

Copies to:-

1. File.
2. War Diary.
3. War Diary.
4. O.C. "A" Company.
5. O.C. "B" Company.
6. O.C. "C" Company.
7. O.C. "D" Company.
8. Headquarters [illegible].
9. Quartermaster.
10. Regimental Sergeant Major.

Appendix F

All Coys. Q.M. T.O. R.S.M. Off. i/c HQ.

Ref. VALENCIENNES 1/100,000.

1. Bn will move to-morrow to ECAILLON area. Bn will parade at 0930 hrs, ready to move off, head of column 200 yards South of L in LOURCHES, facing S.W.

Order of march C
D
Drums
A
B
HQ

Dress etc same as today.

2. Reveille 0700 hrs. Breakfasts 0800 hrs. Valises, Coy. stores, Blankets at Q.M. stores by 0830 hrs. Mess cart for officers mess stores at 0845 hrs. Loading party at Q.M. stores 0830 hrs.

3. All billets must be left clean.

4. A foot inspection must be held afternoon.

5. Same advance party as to-day to report to 2nd Lt JACKSON at CHURCH, LOURCHES at 0730 hrs. Party to report to Lt HARVEY at 0845 hrs at CHURCH ECAILLON, and provide guides to Bn, to arrive cross roads 200 yds N. of T. in AUBERCHICOURT at 1145 hrs.

18-11-18

[illegible signature]
2nd i/c

To:- Coys. Q.M. T.O. Loas Peairy (2) R/RSM.

1. The march will be continued tomorrow 18.11.18. Bn will parade ready to move off at 0745 hours. Head of column facing W. opposite 'A' Coy Officers' Mess
Order of March

HQ.
B.
C
Drums
D
A

Bn is moving to LOURCHIES area
Dress etc same as today.

2. Reveille 0545. Breakfasts 0615. Blankets, valises, Coy stores at QM Stores by 0700 hours. Mess cart will call for Officers' Mess stores at 0700 hrs

3. Same advance party as today to report to Lt HARVEY at 0900 hrs at first road junction S of R in LOURCHIES. Party will rendezvous at 'C' Coy Officers' Mess at 0720 hrs

4. Same loading party as today at 0700 hrs at Q.M Stores

21.40 hours
17.11.18

[signature] Re
a/adjt

Secret 8th (S) Bn R.W. Kent Rgt Copy No.

Order No 39

In the Field. 25th Novr '18

1. The march will be continued tomorrow
2. Bn will parade facing N.W. at 1015 hrs on the road outside B.H.Q. head of column at cross roads by 'A' Coy billet

Leather jerkins will not be worn.
Order of march A. B. Drums, HQ. C. D.
3 Blankets, valises, Coy Stores at QM stores by 0900 hrs. Mess cart for mess kit at 0930 hrs.
4 Usual advance party under Sec Lt JACKSON will rendezvous at 'B' Coy HQ. at 0700 hours.
Coys may send 1 Officer per Coy & 1 N.C.O per platoon in addition.

[signature]
Lt
a/Adjt

25-11-18

SECRET

VR 38

WAR DIARY

of

8th S Battn. Royal West Kent Rgt.

from 1st Decr. 1918
to 31st Decr. 1918

(Volume.)

*

To:- D.A.G.
G.H.Q Base
(through H.Qs
72nd Inf. Brigade)

1

8th S.B. Royal West Kent Regt

Instructions regarding War Diaries and Intelligence Summaries are contained in F. S. Regs., Part II. and the Staff Manual respectively. Title pages will be prepared in manuscript.

WAR DIARY
or
INTELLIGENCE SUMMARY.
(Erase heading not required.)

December, 1918.

Army Form C. 2118.

Place	Date	Hour	Summary of Events and Information	Remarks and references to Appendices
NOMAIN	1st Dec		Church Parade in School-House. Very cold day.	C.T.D.
"	2nd	"	Usual Training and Football	C.T.D.
"	3rd	"	Usual Training and Football. Advance parties returned from TOURNAI as	C.T.D.
			move now postponed sine die. Re-organization of Battalion (see Appendix A)	
"	4th	"	Usual Training. Guard mounting drill.	C.T.D.
"	5th	"	Formal guard mounting drill. Each Company with a double guard. Lecture	C.T.D.
			by Battalion Education Officer on the "Scheme of Education". Football & boxing.	
"	6th	"	Battalion Parade to watch guard mounting parade. Lecture by Capt THOMPSON MC	C.T.D.
			on "New Zealand".	
"	7th	"	Lorry to take 85 of the Battalion to TOURNAI to represent the Battalion on the	C.T.D.
			route of H.M. The King's visit. Usual Training & football.	
"	8th	"	Church parade & Recreation	C.T.D.
"	9th	"	Battalion parade and march past. Recreation.	C.T.D.
"	10th	"	Usual Training and football.	C.T.D.
"	11th	"	Usual Training. The B.G.C. (Gen R.W. MORGAN) addressed the Battalion in the School House	C.T.D.
"	12th	"	Two lorries for Lille.	C.T.D.

(A9475) Wt W2358/P360 600,000 12/17 D. D. & L. Sch. 52a. Forms/C2118/15.

2

Army Form C. 2118.

Instructions regarding War Diaries and Intelligence Summaries are contained in F. S. Regs., Part II. and the Staff Manual respectively. Title pages will be prepared in manuscript.

WAR DIARY
or
INTELLIGENCE SUMMARY.
(Erase heading not required.)

3rd S. Bn R. West Kent Regt — December 1918.

Place	Date	Hour	Summary of Events and Information	Remarks and references to Appendices
NOMAIN.	13th Dec.		Usual Training. Sports	C.T.D.
"	14th "		Usual Training.	C.T.D./
"	15th "		Usual Training and football.	C.T.D./
"	16th "		Usual Training and football.	C.T.D./
"	17th "		Advance party of 2 officers and 1 platoon per Coy went to TOURNAI.	C.T.D./
TOURNAI.	18th "		Arrived at TOURNAI. Barracks have the making of a good place, but are in a most filthy condition. (Appendix B)	C.T.D./
"	19th "		Cleaning up.	C.T.D./
"	20th "		B.G.C. inspected the Barracks. Cleaning up.	C.T.D./
"	21st "		Cleaning up.	C.T.D./
"	22nd "		Church parade in the Y.M.C.A	C.T.D./
"	23rd "		Company Training and fatigues. Very wet.	C.T.D./
"	24th "		Preparation for Christmas.	C.T.D./
"	25th "		Church Parade in the Y.M.C.A. Christmas dinner. Battalion Concert.	C.T.D./
"	26th "		Usual Training. Cleaning up of billets.	C.T.D./
"	27th "		Usual Training	[illegible]

(A9473) Wt W2358/P360 600,000 12/17 D. D. & L. Sch. 52a. Forms/C2118/15.

3

Army Form C. 2118.

8th S. Bn R. West Kent Regt.

Instructions regarding War Diaries and Intelligence Summaries are contained in F. S. Regs., Part II. and the Staff Manual respectively. Title pages will be prepared in manuscript.

WAR DIARY
or
INTELLIGENCE SUMMARY.
(*Erase heading not required.*)

December 1918.

Place	Date	Hour	Summary of Events and Information	Remarks and references to Appendices
TOURNAI.	28th Dec.		Usual Training	C.T.D.
"	29th "		Church parade.	C.T.D.
"	30th "		Usual Training.	C.T.D.
"	31st "		Usual Training.	C.T.D.

C. Macaskie ......Capt. & Adjt.
8th (S) Battn. Royal West Kent Regt.
5-1-19

(A9475) Wt W2358/P360 600,000 12/17 D. D. & L. Sch. 52a. Forms/C2118/15.

Appendix A

Battalion Orders
by
Lieut-Col. [illegible] W[illegible], D.S.O.,
Commanding 8th.S.[illegible] Royal West Kent Regiment.
In the Field, 2nd.Decr.1918.
-:-:-:-:-:-:-:-:-:-:-:-:-:-

DETAIL:-
Orderly Officer for tomorrow:- 2nd.Lieut. [illegible]
Next for duty:- 2nd.Lieut. [illegible]
Company for duty tomorrow:- "[illegible]" Company.

766. PROMOTION:- (Officers):-

The following extract from London Gazette Supplement dated 27.11.1918 is republished for information:-

[illegible] Royal West Kent [illegible], Sec. [illegible] to be [illegible].
([illegible] 1st.191[illegible])

767. PROMOTION [illegible]

[illegible] Pte [illegible] "[illegible]" Company appointed [illegible] Corporal, and [illegible] this day.

768. LEAVE TO THE U.K.,

The following granted leave to the United Kingdom from the dates as shown against their names, and are each entitled to 14 days Ration Allowance only:-

11[illegible]	L/[illegible]	W[illegible]	T. "[illegible]" Coy	27.11.18 to 11.1[illegible]	
4126	Pte	Turner	[illegible]	"	1.12.18 to [illegible]
202586	Pte	Shorell	[illegible]	"	3.12.1[illegible] to 1[illegible]
1[illegible]244	"	[illegible]	W. "[illegible]"	"	[illegible] to 1[illegible]
11[illegible]		[illegible]	[illegible]	"	[illegible].12.1[illegible] to 1[illegible]
[illegible]	"	[illegible]	[illegible]	"	4.12.18 to [illegible]
73[illegible]	"	[illegible]	[illegible]		[illegible] to 1[illegible]
11[illegible]	Cpl	Brewer	[illegible]		[illegible] to [illegible]
[illegible]	Pte	[illegible]	[illegible]		[illegible] to 1[illegible]
[illegible]	"	[illegible]	[illegible]	"	[illegible] to [illegible]
7[illegible]	"	Martin	[illegible]	"	[illegible] to [illegible]
[illegible]	"	Bates	[illegible]	"	[illegible] to [illegible]
[illegible]	"	Simmons	[illegible]	"	[illegible] to [illegible]
740[illegible]	"	Simmons	W. "[illegible]"	"	[illegible] to [illegible]

769. STRENGTH:-
(a) Increase:-

2nd.Lieut. [illegible] embarked and disembarked 24.11.18, joined Battalion for duty 29.11.18. Taken on strength accordingly and posted to "A" Company.

[illegible] Pte [illegible] [illegible] "[illegible]" Coy hospital to duty 29.11.18.

1[illegible]	[illegible]	Davis	[illegible] "[illegible]" Coy	Re-joined Battn. for duty from
11[illegible]	"	[illegible]	[illegible] "A" "	224th. Employment Coy. Taken
[illegible]	"	Richardson	W. "[illegible]" "	on strength with effect from 29.11.1918.

(b) Decrease:-

[illegible]	[illegible]	Greenaway	[illegible] "[illegible]" Coy	To Base for transfer to Home
[illegible]	Sgt	[illegible]	W. "D" Coy	Establishment on exchange
[illegible]	"	Jansen	W. "[illegible]" "	30.11.18. Struck off
[illegible]	Cpl	[illegible]	[illegible] "D" "	strength accordingly. Authy:
1[illegible]	"	[illegible]	[illegible] "[illegible]"	[illegible], 3rd. Echelon G.H.Q.
[illegible]	"	[illegible]	W. "A"	[illegible]/134/[illegible] of 19.11.1918.

[illegible]	L/[illegible]	Wheldon	A. "B" Coy	Sick 27.11.18
202[illegible]	Pte	Wainscott	[illegible] "A" "	Sick 28.11.18
1[illegible]	"	Rodwell	[illegible] "A" "	Sick 28.11.18
200[illegible]	"	[illegible]	[illegible] "A" "	Sick 28.11.18.

(over.)

58. STRENGTH-(b)-decrease-cont'd.

17808	Pte	Wells	W.	[illegible]	[illegible] Sick	26.11.18
23521	L/C	Clarke	[illegible]	[illegible]	" Sick	27.11.18
200[illegible]	Pte	[illegible]	[illegible]	[illegible]	" Sick	2[illegible].11.18
[illegible]	"	[illegible]	S.	[illegible]	" Sick	2[illegible].11.18
[illegible]	Cpl	[illegible]	E.	[illegible]	" Sick	2[illegible].11.18
[illegible]	Pte	Williams	E.	[illegible]	" Sick	28.11.18
202[illegible]	"	Barber	W.	[illegible]	" Sick	2.12.18
16964	"	Field	E.	[illegible]	" Sick	1.12.18
20[illegible]	"	Colegate	W.	[illegible]	" Sick	1.12.18
205[illegible]	"	Amhurst	E.	[illegible]	" Sick	1.12.18

[illegible]. ADDITIONAL PAY.-

No. 6114 Sergeant Luckhurst J. "D" Company performed duties of Sergeant Cook from 24 - 30.11.1918 inclusive; additional pay granted at 6d. per diem.

[illegible]. BATTALION ORGANISATION - 2/12/1918.

Headquarters.-

	Commanding Officer-	Lt.Col. E.J. WENYON, D.S.O.,
	Second-in-Command-	Major [illegible] BROWN, M.C.,
	Acting Adjutant-	2/Lieut.C.[illegible] MACASKIE.
	Intelligence Officer-	Lieut.G.S. BOWEN, M.C.,
Transport.-	Transport Officer-	Captain [illegible] ARNAUD.
	Asstnt Tpt.Officer-	2/Lieut.[illegible] OUTRAM.
	Transport Sergeant-	[illegible] Sgt G.Sheppard.
Q.M.Stores-	Quartermaster-	Q.M. & Lieut. W.J. GREEN.
	R.Q.M.Sergeant-	3818 RQM Sergt. [illegible] Dunk, DC[illegible]
Staff N.C.O's-	O. R. Clerk-	[illegible] Sgt W.G.Carr.
	Sergeant Cook-	6114 Sgt J.Luckhurst.
	Sergeant Drummer-	200078 Sgt [illegible] Underdown.
	Provost Sergeant-	240748 Sgt G.[illegible].
[illegible] Instructors-	Lewis Gun-	Captain F.PROCTOR.
		[illegible] Sgt [illegible]
		[illegible] L/Sgt A.Cook, D.C.M.,
		[illegible] Sgt [illegible] Charles.
	Musketry-	7250 L/Sgt [illegible] Hillman.
	Gas-	
	Educational Officer-	2/Lieut.[illegible] FITCH.

Companies:- "A" COMPANY.-

	Company Commander-	Captain J.M.SELFE, M.C.,
	Second-in-Command-	2/Lieut.C.G.TILBY.
	Comp[illegible].Sgt.Major-	5713 C.S.Major G.Buck, M.[illegible]
	Coy.Qr.Mr.Sergt-	203332 A/C.Q.M.Sgt. D.Gra[illegible]
No.1 Pltn.-	Platoon Commander-	Lieut.R.A.QUARTERMAIN.
	Platoon Sergeant-	2340 Sgt W.Ready.
No.1 Sectn.-	Section Commander-	[illegible] Cpl C.Igon.
	Sectn.2-i/Command-	19685 L/C B.Sparrow.
No.2 Sectn.-	Section Commander-	1351 L/C [illegible].Day.
	Sectn.2-i/Command-	25514 Pte T.Culliven.
No.3 Sectn.-	Section Commander-	19643 L/Cpl [illegible]
	Sectn.2-i/Command-	1991[illegible] Pte L.Hill.
No.4 Sectn.-	Section Commander-	19673 L/Cpl H.Richardson.
	Sectn.2-i/Command-	242251 Pte J.Triggle.
No.2 Pltn.-	Platoon Commander-	Lieut.D.G.GODDEN.
	Pltn.2-i/Command-	Lieut.E.O.GOULDEN, [illegible]
	Platoon Sergeant-	2761 Sgt A.Sharp[illegible]

No. 5 Sectn. Section Commander- 11140 L/Cpl R.Dixon.
Sectn.2-i/Command- 29634 Pte F.Copping.

No. 6 Sectn. Section Commander- [illegible] L/Cpl [illegible]
Sectn.2-i/Command- [illegible] L/Cpl [illegible]

No. 7 Sectn. Section Commander- [illegible] L/Cpl W.[illegible]
Sectn.2-i/Command- [illegible] Pte [illegible]

No. 8 Sectn. Section Commander- [illegible] L/Cpl [illegible]
Sectn.2-i/Command- [illegible] Pte [illegible]

No. 3 Pltn. Platoon Commander- [illegible]
Platoon Sergeant- [illegible]

No. 9 Sectn. Section Commander- [illegible] Cpl [illegible]
Sectn.2-i/Command- [illegible] L/Cpl [illegible]

No. 10 Sectn. Section Commander- [illegible] L/Cpl W.[illegible]
Sectn.2-i/Command- [illegible] Pte [illegible]

No. 11 Sectn. Section Commander- [illegible] L/Cpl [illegible]
Sectn.2-i/Command- [illegible] Pte [illegible]

No. 12 Sectn. Section Commander- [illegible] L/Cpl [illegible]
Sectn.2-i/Command- [illegible] L/Cpl [illegible]

No. 4 Pltn. Platoon Commander- [illegible]
Plt.2-i/Command- [illegible]
Platoon Sergeant- [illegible] Sgt [illegible], M.M.,

No. 13 Sectn. Section Commander- [illegible] Cpl [illegible]
Sectn.2-i/Command- [illegible] Pte [illegible]

No. 14 Sectn. Section Commander- [illegible] L/Cpl [illegible]
Sectn.2-i/Command- [illegible] Pte [illegible]

No. 15 Sectn. Section Commander- [illegible] Cpl [illegible], M.M.,
Sectn.2-i/Command- [illegible] L/Cpl [illegible]

No. 16 Sectn. Section Commander- [illegible] Cpl W.Thompson.
Sectn.2-i/Command- [illegible]

[illegible] Company.

Company Commander- [illegible]
Second-in-Command- [illegible]
Compy.[illegible] [illegible]
Coy.[illegible] [illegible]

No. 5 Pltn. Platoon Commander- 2nd.Lieut.[illegible]
Platoon Sergeant- [illegible] Sgt [illegible], M.M.

No. 1 Sectn. Section Commander- [illegible] L/Cpl [illegible]
Sectn.2-i/Command- [illegible] Pte [illegible]

No. 2 Sectn. Section Commander- [illegible] Cpl [illegible]
Sectn.2-i/Command- [illegible] L/Cpl [illegible]

No. 3 Sectn. Section Commander- [illegible] Cpl [illegible]
Sectn.2-i/Command- [illegible] Pte [illegible]

No. 4 Sectn. Section Commander- [illegible] L/Cpl [illegible].Payne.
Sectn.2-i/Command- [illegible] Pte [illegible]

No. 6 Pltn. Platoon Commander- 2nd.Lieut.[illegible]
Platoon Sergeant- [illegible] Sgt [illegible]

(over)

Battalion Orders dated [illegible].12.1918 contd., Sheet -[illegible]-

771. BATTALION ORGANIZATION- 2/12/1918-contd.,

No. 5 Sectn.	Section Commander-	2298 Cpl S.Pankhurst.
	Sectn.2-i/Command-	20[illegible] L/Cpl A.Woolmore.
No. 6 Sectn.	Section Commander-	17[illegible]5 L/Cpl E.Masson.
	Sectn.2-i/Command-	50[illegible]6 Pte S.Goodchild.
No. 7 Sectn.		
No. 8 Sectn.	Section Commander-	10[illegible] Cpl F.Apps.
	Sectn.2-i/Command-	20[illegible]0 Pte J.Dempsey.
No.7 Pltn.	Platoon Commander-	2nd.Lieut. W.E.W.THOMAS.
	Pltn.2-i/Command-	2nd.Lieut.J.E.W.[illegible]ARGENT.
	Platoon Sergeant-	3993 Sgt F.Crow.
No. 9 Sectn.	Section Commander-	[illegible] Pte E.Crabb.
	Sectn.2-i/Command-	204592 Pte [illegible].Hewitt.
No.10 Sectn.	Section Commander-	205101 L/Cpl W.Wheatley.
	Sectn.2-i/Command-	13[illegible] Pte P.Smith.
No.11 Sectn.		
No.12 Sectn.	Section Commander-	15[illegible] L/Cpl A.Wells.
	Sectn.2-i/Command-	39814 Pte G.Newman.
No. 8 Pltn.	Platoon Commander-	2nd.Lieut.J.E.JORDAN.
	Platoon Sergeant-	20014 L/Sgt [illegible]
No.13 Sectn.		
No.14 Sectn.	Section Commander-	4741 L/Cpl G.Cook.
	Sectn.2-i/Command-	90[illegible] L/Cpl [illegible]
No.15 Sectn.	Section Commander-	6008 Cpl P.Vile.
	Sectn.2-i/Command-	77[illegible] Pte [illegible].Packham.
No.16 Sectn.	Section Commander-	1[illegible]43 L/Cpl [illegible]
	Sectn.2-i/Command-	39[illegible] Pte [illegible]
"C" Company.	Company Commander-	Captain [illegible]
	Second-in-Command-	Capt. A.[illegible], D.S.O.,
	Compy.Sgt.Major-	2[illegible]6 C.S.Major S.Philp.
	Coy.Q.M.Sgt-	[illegible] C.Q.M.Sgt A.E.Judd.
No.9 Pltn.	Platoon Commander-	[illegible].JAMES.
	Pltn.2-i/Command-	[illegible].PEARSE.
	Platoon Sergeant-	3[illegible] [illegible], M.M.,
No. 1 Sectn.	Section Commander-	20[illegible] Pte [illegible].Collier.
	Sectn.2-i/Command-	1[illegible] Pte [illegible]
No. 2 Sectn.	Section Commander-	[illegible] L/Cpl W.[illegible]
	Sectn.2-i/Command-	20[illegible] Pte [illegible]
No. 3 Sectn.	Section Commander-	[illegible]120 Cpl [illegible]
	Sectn.2-i/Command-	[illegible] Pte [illegible]
No. 4 Sectn.	Section Commander-	[illegible] Pte [illegible]well.
	Sectn.2-i/Command-	[illegible] Pte [illegible]

[illegible] BATTALION ORGANIZATION [illegible] - Contd.

No.11 Pltn. Platoon Commander - 2nd.Lieut.W.[illegible]
Pltn.2-i/Command - [illegible]
Platoon Sergeant - [illegible] Sgt [illegible]
[illegible] Pltn.Sergeant - 7622 Sgt [illegible]

No. 9 Sectn. Section Commander - 20387 Cpl [illegible]
Sectn.2-i/Command - [illegible] Pte [illegible]

[illegible] Sectn. Section Commander - [illegible] Cpl W.[illegible]
Sectn.2-i/Command - [illegible] L/Cpl [illegible]

No.11 Sectn. Section Commander - 202[illegible] L/Cpl W.[illegible]
Sectn.2-i/Command - [illegible] Pte [illegible]

No.12 Sectn. Section Commander - 3160 L/Cpl [illegible]
Sectn.2-i/Command - 240772 Pte L.Morg[illegible]

No.12 Pltn. Platoon Commander - [illegible] CHAUNCY.
Pltn.2-i/Command - [illegible]
Platoon Sergeant - [illegible] Sgt [illegible]

[illegible] Sectn. Section Commander - [illegible] Cpl [illegible]
Sectn.2-i/Command - [illegible] L/Cpl [illegible]

No. [illegible] Sectn. Section Commander - [illegible] Cpl [illegible]
Sectn.2-i/Command - [illegible] L/Cpl [illegible]

[illegible]

[illegible]

2nd.Lieut.[illegible]

[illegible] Sectn. Section Commander - 21[illegible] Sgt [illegible]
Sectn.2-i/Command - [illegible] Cpl [illegible]

[illegible] Sectn. Section Commander - 20[illegible] L/Cpl [illegible]
Sectn.2-i/Command - 38[illegible] Pte [illegible]

No. 3 Sectn. Section Commander - [illegible] L/Cpl [illegible]
Sectn.2-i/Command - 7[illegible] Pte [illegible]

Battalion Orders dated 3-12-1918 contd., Sheet 6. 6

XVII. BATTALION ORGANIZATION - 3-12-1918-contd.,

No. 4 Sectn. Section Commander- 23596 Cpl [illegible]
Sectn. 2-i/Command- 29870 Pte [illegible]

No. 2 Pltn. Platoon Commander- 2nd.Lieut. [illegible] SMITH.
Platoon 2-i/Command- 2nd.Lieut. [illegible]
Platoon Sergeant- [illegible] Sgt [illegible] M.M.,

No. 5 Sectn. Section Commander- [illegible] Cpl [illegible]
Sectn. 2-i/Command- [illegible] L/Cpl [illegible]

No. 6 Sectn. Section Commander- [illegible] L/Cpl [illegible]
Sectn. 2-i/Command- [illegible]

No. 7 Sectn. Section Commander- [illegible] L/Cpl [illegible]
Sectn. 2-i/Command- [illegible] Pte [illegible]

No. 8 Sectn. Section Commander- [illegible] Cpl [illegible]
Sectn. 2-i/Command- [illegible]

No. 3 Pltn. Platoon Commander- [illegible]
Platoon Sergeant- [illegible] L/Sgt [illegible]

No. 9 Sectn. Section Commander- [illegible]
Sectn. 2-i/Command- [illegible] L/Cpl [illegible]

No. 10 Sectn. Section Commander- [illegible] L/Cpl [illegible]
Sectn. 2-i/Command- [illegible]

No. 11 Sectn. Section Commander- [illegible] L/Cpl [illegible]
Sectn. 2-i/Command- [illegible] Pte [illegible]

No. 12 Sectn. Section Commander- [illegible] Cpl [illegible]
Sectn. 2-i/Command- [illegible] L/Cpl [illegible]

No. 4 Pltn. Platoon Commander- [illegible]
Pltn. 2-i/Command- [illegible]
Platoon Sergeant- [illegible] M.M.,

No. 13 Sectn. Section Commander- [illegible]
Sectn. 2-i/Command- [illegible] Pte [illegible]

No. 14 Sectn. Section Commander- [illegible]
Sectn. 2-i/Command- [illegible]

No. 15 Sectn. Section Commander- [illegible]
Sectn. 2-i/Command- [illegible]

No. 16 Sectn. Section Commander- [illegible]
Sectn. 2-i/Command- [illegible]

[illegible]
[illegible]

Appendix B

SECRET. 8TH.S.BATTN.ROYAL WEST KENT REGT. Copy No. 2
ORDER NO.40.
IN-THE-FIELD. 17TH.DECEMBER 1918.

1. The Battalion will move by March Route to TOURNAI tomorrow, 18th December 1918.

2. Battalion will parade on road outside "D" Coys' billets, facing S.E. ready to move off at 0830 hours. Head of column at "D" Coys' billets.
Order of March.
[illegible]
H.Q.
"[illegible]" Coy.
[illegible]
"A" Coy.
"[illegible]" Coy.
Dress. Full Marching Order as demonstrated today.
100 yards intervals between Companies on the march.

3. Officers' valises and blankets will be dumped at Battalion Guard Room at 0730 hours.
Mess cart will call for Officers' mess kit at 0745 hours.

4. Breakfasts 0630 hours.
Sick parade 0700 hours.
Dinners to be prepared en route.

5. Duty Company "A" Coy. will detail a guard to mount as soon as possible after arrival in barracks.
Prisoners will march with H.Q.Grs. and on arrival will be handed over to the Guard.

6. Transport will follow the Battalion, 100 yards interval will be kept between the head of the Transport and the rear of the Battalion.

7. Each Company will detail one man (wearing leather equipment) to report to Transport Sergeant at 0800 hours for duty as brakesmen.

8. Certificate that billets have been left clean will be rendered by 2000 hours 18.12.18.

9. Instructions re loading party for lorries and accommodation on lorries for any men possessing medical certificate of unfitness to march will be wired later.

Sd. C.F.C. MACASKIE 2nd.Lieut.,
Issued at 2030 hrs. A/Adjutant 8th.S.Bn.Royal West Kent Regt.

Copies to:-
1. File.
2. War Diary
3. War Diary
4. O.C. "A" Company.
5. O.C. "B" Company.
6. O.C. "C" Company.
7. O.C. "D" Company.
8. Headquarters' Mess
9. Transport Officer.
10. Quartermaster.
11. [illegible] Heath.

SECRET.

24

16/3

WAR DIARY

of

8th S. Bn. R. W. Kent Regt.

from 1.1.1919

to 31.1.1919

(Volume. –)

VR 39

To:-

D.A.G., 3rd Echelon
(through Headquarters,
72nd Infantry Brigade).

Army Form C. 2118.

Instructions regarding War Diaries and Intelligence Summaries are contained in F. S. Regs., Part II. and the Staff Manual respectively. Title pages will be prepared in manuscript.

8th S. Bn Royal WAR DIARY West Kent Regt or INTELLIGENCE SUMMARY.

January, 1919

(Erase heading not required.)

Place	Date	Hour	Summary of Events and Information	Remarks and references to Appendices
TOURNAI	1-1-19		Usual Daily Programme. 0725 Breakfast Roll Call 0730 Breakfast 0900 Parades Guard Drill P.T Arm Drill General Barrack Square work. Education 0930-1030 H.Q A & B Coys 1100-1200 C & D Coys. Sports: Football, Boxing, Tug-of-War, Cross-Country Running	FC
	2.1.19		Usual Daily Programme. Demobilized 3 O.R.	FC
	3.1.19		Usual Daily Programme. Demobilized 1 O R	FC
	4.1.19		Usual Daily Programme. Demobilized 1 O R	FC
	5.1.19		Usual Daily Programme Col Wenyon to Brussels on 72 hours leave. Major Brown in command	FC
	6.1.19		Usual Daily Programme	FC
	7.1.19		Usual Daily Programme. Demobilized 1 O.R	FC
	8.1.19		Usual Daily Programme Col Wenyon returned from Brussels Major Brown to Aldershot on Senior Officers' Course	FC
	9.1.19		Usual Daily Programme	FC
	10.1.19		Battalion becomes Duty Battalion for the Brigade. All available men on guard or on fatigue	FC
	11.1.19		Usual Duties Demobilized 3 O.R	FC
	12.1.19		Usual Duties. Demobilised 2 O.R	FC
	13.1.19		Usual Duties Demobilized 1 O.R	FC

(A9475) Wt W2336/P360 600,000 12/17 D. D. & L. Sch. 52a. Forms/C2118/15.

Instructions regarding War Diaries and Intelligence Summaries are contained in F. S. Regs., Part II. and the Staff Manual respectively. Title pages will be prepared in manuscript.

Army Form C. 2118.

January 1919

8th S Bn Royal **WAR DIARY** West Kent Regt

or

INTELLIGENCE SUMMARY.

(Erase heading not required.)

Place	Date	Hour	Summary of Events and Information	Remarks and references to Appendices
TOURNAI	14.1.19		Usual Duties. [struck out] Demobilized 4 O.R	7C
	15.1.19		Usual Duties Demobilized 3 O.R	7C
	16.1.19		Usual Duties	7C
	17.1.19		Bn relieved by 1st N. Staffs Regt from Duties. Usual Daily Programme	7C
	18.1.19		Usual Daily Programme. Demobilized 5 O.R	7C
	19.1.19		Usual Daily Programme. Demobilized 6 O.R	7C
	20.1.19		Usual Daily Programme Demobilized 7 O.R	7C
	21.1.19		Usual Daily Programme. Demobilized 6 O.R	7C
	22.1.19		Usual Daily Programme Demobilized 3 O.R	7C
	23.1.19		Usual Daily Programme	7C
	24.1.19		Usual Daily Programme	7C
	25.1.19		Usual Daily Programme	7C
	26.1.19		Usual Daily Programme. Demobilized 9 O.R Heavy snowfall	7C
	27.1.19		Usual Daily Programme Demobilized 18 O.R Still snowing	7C
	28.1.19		Usual Daily Programme Snow still lying Very Cold Demobilized 1 O.R	7C
	29.1.19		Usual Daily Programme Snow still lying Very cold Demobilized 12 O.R	7C

(A9475) Wt W2358/P360 600,000 12/17 D. D. & L. Sch. 52a. Forms/C2118/15.

Army Form C. 2118.

Instructions regarding War Diaries and Intelligence Summaries are contained in F. S. Regs., Part II. and the Staff Manual respectively. Title pages will be prepared in manuscript.

8th S. Bn Royal West Kent Regt WAR DIARY January ~~Feb~~ FC 1919 or INTELLIGENCE SUMMARY.

(Erase heading not required.)

Place	Date	Hour	Summary of Events and Information	Remarks and references to Appendices
TOURNAI	30.1.19		Usual Daily Programme. Very cold. G.O.C. inspected Barracks Demobilized 15 O.R	FC
	31.1.19		Battalion assumed duties as Duty Battalion. Total fatigues, guards, etc 295	
			Total available parade strength 195. 1st Bn N. Staffs Regt supplied balance of	
			men required Demobilized 14 O.R	FC
	~~1.ii.19~~		~~Usual Duties. Very cold Demobilized 15 O.R~~ FC	~~FC~~
	~~2.ii.19~~		~~Church Parade but only 52 on parade remainder on duties Demobilized 14 O.R~~	~~FC~~ FC

F C McChanny
Lieut. for Capt. Adj.
8th (S) Battn. Royal West Kent Regt

SECRET.

VR 40

War Diary

8th S Bn Royal West Kent Regt

for

February 1919

(Volume)

To:- D.A.G. Base,

Through Headquarters

72nd Inf. Bde.

Instructions regarding War Diaries and Intelligence Summaries are contained in F. S. Regs., Part II. and the Staff Manual respectively. Title pages will be prepared in manuscript.

February, 1919

8th S. B. Royal West Kent Regt. **WAR DIARY** *or* **INTELLIGENCE SUMMARY.**

(Erase heading not required.)

Army Form C. 2118.

Place	Date	Hour	Summary of Events and Information	Remarks and references to Appendices
TOURNAI	1-2-19		Usual Duties. Very cold weather continues. Demobilized 15 OR	CHH
"	2-2-19		Church Parade attendance 52 – remainder on Guards and fatigues. Demobilized 14 OR	CHH
"	3-2-19		Usual Duties. Demobilized 1 off. 13 OR	CHH
"	4-2-19		Usual Duties	CHH
"	5-2-19		Usual Duties – Baths.	CHH
"	6-2-19		Usual Duties – 14 OR Demobilized. Warning Order that 10 off. and 200 OR are required to	
			proceed to join the 10th Bn. 2nd Army	CHH
"	7-2-19		Bn. relieved as Duty Battalion by the 1st N. Staff. Regt. Baths. Coy Training. Education.	
			8 OR. Demobilized	CHH
"	8-2-19		Cleaning Barracks. Lecture by Capt. Penton on the "Rhine Army". 13 OR Demobilized.	CHH
"	9-2-19		Church Parade. 12 OR Demobilized.	CHH
"	10-2-19		Education and Coy Training. R. A. Band in afternoon and evening. 2 off. 14 OR. Demobilized	CHH
"	11-2-19		Men selected for "Draft" under Capt. Penton. Kit inspections etc.	CHH
"	12-2-19		Usual training and fatigues. Capt. Proctor appointed Bn. Demobilization Officer	CHH
"	13-2-19		Usual training etc. Lecture by Lord Denbigh. 1 off. 18 OR Demobilized.	CHH
"	14-2-19		Usual Duties. 14 OR. Demobilized	CHH

ORDERLY ROOM
No. A/.............
28 FEB 1919
8th (Service) Bn. Queen's Own Royal West Kent Regiment

Instructions regarding War Diaries and Intelligence Summaries are contained in F. S. Regs., Part II. and the Staff Manual respectively. Title pages will be prepared in manuscript.

February, 1919

8th S. B. Royal West Kent Regt.

WAR DIARY or INTELLIGENCE SUMMARY.

(Erase heading not required.)

Army Form C. 2118.

Place	Date	Hour	Summary of Events and Information	Remarks and references to Appendices
TOURNAI	15-2-19		Guards and Fatigues 15 OR demobilized. Thaw commenced	[illegible]
"	16-2-19		Col. Wenyon left for Paris leave. Capt. Penton in command. 150 men of 3 R B arrived to take over fatigues in order to enable us to practise the Ceremony of Presentation of Colours.	[illegible]
"	17-2-19		Practise of Ceremony 26 OR demobilized. Snow finally disappeared and weather very much milder	
"	18-2-19			
"	19-2-19			[illegible]
"	20-2-19		Final Practise of Ceremony 17 OR demobilized	[illegible]
"	21-2-19		Presentation of Colours. 27. OR demobilized. For full description of Ceremony see Appendix A	[illegible]
"	22-2-19.		Resumed usual duties	[illegible]
"	23-2-19		Church Parade attended by Corps Commander. Bn parade strength 10 files only	[illegible]
"	24-2-19		Guards and Fatigues. Col. Wenyon returned from Paris and resumed command	[illegible]
"	25-2-19		Guards and Fatigues. Bn re-organized on the basis of 'Draft' and 'Cadre' Coy. Capt. Penton in command of 'Draft' Coy. Capt. Thompson of 'Cadre' Coy.	[illegible]
"	26-2-19		Re-organization continued. 'Cadre' establishment definitely fixed	Appendix B [illegible]
"	27-2-19		Re-organization complete. 7. OR. demobilized	[illegible]
"	28-2-19		8. OR demobilized. This completes demobilization for the present. all men who can be spared having been demobilized. Some are retained over 'Cadre' strength until the 'Draft' goes and animals are demobilized	[illegible]

(A9475) Wt W2358/P360 600,000 12/17 D. D. & L. Sch. 52a. Forms/C2118/15.

[signature] Capt. & Adjt.
8th (S) Battn. Royal West Kent Regt.

Appendix A

PRESENTATION OF COLOURS
on the
CHAMPS de MANOUVRES, TOURNAI,
on
Friday, 21st February, 1919.

The following troops were on parade:-

<u>9th Bn. EastSurrey Regiment:</u>

Lieut-Colonel E.A.CAMERON, C.M.G., D.S.O.

<u>8th Bn. Royal West Kent Regiment:</u>

Captain C.F.PENTON.

<u>12th Bn. Sherwood Foresters (Pioneers).</u>

Lieut-Colonel F.J.ROBERTS, M.C.

the latter Battalion taking the place of the 1st Bn. North Staffordshire Regiment, which, being a Regular Battalion, was already in possession of Colours.

The parade was under the Command of Brigadier-General R.W.Morgan, C.M.G., D.S.O., Commanding 72nd Infantry Brigade, who had with him the Brigade Major (Captain T.B.Hankey, M.C., A.M.) and Lieut. F.S.W.Shute, M.C.

The presentation was to have been made by General Sir Henry HORNE, K.C.B., K.C.M.G., Commanding First Army, but he was, unfortunately, indisposed, and deputed Lieut-General Sir Arthur HOLLAND, K.C.B., D.S.O., Commanding First Corps, to take his place.

The consecretation was performed by the Rev. C.CHARKE, and Rev. J.C.SHARPE, Chaplains attached to the Brigade.

The Brigade was drawn up in three sides of a square, the 9th Bn. East Surrey Regiment forming the right face, 8th Bn. Royal West Kent Regiment the centre, and 12th Bn. Sherwood Foresters, the left face.

Punctually at 11.00 hrs. Sir Arthur HOLLAND arrived, accompanied by Major-General A.C.DALY, C.B., Commanding 24th Division, and the Corps and Divisional Staffs.

The weather, which had been very wet during the night and early morning, now became brilliantly fine, and a bright sun was shining.

The Corps Commander was received with a General Salute, and the Consecration Service then commenced. On its conclusion, the Colours were handed to the Presenting Officer by the Seconds-in-Command, and were received from him by the Senior Subalterns kneeling on the right knee, in the following order:-

<u>9th Bn. East SurreyRegt.</u>

Second-in-Command: Major J.C.BROWN, M.C.

Senior Subaltern: Lieut E.G.BIRTLES, M.C.

12th Bn. Sherwood Foresters.

Second-in-Command: Major J.H.PEARSON, D.S.O., M.C.

Senior Subaltern: Lieut. P.J.ROGERS.

8th Bn. Royal West Kent Regiment.

Second-in-Command: Captain F. PROCTOR.

Senior Subaltern: Lieut. R.C.GOUDEN, M.C.

The presenting Officer then addressed the parade as follows:-

"Brigadier-General Morgan, Officers, Warrant Officers, Non-commissioned Officers, and Men of the 72nd Infantry Brigade. The first thing I have to do, is to apologise for the absence of the Army Commander. He had fully intended to come, and had been looking forward to the privilege of presenting these Colours, but I am sorry to say he is unwell, and consequently has been unable to come. I have, therefore, the privilege of being here, in his place, and the honour of presenting the King's Colour to the Battalions now on parade, an honour enhanced in this case by the fact that the presentation takes place at the moment of victory, and to Battalions which have fought in this, the greatest war in the history of the British Empire.

The Colours which I have entrusted to your keeping, are the symbol of your allegiance to your King and to your Country, and, as such, they will I know full well, be honoured and guarded by you on all occasions and at any price, and that you by your deeds and by your conduct, will worthily uphold the glorious traditions of your Regiments, not only in War, but equally in peace. I want you to remember that the trials which will face you in peace, are as great, and more insidious than the trials which you have so heroically overcome during this War, but if, when you return to civil life, you face these trials with the same loyalty, steadfastness and self-sacrifice which have been the mainsprings of your actions, and the foundations of your success out here, then I am convinced that no stain will be placed on the fair fame of your Regiments by any act of yours.

The 72nd Infantry Brigade has a magnificent record throughout this War. It first fought at LOOS in 1915, after a long and trying march up from the Coast. It was next engaged in the attack on GUILLEMONT, and in the heroic defence of DELVILLE WOOD. It was then transferred to the 1st Corps, and performed fine service during the VIMY RIDGE operations, when, just prior to the attack, it held the Canadian assault trenches and endured with the utmost steadiness the brunt of the German artillery counter preparation. The Brigade then moved North and took a distinguished part in the Battle of MESSINES and in the Third Battle of YPRES. In the Great German Offensive in 1918, the 72nd Infantry Brigade played a glorious part, holding up many overwhelming attacks, and, by its courage and fighting spirit, saving the situation on many occasions.

To such gallant Battalions, I, with absolute confidence, entrust these Colours, in the name of His Majesty the King, asking you to remember that as they represent all that is most glorious in the past history of your Regiments, so they must be an inspiration enabling you to add to your Country's glory in the future.".

Brigadier-General Morgan, in a brief speech of thanks, said:-

"Sir:- In the name of the 72nd Infantry Brigade, and on behalf of the Battalions on parade to-day, I beg to thank you for the honour done to them in the presentation of Colours, and for the reference to their services in your address. The third Battalion of the Brigade, 1st Bn. North Staffordshire Regiment, being a regular Battalion and already in possession of Colours, is not represented on parade, its place being taken by the 12th Bn. Sherwood Foresters, the Divisional Pioneer Battalion.

These Battalions are justly proud of their record in the War, and speaking for myself, I have always felt it a very great honour to have them under my Command.

All may soon cease to exist as Units, but the Colours will remain as a lasting symbol of their loyalty and devotion to His Majesty: and, should it ever be found necessary to re-form the Battalions, the flags which you have just presented to them will form a rallying point round which will again be displayed that lofty sense of duty, comradeship and devotion, which has ever distinguished the 9th Bn. East Surrey Regiment, the 8th Bn. Royal West Kent Regiment, and the 12th Bn. Sherwood Foresters".

Battalions then moved to the Saluting Base and marched past, after which the Brigade formed up in line, advanced in Review Order and gave a General Salute.

Sir Arthur HOLLAND congratulated all ranks on their turn-out and steadiness in the ranks.

The parade was then dismissed.

---

appendix B

Roll of Cadre Establishment.
8th S.Bn. Royal West Kent Regiment.

Commanding Officer	Lieut-Colonel H.J. Kenyon, D.S.O.
Adjutant.	Captain C.F.C. Lucaskie.
Quartermaster.	Lieut. W.J. Green.
Lewis Gun Officer.	Captain F. Proctor.
Quartermaster-Sgt.	R.Q.M.S. W. Dunk, D.C.M. No. 3818
Orderly Room.	Sgt. F.B. Swain. No. 2886.
Transport Sergeant.	Sergt. J. Sheppard. No. 1369.
Transport Drivers:	20235 Pte. Burden, J.
	5415 Pte. Downs, G.
	3106 Pte. Davis, A.
	7048 Pte. McLean, F.
	3662 Pte. Patrick, P.
	19702 Pte. Wigley, J.
	8722 Pte. Evans, W.
	2596 Pte. Hill, A.E.
	10160 Pte. Hickmore, B.
Batmen:	4196 Pte. Norman, F.
	208870 Sig. Humphrey, W.
	202362. Sig. Airey, H.
	~~20413 Pte. Tooby, G.~~ 38684 Pte LAWTON, A
Pioneer:	21287, Pte. Booth, J.
Signallers:	2535 L/C. Pitt, G.
	202564 Sig. Hough, F.
Lewis Gun Sergeant.	4387, Sgt. Wragg.
C.Q.M.S.	892 C.Q.M.S. Cooper.
"A" Company:	8568 Cpl. Ison, C.P.
	11140 L/C. Dixon, F.
	7435 Pte. Simmons, R.G.
	17995 Pte. Legg, H.
	19533 Pte. Parnell, C.
	7601 Pte. Rattray, D.
"B" Company:	20882 Cpl. Poyser, T.
	202407 Pte. Pole, T.H.
	20896 Pte. Johnston.
	19008 Pte. McNamara.
	~~3931 Pte. Heckham, G.~~ 19666 Pte NOBLE, O.
	19665 Pte. Moyes, R.
"C" Company:	10907 Cpl. Morley, W.
	7391 Pte. Martin, J.
	16416 Pte. Todd, T.
	18905 Pte. Banks, J.
	205850 Pte. Roberts, P.
	7430 Pte. Hall, P.
"D" Company:	240904 Cpl. Goodwin, W.
	8115 L/C. Harris, H.
	203589 Pte. Allen, C.
	11247 L/C. Wissenden, P.
	11764 Pte. Fagg, A.
	205848 Pte. Sorrell, E.

C.F.C. Lucaskie Capt
for ....Lt-Col.,
Cmdg. 8th (S) Battn. Royal West Kent Regt

SECRET.

Vol 41

War Diary
of
8th S. Bn. Royal West Kent Regt.
for
March 1919.
(Volume)

To:
D.A.G.,
Base, (through)
Headquarters,
72nd Inf. Bde.

Instructions regarding War Diaries and Intelligence Summaries are contained in F. S. Regs., Part II. and the Staff Manual respectively. Title pages will be prepared in manuscript.

WAR DIARY

or

~~INTELLIGENCE SUMMARY.~~

(*Erase heading not required.*)

Army Form C. 2118.

Place	Date	Hour	Summary of Events and Information	Remarks and references to Appendices
TOURNAI	1/3/19		Guards & Fatigues.	
do	2/3/19		do do No Church Parade due to no men being available. Transferred 5 Riding Horses to 7th East Surreys. Sent off 15 Animals by Rail & 5 to be sold locally.	
do	3/3/19		Guards & Fatigues. Demobilized 15 Animals.	
do	4/3/19		do do. 7th East Surreys left the Brigade for the Rhine Army	
do	5/3/19		do do. Orders for reduction to Cadre A received.	
do	6/3/19		do do. Very Wet	
do	7/3/19		do do. Lt Col Kenyon left on Leave to UK. Captn CF Penton in command.	
do	8/3/19		do do.	
do	9/3/19		do do.	
do	10/3/19		do do. Capt CF Penton left on Leave to UK. Captn SG Thompson MC in command	
do	11/3/19		do do.	
do	12/3/19		do do.	
do	13/3/19		do do. Definite Orders received to send Draft to 10th Battn on 15th.	
do	14/3/19		do do.	

(A9475) Wt W2358/P360 600,000 12/17 D. D. & L. Sch. 52a. Forms/C2118/15.

Instructions regarding War Diaries and Intelligence Summaries are contained in F. S. Regs., Part II. and the Staff Manual respectively. Title pages will be prepared in manuscript.

WAR DIARY
or
~~INTELLIGENCE SUMMARY~~.
(Erase heading not required.)

Army Form C. 2118.

Place	Date	Hour	Summary of Events and Information	Remarks and references to Appendices
TOURNAI	15/3/19.		Guards & Fatigues.	
do	16/3/19		do do . Voluntary Church Parade. Lts TILEY, GOULDEN, & GODDEN, and 2nd Lt PEARSE and 2 O.R's demobilized	
do	17/3/19		Guards & Fatigues. Draft of 5 Officers and 131 OR's left to join 10th Battn Capt Drumgold in charge with Lts BOWEN, BINNEY, JAMES & 2nd Lt BEYNES. Capt PENTON & 2nd Lts BRUNGER, JACKSON, GIBBONS & SMITH to proceed direct from England on completion of Leave	
do	18/3/19		Guards & Fatigues.	
do	19/3/19		do do	
do	20/3/19		do do	
do	21/3/19		Evacuated Infantry Barracks Cadre billeted in Chaussé de Lille. H Q remains at 21 Rue de l'esplanade.	
do	22/3/19		Fatigues	
do	23/3/19		Guards & Fatigues.	
do	24/3/19		Guards & Fatigues.	
do	25/3/19		do do	

Instructions regarding War Diaries and Intelligence Summaries are contained in F. S. Regs., Part II, and the Staff Manual respectively. Title pages will be prepared in manuscript.

WAR DIARY
or
~~INTELLIGENCE SUMMARY~~.
(Erase heading not required.)

Army Form C. 2118.

Place	Date	Hour	Summary of Events and Information	Remarks and references to Appendices
TOURNAI	26/3/19.		Battalion moved from TOURNAI to Billets in LAMAIN, Transport personnel remained behind.	
LAMAIN	27/3/19.		Fatigues.	
do	28/3/19		do. Transport rejoined	
do	29/3/19.		do Lt PC BRUNGER & 32 OR's left to join 10th Battn. Capt. the Revd Sharpe left for Demobilization. Heavy fall of snow	
do	30/3/19.		Fatigues. Lt Michie & 19 OR's demobilized	
do	31/3/19		Fatigues.	

[signature] ......Lt.-Col.,
Cmdg. 8th (S) Battn. Royal West Kent Regt.

(A9475) Wt W2358/P360 600,000 12/17 D. D. & L. Sch. 52a. Forms/C2118/15

APRIL 1919

8th Bn Royal West **WAR DIARY** Kent Regt
or
INTELLIGENCE SUMMARY.
(Erase heading not required.)

Army Form C. 2118.

Instructions regarding War Diaries and Intelligence Summaries are contained in F. S. Regs., Part II. and the Staff Manual respectively. Title pages will be prepared in manuscript.

No. 42

Place	Date	Hour	Summary of Events and Information	Remarks and references to Appendices
LAMAIN	1-4-19 to 3-4-19		All men on "employment". No parades except for Draft men & mornings on by training	CHL
do	4-4-19		Inspection of Indents etc by Ordnance Board	CHL
do	5-4-19 to 9-4-19		Usual routine	CHL
do	10-4-19		2 Lts GOBELL, HERD and LANE and 29 OR left to join 10th Bn Royal West Kent Regt	CHL
do	11-4-19		Party left for lorry ride - 2 days to Ypres. Capt. PROCTOR left on leave to U.K.	CHL
do	12-4-19 to 15-4-19		Usual routine	CHL
do	16-4-19		2 Lts BAINES, JORDAN and Lt OUTRAM left for demobilization. Lorry to SOMME battlefields	CHL
do	17-4-19 18-4-19		Usual routine	CHL
do	19-4-19		Capts. SELFE and ORCHARDSON returned from U.K. leave	CHL
do	20-4-19 21-4-19		Usual routine	CHL
do	22-4-19		10 OR left to join 10th Bn Royal West Kent Regt	CHL
do	23-4-19		Lorry for 3 days trip to Ostend	CHL
do	24-4-19		12 OR demobilized	CHL
[illegible]	25-4-19, 26-4-19		Usual routine	CHL
	27-4-19		Capt. PROCTOR returned from leave	CHL
	28-4-19 to 30-4-19		Usual routine	CHL

ORDERLY ROOM
No. A/
6 MAY 1919
8th (Service) [illegible] Queen's Own
Royal West Kent Regiment

C.H. [illegible]
Capt. & Adjt

(A9475) Wt W2358/P560 [illegible] D. D. & L. Sch. 52a. Form [illegible]

www.ingramcontent.com/pod-product-compliance
Lightning Source LLC
Chambersburg PA
CBHW080849230426
43662CB00013B/2056